A World Traveler

A World Traveler

Traveler

The Life of

Thomas A. Ries

This book is dedicated to a special group of people known as expatriates. These people live and work in countries around the world. They leave their home countries and lead a new life in a new environment. This means adapting to the laws, regulations, customs and, in many cases, a new language. Not everyone can function in a foreign country, especially when faced with drastic new challenges. In the evenings, their conversations will touch on experiences in many world areas, much like people talk about experiences in their local communities. Often, when they visit their home country, they find that they cannot speak freely about their international life as people back home will think that they are showing off. I have lived and worked with many expatriates during my career and am happy to be a member of this special group.

I would like to dedicate a special thank you to family members who have supported me with love over many years. I have been blessed with four fantastic daughters who have given me seven wonderful grandchildren. All of my daughters are warm, caring mothers who have given my grandchildren a solid foundation to lead meaningful lives. What a wonderful gift! My first-born daughter, Grace Arteaga, and her husband Jorge have given me great support in dealing with medical issues. Their daughter Nina has earned a bachelor's degree at the school of the Museum of Fine Arts at Tufts University in Boston

My second-born daughter, Debbie Ost, has raised two fine young men; Andy, who has earned a bachelor's degree in psychology from the University of Washington, and his brother, Dante, who has earned a bachelor's degree in management, also at the University of Washington. Debbie has joined me in several travel adventures, including a fantastic visit to Hawaii which she was able to organize for all of us.

My third daughter, Tonia Ries, has one son, Tim, who earned a PhD in mathematics at the University of Texas. Tim is married to Soledad who also has a PhD in Mathematics. She is from Uruguay, and they are expecting a baby this August, which will be my very first great grandchild. Tim works for Google as an engineer and is now fluent in Spanish.

My youngest daughter, Alexandra Leach, has two boys and one girl in her family. Sam is a Boston University graduate starting his career in technology. Jack and Kate are twins. Jack is earning a degree at Northeastern University and his twin sister Kate is enrolled at Tulane University here in New Orleans.

I would like to thank those who have supported me in writing this book. First to Tonia, for formatting all of the material and for checking for errors in spelling or grammatical errors. She has spent hours compiling and organizing what I have written. Alex and her husband Mark have shown me how to scan and upload photos. Alex has typed a lot of the materials in the appendix from some hard-to-read original documents. Both Sam and Kate have helped to upload and insert pictures.

My niece, Kym Zwonitzer, has supported me in finding a lot of material and family history. My mother, Grace Ries, researched both the Ries and Thomas ancestry, and Kym has followed in my mother's footsteps with a wealth of material in her possession.

My thanks to all of you who have given so much support and encouragement in the development and publication of this book.

Tom Ries
New Orleans
July, 2024

Table of Contents

Prologue 11

Early Life 1932-1952 13

    The Beginnings 13

    The Ries Family 17

    The Thomas Family 20

    Snowy Range 23

    Early Jobs 26

Musician 1952-1964 35

    Don Hoy Orchestra 35

    Russ Carlyle Orchestra................................. 36

    Air Force Band.. 37

    Family Visit... 46

    Return to USA 47

    1958 Mexico Trip With My Parents 50

    Don Glasser Orchestra 52

    First Marriage... 54

    Christiani Brothers Circus............................ 55

    Rocky Mountain Accounting Company............... 60

    Musician Again 63

    Clyde McCoy Orchestra............................... 64

Businessman 1964-1990 69

    North American Van Lines 69

    Bronnbach 71

    Second Marriage 73

    Home Pack 76

    Frankfurt, Germany.................................... 79

HHG Shipping and Spedition 82

Massport 85

Russia 90

Trade Mission to Rome 92

ITT Corporation 94

Nigeria 98

Italian Nigeria Shipping Line 99

ITT Mailbag 100

Port Harcourt 103

Containerized Exchanges 109

Coaxial Cable Problem 111

Delayed Flight 118

Abonnema 120

Caribbean Cruise 126

Iraq 127

ITT Europe 131

East/South Africa 136

Mozambique 141

Form M 146

ITT-TDS 149

Woodslanding 151

Professor 1992-2012 159

University of Northern Colorado 159

Preston University 160

Newport International University 168

Regis University 169

EC Council University 171

Tim's Award Trip 183

Woodslanding Construction 184

Nina's Award Trip 187

Andy's Award Trip 189

Ackitoberfest 191

Planning for Retirement 194

Retirement **197**

Montauk 197

New Orleans 203

Sam's Award Trip 204

Musician Again 210

Appendix A: Ries Family **221**

Grace Ries Visits Europe in 1956 221

Statement of Mary Ries 260

Appendix B: Thomas Family **263**

Biography of Charles S. Thomas 263

A Poem by Meroa Thomas 276

Prologue

My greatest desire has always been to share my life with someone. I have not been able to share experiences with a caring life partner, but I have been blessed with four wonderful daughters. This will be an attempt to put my life into a text that anyone who is interested in knowing me can read.

My life has been rich and rewarding. I have had careers in Music, Business, and Education. These have allowed me to visit all 50 American states and 110 foreign countries on six continents. I have experienced high society and have also been exposed to those living in poverty. I have dined in the best restaurants and have experienced hunger in mud huts in Africa. I have flown first class on many flights, but I have also spent hours traveling in trucks on muddy, bumpy, and poor roads to get to villages in many countries.

I have been able to research my ancestry and to find relatives in Germany and Wales, the birth places of my two grandfathers. My travels have allowed me to experience many cultures, and I have made friends around the world. I have lived in the United States, Germany, France, Belgium, and the Netherlands. My work experience has been on a high intellectual level in both business and education. I have also worked alongside people who had little or no education. They live in different worlds, and it was rewarding to be able to experience the various levels of society.

My first marriage produced two beautiful daughters that I love very much. It came to an end when my wife decided that her godmother was more important than her husband. She took my children and went to live with her godmother in Mexico. I was only able to see my daughters twice when they were young.

My second marriage also produced two beautiful daughters. However, our home life was filled with a lot of ongoing criticism and did not contain the love and caring that a person seeks. This was a difficult time and today I realize that I was able escape with travel and trips that were required by my employment.

I thank both of my wives for doing a great job with my children, I love and am proud of my four daughters. They are all exceptional women, successful and wonderful mothers. They have all given me healthy grandchildren who are all a blessing.

Early Life 1932-1952

The Beginnings

My life began on October 17, 1932, when I was born in Cheyenne, Wyoming. My father, Anthony Martin Ries, was with the postal service and my mother, Grace Lilian Ries (née Thomas), was a housewife. I had one sibling, a sister, Charlene Grace Ries, who was seven years older.

We lived at 109 West Pershing in a white house. Some of my first memories were of riding my tricycle around the block, which was a huge excursion. There were only a few houses on the block when I was a child, and therefore we had a lot of places to play. I can remember digging a cave into the ground where the home of Sol Berstein was later built. I also remember playing in the new house next door, which was to become the Yoder house.

My parents were married in 1923 and bought a house shortly after they were married. When they purchased this house there were only two other houses north of the Capitol building, which was located on 25th Street. Pershing was one block north of 30th, so they were out in the country. There used to be a beaver dam on Pershing, and there was a creek feeding this dam. I heard stories about a beaver being caught by a policeman in a bushel basket and being placed in the rear seat of the police car. Evidently, the beaver smashed the basket and was loose in the police car. Wish I could have seen that one, but that was before my time.

109 West Pershing Blvd.

The house had an open front porch which they

sealed with a door and windows. There were two bedrooms, a combined dining & living room, a kitchen, and a bathroom on the main floor. When I was born, my father finished off the attic and made a staircase, so my sister moved upstairs, and I was placed in the rear bedroom. The basement was unfinished but during WWII there was a critical housing shortage, so my father finished off the basement and made it into an apartment which they rented to the military. I can remember Jess Winsenreed and his wife living there. Dad made a small bathroom and put a shower and a stove in the laundry room. I grew up in this house and remember that there were closets everywhere that my father had built.

My two childhood playmates were Dick Pickett and Harry Cole. We were known as Tom, Dick & Harry. There were articles appearing in the local newspaper, which I believe was the work of my mother. Harry and I were in the same grades growing up and Dick was one grade behind us in school. Dick's father was a judge, Dick became an attorney and Harry became a doctor. I retired as a university professor.

I remember that I had a tricycle and was allowed to ride it around the block we lived on. There were only 2 houses on our block when I was young, and part of my journey would be on a

Tom, center, in Second Grade

dirt path. Oh, how I struggled through those obstacles. However, I had my faithful companion with me, Sparky a fox terrier. He was always by my side and was my guardian angel. He was always there to help me when I felt bad.

I attended the Gibson Clark Elementary school. This was a three-block walk from our house. I would cross Central, walk through a vacant lot between 29th and 30th, and then pass the senior high school before arriving at my school which was on the block between 28th and 29th. It was a two-story red brick building. This was my school from kindergarten through the sixth grade. We walked every day; there was never a snow day. We walked though deep snow and blizzards in subzero weather.

Because of the weather, we would always dress in heavy warm coats, sweaters, scarves, and would wear galoshes over our shoes; these were stored in the rear staircase of our house. When you entered the back door there were three steps in a stairway to the kitchen. You would lift the second step and there were the galoshes! This was before zippers were invented, so everything had snaps or buttons. The naughty boys would play "rip the fly" by sharply jerking the front of other boys' pants which would open his fly. We also wore caps with earmuffs to keep our ears from freezing and heavy gloves or mittens for our hands. Those were cold walks.

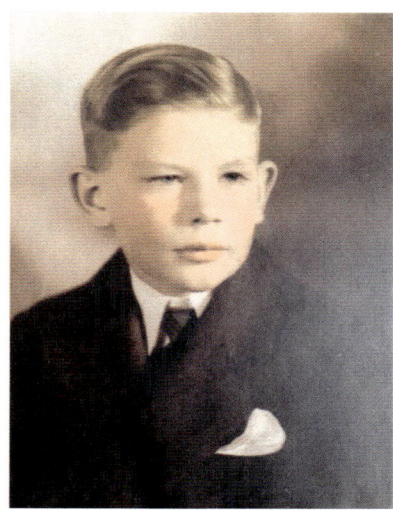

Tom, 9 years old

I can remember my second-grade teacher, Mrs. Vogelsang, whom I adored. The principal was Mrs. Hinkston, who everyone feared. One day when I went to school, I put my tongue on the outside water fountain, and it froze. They had to pour water on it before I could get away and, even then, I lost skin. I will never do that again! There was a lady who sold candy in the basement of a house on Warren between 27th and

28th. There was penny candy, and a candy bar was only 5 cents. Oh, how we would all rush to that treasure cove!

From an early age, I had to wear glasses. In those days they were made of real glass and breakable. One day I broke my glasses after school. The next morning, I had to sit in class without glasses and could not read the blackboard. My father always walked to work, and he was able to obtain a new pair of glasses. He walked to the school from his downtown office and brought them to me at noontime in school. I was happy as I could again read the blackboard. Later that afternoon, I put them in the drawer under my seat and broke them again! Needless to say, my father was not pleased.

I remember that each classroom had a pencil sharpener which we could all use. We only had pencils in the lower grades. In the upper elementary grades, there were ink wells in the desk and we would use pens that we dipped into the ink wells. The lasting memory I have of Gibson Clark was when we were all told to gather in the central hallway between the classrooms. Mrs. Hinkston turned on a radio and we all heard President Roosevelt talk about Pearl Harbor and declare war on Japan. This was very scary for a 9-year-old child. I did not understand everything, but I knew from everyone's reaction that it was bad.

During the war years there was rationing of gasoline, sugar, meat, milk, butter, oil, and many other products. We all had ration books and had to present a coupon in order to buy rationed materials. No one was allowed to talk about relatives in the military,

Tom as a teenager in downtown Cheyenne

where they were, what they were doing etc., under severe penalties. We never knew where our relatives were, and all of the mail was sent to an APO box. The news we received was only by radio and was at least a week old from the battle zones. When I see what the news media does today, I can only say that they would have been shot for some of their reports.

We used butter substitutes and powdered milk. We were also not able to have as many sweets as children always want. Rubber tires were a precious commodity and many of the cars had worn tires. There were no new cars, all were used models. There were a lot of Model A Fords and the older models of other cars. They all had straight windshields, and many had wipers you operated by a lever inside the car. My uncle Lew was able to buy a new Mercury in 1941 and he let my father buy his old 1936 Plymouth, which is the car I remember.

Sometime in the early 1930's my mother and I were in this old car in downtown Cheyenne. I do not remember this, but we were hit by another car and our car turned over. My mother suffered back injuries, which continued for the rest of her life.

The Ries Family

The Ries family originated in a small German town on the Tauber River called Gamburg. There is a house there that my great-grandfather built. In the stone over the door is inscribed: "18 Anton Ries 42," the year it was built. He married the daughter of the local innkeeper, and they came to America in the 1850s. They settled in Milwaukee, Wisconsin and raised their family there. He was a skilled cooper (made wooden barrels for wine and beer) and had a large family. My grandfather got a job working for the Union Pacific railroad as a car inspector and was sent west. His first children were born in Omaha and my father was born in Lincoln, Nebraska. Then the family moved to Cheyenne, Wyoming still employed by Union Pacific this time as a car repairman.

My father's family lived at 322 East 22nd street. This was an old house, and it was yellow. There was a trap door in the kitchen which led down to a root cellar. They used an ice box, and the iceman would deliver a big block of ice which

322 East 22nd Street, Cheyenne

was placed in the top. The root cellar was used to store potatoes, onions, apples, and other vegetables. It was very scary to go down there; there were old wooden stairs, and the cellar was all dirt. The toilet was the European style with a shelf inside. One could look and see what they had left behind before flushing. One day I used the toilet only to urinate. When I came out my Aunt Francis wanted to know if I had wiped myself real good. I had no idea what she was talking about as boys do not do this.

Her sister, Frieda, worked in the office of the Secretary of State. I remember her as a loving, caring lady. We all loved Frieda, but Francis was a much different type. She had fallen out of her highchair as a child and limped. She wanted everyone to treat her special, which became old after a while. I only remember my Grandmother Ries a little. I know she was always in a dark room lying on the couch. She had an accent, and she died in 1939 when I was only 7 years old. I never knew my Grandfather Ries as he died before I was born.

Frieda and Francis always traveled as a team. You never saw one without the other. They always took my sister to lunch at the Plains Hotel every Saturday. They would take her shopping, and I remember my mother being upset from time to time. Later, when Charlene married and moved away, they took me to the Plains Hotel for lunch. Evidently this did not work out too well as it only happened a few times instead of becoming a weekly ritual.

My father also had a brother, Grover Cleveland Ries. He was older and had two sons, Carl and Grover Junior. I have vague memories of Grover Jr. He went into the US army during WW

II, and he never came home as he was killed in battle in Italy at Monte Cassino fighting German forces. I remember my Aunt Ann placing a gold star in her window. They lived at 720 East 18th Street. Carl and my sister were the same age; I was called tagalong by them. Aunt Ann was born a Ketchum and had one sister, May.

Aunt May had a ranch on the military highway behind the Air Force base. Her son, Mark Cox, was a very wealthy rancher and had ranches in Colorado, Wyoming, Argentina, and Spain. I was told that one of his horses won the Kentucky Derby. At one point Mark drove a Rolls Royce. The home ranch is located on the Happy Jack Road west of Cheyenne. Mark also used to go big game hunting in Africa. In later years, we had a conversation about Mozambique and shared experiences we had in that country. Mark had hunted there and I went there while working for the ITT Corporation.

Grover Sr. worked on the railroad and sorted mail. I have been told that he operated the first ever motion picture theater in Cheyenne. Aunt Ann was an accomplished musician and played cello and piano. She also suffered from arthritis and one day

Left to right: Tom's aunt Frieda, her mother Mary Glaub Ries, unknown, and Vera Kruegher

Grover came home and found her hanging in the coal shed behind their house. This was a family tragedy.

From stories I heard, both Grover and my father had to go to Cheyenne bars and bring their father (my grandfather) home. He evidently had a drinking problem. I never knew my grandfather Ries as he was killed in an accident in the railroad yards in 1907 where he worked. As wine was shipped in railroad cars, sometimes the workers would go under the car and turn on the tap. I heard about this happening, but this was kept quiet when I asked if this is what happened to my grandfather. All I know is that he had been hit by a train.

The Thomas Family

My grandfather, Charles Samuel Thomas, was born in 1859 in Llangynog, Wales. The family settled in Cleveland, Ohio. My grandfather left Cleveland for Denver and went to work for Chamberlian & Archer who were meat dealers in Denver, Colorado. In 1880 he came to Cheyenne working for James Tynan who dealt in hides supplies and cattle. While working there he was homesteading on a ranch. Two years later he purchased the business and hired Jim Barnes as manager for his ranch. His interest in cattle increased and, in 1886, he moved to his ranch.

On a trip to Stockville, Nebraska, he met his wife and took her back to his Wyoming ranch. In 1900 they were visiting family in Stockville when a storm developed. My grandmother and her 9-year-old son took shelter in a cyclone cellar when my mother was born.

The men were all out in the fields so my Uncle Bob, the 9-year-old boy, assisted with the birth. Must have been quite the event. They had the Wyoming ranch until 1908 when the Homestead Act was passed, and people began to come west and settle. The Thomas family moved to Cheyenne and my grandfather became a banker, establishing the Citizens National Bank. In the

Citizens National Bank, built by C. S. Thomas. A 6-story building, it was the tallest building in Cheyenne.

1920s he sold the bank and invested in the stockyards in Memphis, which was a bad investment. He then purchased property in Cheyenne and became a landlord.

My mother's family lived at 408 East 25th Street. This was a large house and was in a better neighborhood. They also had a basement that was dirt-walled. You went down an old stairway made of logs and wood. Other than the furnace and water heater, nothing else was in that dirt basement. My grandmother would store her potatoes, vegetables and canned goods in an opening dug into the dirt on one side. I can remember my Grandfather Thomas. He was an elegant man with snowy white hair in a crew cut. He used to go fishing with my father and me. I remember him wearing a mosquito net over his head and face. We did not have sprays in those days and the mosquitoes could be very fierce. In the end I remember that he was confined to a bed where I last saw him. He died in 1945. My grandmother passed away in 1948. There is a family picture with all of us taken in front of their home on their 50th Wedding Anniversary. I was a young boy at the time.

My mother was the only daughter; however, she had a lot of brothers. My idol was my Uncle Lew. Uncle Bob ran the Rainbow Tourist Court which is now the Atlas Motel. I used to go

In front of the Rainbow Tourist Court in 1941. Front row, l to r: Mildred Thomas, Charlene Ries, Grace Ries, Meroa Thomas, Charles Thomas. Middle: Thomas Ries. Back: Eva Thomas, Francie Thomas, Lewis Thomas, Tony Ries, Griffith Thomas, George Thomas

there and play with my younger cousin, Johnny Thomas. We would go bird hunting with our BB guns. In those early days Cheyenne was much smaller than it is now, and there were big open fields behind the Rainbow Tourist Court. I remember Johnny having a pet alligator and I remember it growing to a large size. They finally had to get rid of it. Lew originally owned and operated the Rainbow Tourist Court but sold it to his brother Bob to finance a new venture, the Wyott Manufacturing Company.

The Wyott Company produced a cream dispenser that, upon lifting a handle on the front, would dispense the right amount of cream for a cup of coffee. He sold shares in this new venture and was able to build a factory across the street from the Rainbow Motel. His partner was Tommy Titus, and they named this new company "The Wyott Manufacturing Company." The Wyo stood for Wyoming and the two t's stood for Thomas and Titus. During WW II they won a contract to manufacture valves for US submarines. They won the Army Navy E award for their efforts. The factory ran three shifts on a 24-hour basis. With his cream dispenser and this government contract, Uncle Lew became very wealthy.

Snowy Range

Each summer my father would take a two-week vacation. We would pack everything in the car and drive to the Snowy Range for a two-week fishing vacation. We stayed at Plummer's Cottage Camp. The fishing in those days was excellent. We could catch 40 fish per person per day and were allowed to take home a two-day catch. That meant for our family of 4 we could have 320 fish to take back to Cheyenne. There were very few fishermen, and we had many good fishing places. North Brush, South Brush, and French creeks all had huge beaver dams. We walked to all of these, as access was limited.

In the evenings we would go for a walk. There was an old red bridge located on North Brush creek that we would go to as a destination. It was a 30-to-40-minute walk, each direction. This was the old highway route and was no longer used, so both a small bridge over a canal and the red bridge were in bad shape and could longer be used by a vehicle. Later, the bridge over the canal collapsed so we had to wade through the canal.

The various beaver dams would be named after a family member who would then be responsible for clearing away the brush and other branches to allow fishing on that pond. In those days we would catch a lot of 18-to-24-inch trout. There were not that many people fishing as it was difficult to travel on the gravel roads. The trip from Cheyenne to our cabin would take 18 to

Snowy Range fishing vacation, 1945. Front row: Tony Ries, Grace Ries, Tom Ries with Sparky. Back: Lew Thomas, Francie Thomas, Eva Thomas.

20 hours. Today, it can be done in 1 hour 20 minutes. The old cars were fully loaded and there would even be supplies on the running boards of the old cars.

My father helped build the first cabin in Plummer's Camp. It was number 4. There was no running water; we had to carry water from a hand pump. Garbage was thrown into a pit with a wooden cover on it and there were outdoor toilets. We heated the cabin with a wood stove, and we used kerosene lanterns for light. To catch the millers, we would place a kerosene lamp in a wash basin full of kerosene. The millers and moths would be attracted to the light and would fall into the kerosene and die. One day, one flew over the flame and his wings caught on fire. He fell into the kerosene and the pan caught on fire. My father grabbed the pan and ran for the door. He tripped just as he got to the door, luckily the flaming liquid went out of the door. We almost lost the cabin! In the morning it would be cold, and we would all stay under the heavy covers until my father started a fire and warmed the cabin. Uncle Lew and Aunt Eva also came to the mountains with us. They had a daughter, Francie, who was the same age as Charlene.

As a youngster I was always getting into mischief. I caught garter snakes and put them in a jar. I would wait until my sister went into the outdoor toilet and would release them along the path between the cabin and the toilet. She would scream as she was afraid of snakes. My father then had to accompany her to the toilet with a flashlight and wait outside for her. No one knew what I was doing, and it was only in 1999 that I confessed to her. Her reaction: "I always wondered why I was the only one to find snakes on that path." She forgave me.

One year, Uncle Lew pulled a trailer to the Snowy Range. I was allowed to bring my bicycle! As there were very few automobiles, they allowed me to ride my bicycle from the summit 8 miles down to where we stayed. What fun! It was all downhill and I was a speed demon! I would carry the bike up the hills and then ride down the dirt paths. That was a great summer that I have always remembered.

My mother had another brother, Griffith. He was a mail carrier in Cheyenne and during the war he joined the US Navy. He was assigned to submarines. One day they were hit by a depth charge in Tokyo Bay. They were down to the last of their oxygen supply when they were rescued. He did not talk about this, but I understand we were lucky to have him back.

There was another brother, George, who was very intelligent and earned a PhD at the Colorado School of Mines. He was living in St. Louis and had a high position with the Aluminum

June 1 - 1942.

50th Wedding Anniversary of Meroa and Charles Thomas. Back: Lew Thomas, Tony Ries, Francie Thomas, Robert Thomas. Middle row: Charlene Ries, George Thomas, Eva Thomas, Grace Ries, Mildred Thomas. Front: Charles & Meroa Thomas. Bottom front: Tom Ries, Laurabelle Thomas, Johnny Thomas.

Company of America. He was on his way home when he was killed in an automobile accident. Someone was running from the law in a dump truck and would sideswipe cars to avoid being caught. Unfortunately, he hit Uncle George head-on and killed him.

I never knew my Uncle John, but the story went that he, Lew, and Bob were out at Granite Lake fishing one day. John went to crawl under a barbed wire fence. His gun caught on the fence, went off and killed him. They had to carry the body a long distance back to the road and then had to inform my grandmother.

My grandmother Thomas had three other children. There were twins who died of food poisoning when they got sick on some bad milk when my grandparents were coming home from Cheyenne to their ranch. This was an all-day trip by horse and buggy. The ranch was located on Lodge pole creek just north of Burns, Wyoming. Another brother to my mother was Uncle Willy, who fell into a rain barrel one day at the ranch and drowned. I believe he was 3 years old at the time.

Early Jobs

As a young boy, my first job was selling Christmas trees on a vacant lot on Central Avenue. I do not know how old I was but I remember that I knew nothing about money. Someone would buy a tree and I would hold out my hand so they could make change. It worked well as I took in more money than the value of the trees I sold. I guess people felt sorry for this little kid. They were more honest in those days.

My next job was delivering newspapers. They were delivered to our house at 109 W. Pershing and then I would have to fold all of them and put them into big canvas bags which I would carry over my shoulders (one bag in front and another on my back), or over the handlebars of my bicycle when I delivered by bicycle. I would use the bike whenever possible, but when there was a lot of snow I had to walk. I can remember coming home with my feet almost frozen. I would take off my shoes and socks and place my feet on the furnace outlet on the dining room floor. There were times when they hurt from the cold. We did not have central heating and the house was heated by a coal-burning furnace that had a 3-foot square grate in the dining room. The dining room would be warm while other rooms would be cold.

Television was not

High School band

known, and we would listen to the radio in rapture. I remember the Lone Ranger, Red Skelton, Fibber McGee & Molly, etc. We would rush home to hear the next adventure. On Saturday afternoon I would need 25 cents to go to the movies. We would see the latest news, a cartoon, and always an adventure of Superman or some other hero that would leave you wondering how he would survive some action and leave you wanting to return the following Saturday. Usually, there was a double feature, so it was a long movie visit.

Later, when I was older, I would drive the panel truck and deliver newspapers to the young boys for them to deliver. In 1949, there was a bad snowstorm. I remember that I buried the truck in a snow drift, and I believe that was the end of that job. During that snowstorm, Cheyenne experienced snow drifts up to 35 feet deep. We had to exit our house via the second-story window as all of the doors and windows were blocked on the first floor.

When I was in the Johnson Junior High I would walk back and forth. This was about a 20-minute walk, and I would always pass through the Capitol Building. My Aunt Frieda was the secretary in the Secretary of State office, so I would stop and get warm on a cold day. In the winter, we walked no matter what the temperature. In those days they did not close for a snowstorm or bitter cold temperatures. Even when it was 20 degrees below zero, we would walk back and forth, sometimes in deep snow.

I joined the Junior High School band and played the baritone horn. One day I was asked if I would change to the tuba, and I said yes. That was the beginning of my musical career. In high school, I also learned how to play the string bass as that was required for the dance band. I played in the Cheyenne City Band and also the Eagles Lodge band.

I can remember the day that we received the news about my cousin, Grover Jr., being killed at Monte Cassino in Italy. I wanted to kill every German in the world, I was so mad. We all went over to the home of Uncle Grover and Aunt Ann. There was a lot of sadness and Aunt Ann hung a Gold Star in her front window. The effects of WWII were deep with all of us in Cheyenne, Wyoming on that day.

I always worked and held many various jobs while I was in school. After leaving the newspaper delivery business I worked as a janitor for the Spear Lumber company and for an insurance office. I helped Tony Scoolas make candy, I stocked shelves at Woolworths, I was a warehouseman for Asher Wyoming a wholesale grocery, and delivered freight for a local freight company to addresses in Cheyenne. When I was a senior in High School, I worked from 11 pm to 7 am for the Colorado & Southern Railroad, sorting, loading, and unloading mail for the trains. After the mail was done, I would check all of the empty box cars located along the C & S tracks and sidings. To do this, I drove a tractor that we used for handling the mail. This was a little risky at times, as there would be bums sleeping in the rail cars or young couples using them as a bedroom. More than once, I had to handle some unhappy people and some would make threats.

During my school years, I also earned money by playing

with local dance bands on the weekends. Because of all of these activities, I had little time for dating the local high school girls. I would play in the band while they were attending the high school proms and other social activities. I was nineteen before I had my first real date.

I remember the first time I played with a dance band. It was in a club on the Happy Jack Road where it intersected with the military highway. My fingers all had blisters on them and were bleeding. I was in a lot of pain and then I remember the club manager complaining that he could not hear the bass notes. I learned to place band-aides on my fingers before I developed strong skin that would withstand the pulling on the strings.

In 1949 Cheyenne had a major snowstorm. It snowed for 6 days, and there were snow drifts 30 feet high on Pershing Boulevard. There were people stuck in trains out in the countryside that could no longer move. We had to go out of the house via the second-story windows as both the front and back doors were covered by the snow. I walked from our house to the Dairy Gold Dairy that was located on 8th Avenue and came back with a sled full of milk, butter, and cheese that I gave to all of the neighbors who were snowed in. I was a hero, but I remember that it was a very cold exhausting walk. After the snow stopped it took over a week for the streets to be cleared and for traffic to flow again. Many cars could only be located by the tips of their radio antennas protruding out of the snow drifts.

Cheyenne had a population of 20,000 when I was born and had grown to 30,000 when I was in high school. I ran around with Jerry Daniels and Norbert Giltner. The big entertainment was to drive from the Owl Inn on the North side of Cheyenne to the Hitching Post on the West side. We would all honk at each other and flash our lights. These were both drive inns, and they would attach a tray on your car and serve hamburgers and soft drinks—all served by curb hops with whom we would flirt.

My father did a lot of work around our house. He built cabinets, finished off floors, walls, and ceilings. He also built a lot of cabinets and even constructed a garage. He was a good carpenter and taught me a lot. There was one room in the basement used as a workshop. There were no power tools in those days, so

I learned to use a crosscut saw and a fine-tooth saw. For drilling there was a brace and bit which was turned by hand. Simple tasks took longer and required very close precision when marking and processing materials. I learned a lot and spent some wonderful times with my father. Grandfather Thomas was also very skilled and taught me some skills.

I was fascinated with cars. I learned to drive in a 1936 Plymouth on a country road with my father as my instructor. Later I learned how to drive a truck from Butch Verplanke in a logging truck in the Snowy Range. My first car was a 1939 Buick. I owned 50 percent and my sister the other 50 percent. Then this car was sold and my sister bought a new Ford which I was allowed to drive. When she married and moved away, I bought a 1932 Buick that had 15,000 miles on it and was a beautiful car. I showed off and broke the gear box on a high center. I brought the car home, dug a grease pit in our garage, and prepared to fix it. I also decided to overhaul the engine and put in new rings on the pistons etc. I took the engine apart, tried to reassemble it, and the car never ran right again.

Later I had a 1941 Buick, put

on fender skirts, made a leopard skin dashboard, leopard seat covers, and had dual exhausts installed to make noise. I was the king of the road. My final car in Wyoming was a 1950 Buick, which I drove to Iowa and on the road as a musician and sold when I went overseas in the Air Force. In Germany, I bought a brand-new Volkswagen, and when I returned to the US, I bought a 1955 Ford convertible to which I added fender skirts and a fancy rear tire mount. After that, I settled down and drove normal cars.

I played in the Cheyenne City band. We would rehearse once a week. Jerry Daniels played the Baritone Horn and Jim Newman played trombone; I played the sousaphone. Afterward, the three of us would drive around. As stupid kids, we would race our automobiles. One evening we were on the highway west of Cheyenne and were going to race back to town. I was in a Buick and Jim had a Pontiac. We took off and he was faster and ahead of us. Jim had his girlfriend with him. Suddenly there was a loud bang, and sparks flew. Jim had hit another car. Jerry stayed with him, and I rushed to town for help. Then I had to go to Jim's house and get his father. There were injuries and that was the end of my racing career.

After I graduated from high school, I was appointed as the local manager for Burlington Freightways. At this time, I drove large 18-wheel semi and also made local deliveries with a smaller truck that would fit behind the downtown stores. After some time, I was informed that I could no longer drive their

Cheyenne City Band. Tom, center left, standing with sousaphone.

trucks as my eyesight was not acceptable. Then I loaded and hauled freight for Calhoun Transport.

In 1950, I became a freshman at the University of Wyoming. I majored in music and played in the University Band and Orchestra. In 1950, the University of Wyoming football team played in the Gator Bowl in Jacksonville, Florida. As a member of the band, I went to this game, the first time that U WYO was in a bowl game. We all went on a special train that went from Laramie to Florida and the band would get off and play at every stop along the way. The game was held on New Year's Day, January 1, 1951, and Wyoming won. This was my first real trip outside the state of Wyoming.

I was not a good student and was also working when I attended the University as a freshman. I was a bellhop at the Conner Hotel, which had side benefits. The city of Laramie was well known for its houses of loose ladies. Many military men would come to Laramie and stay at the Conner Hotel. As a bellhop, I had a good side business renting civilian clothes to the military (uniforms were not allowed in the local houses) and also supplying liquor after hours in the hotel. I also made money by playing with dance bands.

My next job was selling used cars. Although I had modest success, I did not enjoy this business. I then found a job at the Laramie Ice House. We would service the freight trains that came through Laramie. The freight cars carrying produce and other perishables had charcoal heaters at each end to keep things from freezing. Our job was to lift these out of their compartments and to put in new charcoal in the winter. In the summer, we would put 50 lb blocks of ice in the compartments to keep

Our first TV

things fresh. I went to work at 11 pm and left at 7 am. Many times, there were no trains so we would simply sleep. Of course, when you had a test the next day then there would be an endless string of trains to service. So much for study time!

For transportation I bought a 1934 Terraplane for $40 and

Alice Harrington Orchestra, 1949 (top), and Carl Vincent Trio, 1950

put used tires on it for $12 (4 times $3 at the junkyard). I had an accident and crumpled a rear fender, so I simply took both fenders off and drove it like a hot rod!

As I said before, I was not a good student so I decided I could earn more money by being a truck driver. I went back to Cheyenne and went to work for the North American Van Line agency, Burke Moving & Storage. I was able to purchase a string bass, so I also played with some local dance bands. I had an old sousaphone that I used when playing with the Cheyenne Municipal Band.

At this time, I was also a scoutmaster for a Boy Scout troop which met every Monday evening in the Methodist Church. In the summer of 1952, my troop was scheduled to go to the Boy Scout camp in Colorado. I informed the people at Burke that I needed to go with my troop. They said no, but I went anyway. I spent 10 days in Colorado with my troop. When I returned to Cheyenne, I found that I had been fired and no longer had a job with the moving company. Now all I had was playing a few gigs with some of the local bands.

Musician 1952-1964

Don Hoy Orchestra

So, what to do? In 1952 I checked a musician's magazine and found that Don Hoy and his Orchestra, based in Des Moines, Iowa, wanted a bass player. I called and got the job. This was the start of my career as a musician.

When I arrived in Des Moines, I found out that this was a part time job. We would play three to five nights a week and traveled all over the state of Iowa. So, I looked for another job. I found employment as a shoe salesman at Burts shoe store. They sold ladies shoes, and this was quite an experience. The women tended to totally ignore the shoe salesmen and would expose a lot when you were sitting on a low stool in front of them. One day a lady went into the stacks (where we keep all of the shoes) and was putting on a girdle to hold up her stockings when I went to get some shoes for another lady. I simply said excuse me, got

Don Hoy Orchestra, Des Moines, Iowa

the shoes I needed and returned to the sales area.

Strangely enough, another musician, Valentino Carrucci, also came to work at Burts selling shoes. We became friends and I wound up renting a room at his home. His musician's name was Val Carol. I remember that every Sunday they would have a big homemade Italian dinner—the food was delicious!

In the winter, Iowa had some terrible ice storms. I would have to take an ice pick and chip at the door to get into the car. Then I would start the car, turn on the heater and defrosters and go back inside to eat breakfast. Even doing this, there were times when I had to chip ice off of the windshield before I could drive to work!

Russ Carlyle Orchestra

In November 1952 I had the opportunity to join the Russ Carlyle Orchestra which was a name band. I drove to Memphis, where we played in the Peabody Hotel and then we drove to Milwaukee where we played in the Empire room of the Sheboygan Hotel.

It was during this engagement that I received a letter from

Russ Carlyle Orchestra, Sheboygan Hotel, Milwaukee, 1952

Uncle Sam telling me that I had been drafted and to report to the army in Denver for a physical. At this time, the Korean War was being fought, and they would send young men for 8 weeks of basic training before shipping them to the killing fields of Korea. Even though I couldn't read the eye chart without my glasses, they passed me and told me to report for duty in January.

Air Force Band

I was anxious about being in the infantry, so I went to Warren Air Force Base in Cheyenne and auditioned for the Air Force Band of the Great Plains. I passed the audition and was given a letter stating that I would be able to be assigned to this band if I joined the Air Force. This would require signing up for four years instead of only two if I were drafted into the army. I signed! So began my career as a bandsman in the United States Air Force. First, I went to Parks AF base in California for basic training and band school. I was then assigned to the band in Cheyenne and could live at home. During this period, I continued to play with local bands and spend time with my family.

In the spring of 1953, an opportunity came to go to Bolling Air Force Base in Washington DC and play with the USAF band under Cornel Howard. I had a 1950 Buick, and my mother was going to attend the Daughters of the American Revolution convention in Washington, so we drove together with another lady from Cheyenne to Washington. I had met a young lady, Mary Lee Williams, who I introduced to my mother. At our home in Cheyenne, there was a roll-top desk that my grandfather Thomas and I had restored. My mother has a large photograph of the DAR convention showing hundreds of women attending the convention. There in the middle of that picture sat the only male, Tom Ries in his Air Force uniform, and next to him was Mary Lee Williams!

One day I was ordered to the orderly room and was told that, since I was from Wyoming, I was to go to the dental clinic and sit in the dentist's chair. We were to receive Senator Lester C.

Hunt from Wyoming and I was the only person on base from Wyoming. Little did they know that my Aunt Frieda used to be his secretary, and that I knew him from my days at Johnson Junior High School. Senator Hunt arrived with the Base Commander and the officer in charge of the dental clinic. When they started to introduce me, Senator Hunt took my hand and said, "Hi Tom, nice to see you again! How is your aunt Frieda?" All of the officers looked on in silence as we chatted about family matters. They were impressed!

About three weeks later, I received an invitation to visit the White House and meet Mamie Eisenhower. My mother, in doing her genealogical work, had discovered that she was a cousin to Mamie via the Doud line. My mother then corresponded with Mamie and told her that I was stationed at Bolling AFB. Mamie had the courtesy of inviting me for tea on a Saturday morning. The band misbehaved on Friday, so we were all restricted to base that weekend. When a car and driver arrived to pick me up, he was told to get lost as I couldn't leave the base. Some phone calls were made, and I was ordered to go but to be back within two hours. There was one very upset Master Sergeant when I returned, but the story went around quickly. The following week an opening in the Air Force Band in Wiesbaden, Germany was offered. I applied and was quickly given that assignment. People wanted me out of Bolling, and this was their chance. I knew too many high-level individuals!

Airman Thomas Ries in Washington

I had always wanted to visit Europe, and this was my chance. I received the approval and was told that I would be going to Europe. I was thrilled. They first sent me to New York where I was able to stay in town for 2 days. Now I have seen the biggest city in the USA. WOW, this was a big adventure for a 20-year-old boy from Wyoming.

For my first trip to Europe, in April 1953 I boarded the USS General H. W. Butner, which was a troopship sailing from Brooklyn to Bremerhaven. The weather was cold, and the North Atlantic was rough. We had to be above deck from 7 am until 5 pm so the ship could be cleaned. There was a lot of seasickness, and there were barrels placed around the ship to catch the vomit. The stairs were slippery, and the smell was terrible. I found a place sitting on a grill that was over the kitchen. I smelled like food, but I was able to keep warm. The crossing took 11 days.

Upon arriving in Bremerhaven, I boarded a train which took me to Wiesbaden. There I was met by two Air policemen who transported me to the 686th Air Force band headquarters located at Camp Lindsey on the Schiersteinerstrasse. I reported and was issued my identification papers and was told I had the night off and to report at 8:00 the next morning. My first free night in a foreign country where I could legally drink beer. I was only 20 years old. I walked down the street, found a bratwurst stand, and enjoyed a brat and a beer before returning to camp.

The next day was my first rehearsal with the band, and I learned that we would be going to Morocco to play in a parade. Now I would see North Africa! WOW. We flew on a C-130 and landed in Casablanca. It was exciting to see the French and Arab sections. I took a picture of an Arab and wound up running through the market as he chased me screaming. I learned later that they did not want an image of them to be made on earth.

Another interesting fact is that this was the Morocco era

USS General H. W. Butner Troopship

Tom and his Alexander tuba

when the movie Casablanca, starring Humphrey Bogart was made. There was a French section, an Arab section, and a Spanish section. The country was full of bars, night nightclubs, and everything was available. This all changed when it became an Islamic nation. The next day we were bused to Rabat and played in a military parade. We then flew back to Wiesbaden.

The 686th Air Force Band was the leading US military band in Europe, and we were sought after for many events. We played for royalty in many countries such as Denmark and the Netherlands and represented the USA at international events in Europe. I played in the ceremonial marching band, the seventeen-piece big band orchestra, the 5-piece brass quintet, and the 5-piece dance band.

I also served as the mail clerk for our squadron and was the only one authorized to enter the mailroom. Omar Boggs and I were on call to handle phone calls where German was required. But my whole life centered around music. We were the leading Air Force Band in Europe and gave concerts to military troops and also played civilian concerts in many European countries. There were many excellent musicians in this band.

One of my first purchases was to buy my own tuba. The Alexander factory produced handmade instruments. I contacted Mr. Alexander, and we discussed what was available. He had a Kaiser tuba which had been used in the movie "Drei Mädels am Rhein." This instrument was unusual because it had a detachable bell, so it could be an upright bell or a bell front. It was a four-valve instrument with four rotary valves complete with three cases, one for the body and one for each of the two bells.

Tom in Casablanca

Perhaps a few words about the conditions in Germany in 1953 would help a reader to understand what I experienced. Germany was an occupied country and was being monitored by 4 nations. The British were in the north, the Russians were in the east, the French were in the west, and the USA was in the south. All of the major cities were in ruins and there was rubble everywhere. The airport in Frankfurt was made of plywood and the train station in Frankfurt was a bombed-out shell. In Mainz, you drove down city streets which had been bulldozed, and there was rubble standing 2 stories high on all sides. In Munich the city center was flat, and you could buy a bratwurst for 20 pfennigs at a makeshift bar. A beer cost 50 pfennigs.

The highways were still in bad shape and most of the bridges on the autobahns were gone, meaning there were numerous detours around the bombed areas. Horse-drawn wagons were being used to move materials, bicycles were used by many, and those that had some money were driving motor scooters. They had a Messerschmitt car which was one person behind another riding inside of what looked like the canopy of an airplane. Another small car opened in the front with two people sitting side by side. All of the Germans had to carry identification, and there were numerous checkpoints.

Two cities had escaped the destruction, Wiesbaden and Heidelberg. When the US occupied Germany, Heidelberg was the US Army headquarters and Wiesbaden was the US Air Force headquarters. I was stationed in Wiesbaden, first at Camp Lindsey and later at the Y80 Airbase, close to Wiesbaden in Erbenheim. The Bridge between Wiesbaden and Mainz had been destroyed, and the Patton pontoon bridge was still being used. Further south, Mannheim was in the American zone but Ludwigshafen was in the French zone. Germans had to have a special pass to move between the different zones. We had to wear uniforms and could move freely between the zones. In a nutshell, life was very difficult, and items were in short supply for the Germans.

Coffee and sugar were very precious items and in high demand. The military issued military script as a currency, and it was forbidden for Germans to possess script. In the PX cigarettes were $1.40 for a carton. The Germans would pay 50 cents a pack so there was a black market as German cigarettes were inferior at that time. One of the band members was living with a German girl who had several children. He developed a route in the local German area with repeat customers. He would travel this route on weekends, take orders, go to the PX store on base, buy things like flour, sugar, vegetables, meat, milk, etc., and then make deliveries the next weekend.

The band squadron moved from Camp Lindsey to the Y80 airbase in Wiesbaden. Here I took on various tasks. First, when there was a German phone call, either me or Omer Boggs would

Tom in Wiesbaden

be called to answer and translate. We also would make announcements in German when we were playing concerts for the German public. Second, I was assigned the duty of mailman. I was the only one allowed to have a key to the squadron mailroom and the only one authorized to pick up the mail at the base post office. Third, I went through driver training and drove the special bus which was modified for the band. It had 62 seats and a trailer for all of the instruments. When we were on tour, it was a challenge to navigate some of the streets in the German villages. I was the only one authorized to drive this special bus.

Over the next three and a half years we would perform at numerous military bases around Europe as well as at many goodwill concerts in civilian settings. We went as far north as Finland and as far south as Sicily at the toe of Italy. We made recordings in Switzerland and traveled often to Paris where our 5-piece combo played for dances and functions at the NATO headquarters. We played on the stage with movie stars such as Gina Lollobrigida, Sophia Loren, Ester Williams, Kim Novak, and Van Johnson. I was kissed on the cheek by Gina! I told her I would never wash that cheek again. She laughed!

We were billeted in the Powers Hotel, which was an officer's hotel, so we were close to the NATO headquarters. I was able to spend many weekends in Paris. We played in the Garden of the Tuileries and also in the

WW II damage in Frankfurt, Germany. Hauptwache, top, and the Markt.

Hotel George V, which was the number one hotel ballroom in Paris. I also had the pleasure of performing with Alain Romain who was a famous pianist playing in Paris. We played at most US airbases in France, the UK, Germany, Italy, and the Benelux countries. Usually, we flew in military aircraft, but we also traveled a lot by bus. The military buses were not very comfortable, and the planes would have metal seats and we had to wear parachutes. The heat came from the ceiling so your head would be warm, and your feet would be freezing from the cold floor.

On one of our trips, I met a young lady from Thailand. On my next trip, she said that she would meet me at the airport. She arrived in a chauffeur-driven limousine, and we drove into Paris. We were to have lunch at her uncle's house. He had a large apartment. There was a grand piano in the entranceway, and we dined at a very long table. Turns out he was the Thai ambassador to France. My mother and father met her when they visited Europe, and I was able to reconnect with her when I visited Bangkok with the ITT company.

In Germany, I had many great experiences. I got to know many German musicians and started playing with various German bands. Everyone thought I was a German when they saw me on the bandstand. I remember the orchestra of Josef Vogt, which was large. I believe there were 15 musicians in that band.

686 Air Force Band, Wiesbaden; Tom Ries playing the String Bass.

Meier Gustal Beer hall Mainz

Another person with whom I had a close relationship was Rudi Steiger who played the accordion. We would play in various bars and restaurants in the city of Wiesbaden. For Fasching I would play in Mainz at the Meier Gustl beer hall. These would be very late nights and we would end them at the Wiesbaden train station drinking "coffee royal"—coffee with Asbach!

With the USAFE band, we played concerts in the Kurpark behind the Kurhaus on many weekends. I would play the tuba with the band when marching and sometimes the string bass for the concerts. There were two other tuba players in the band. We also formed a brass quintet, 2 trumpets, a French horn, a trombone and tuba. With this group we were asked to play in many locations and were always well received. The musicians in the USAFE band were all highly qualified and gifted. We were the face of the Air Force in Europe and were well known. We made recordings with the Swiss Radio network and played for royalty in many countries. I remember playing for the Queen of Denmark when we performed in Copenhagen.

Once I was booked to play with a trio at the Officers club for a lady's lunch. I told the band that I needed to take my bass into town for a repair. I was given permission to leave the base. Under my fatigues I had a business suit to play in. When playing at the club the wife of the officer in charge of our squadron sat next to the orchestra. She assumed that I was a local German musician and didn't recognize me! Whew, that was a close call. I reported back to the band after we played.

Family Visit

In 1956 my mother and father came to Europe to visit me. They sailed on the Maasdam, and I met them in Rotterdam. I had purchased a new Volkswagen for $795 in 1954, but since my parents wanted to tour, I traded that for a 1954 Buick so we would have more room. We visited the Netherlands, Belgium, and France when they arrived. I found them a hotel in Wiesbaden, and they were able to attend many concerts and other functions where I would play.

My mother had researched my father's family history, so we drove to the Tauber valley where we met the family of Ernst Lang who owned and operated The Klosterhof, a small hotel and restaurant in Bronnbach on the Tauber River. Ernst spoke English and had lived in the US for some time. We stayed that night in Gamburg, which was where my grandfather was born. The Klosterhof was undergoing some restoration, so Ernst arranged rooms for us in Gamburg at the Gruener Baum. We were able to visit the graveyard where my mother found some ancestors that were buried there, and we visited the local church where we were able to view the church records. Some of the pages were so brittle that it was necessary to back them with paper sheets before they could be turned. My mother was able to find a lot of

Jo Vogt Orchestra, Hanau

information. I didn't understand all of this at the time but after my parents returned to the US, I could go to Bronnbach, stay overnight for nothing, and drink beer and eat food at no charge. Paradise for a young man.

We made one big trip while they were there, to Venice in Italy. We drove through the Alps and stayed overnight in Como, Italy. In the morning, we were served coffee and my father looked at his cup and said, "this cup is dirty!" It was espresso and you had to add hot milk. We all laughed about that experience. We then started for Venice. Along the way we had car trouble. This was close to the Largo Garda, and we found a repair shop. There we met an Italian Army Colonel and were invited to his home, which was located on the Lake. We spent two days with him and his family while the car was being repaired. My mother corresponded with that family for several years. (Her report of this trip is included in the Appendix.)

After my parents sailed back to America, I had only a few months left in my tour of duty before I could go back to the USA. I was due to be discharged in early February 1957 but was told that I would be returned early so I could be discharged and home for Christmas. Unfortunately, this did not happen. In 1956 there was an uprising in Czechoslovakia against the Russian occupation and as a result we were all ordered to remain on base. All early releases were cancelled and there was a shortage of military transport as everything was being used to transport refugees. So, I was not discharged until January of 1957.

Return to USA

Before coming to Europe, and when I was stationed at Bolling AFB in Washington DC I met a young lady, Mary Lee Williams. I was 20 at the time and felt that I had met the lady of my life. During the time I was stationed in Germany, we corresponded regularly. This also kept me from becoming involved with a lady in Germany. I did have one girlfriend, Erica Heinrichs, who lived in Wiesbaden. We dated, but I never allowed it to become serious. As a result, when I was discharged, in January 1957, instead of going back to Wyoming, I used Marylee's address in Takoma Park, Maryland as the address to have my belongings shipped to by the Air Force.

I rented a room on 14th Street NW and began looking for a job. I checked help wanted ads and found a position as the manager of a Moving and Storage Company in Silver Springs, Maryland. I purchased a 1955 Ford convertible and went to work. The company, Bayne & Scates, had 4 moving vans but only one full-time driver. Located on the District line was a field where workers gathered to find work. Those who worked on moving vans would be in a special location. As I knew how many moves were planned for that day, I would hire enough personnel to meet my needs. Transportation was limited so I would arrive at the office with workers piled on each other in my convertible. I would assign them to the trucks and send them to their moves.

These were exciting times as I was in charge of everything. booking moves, scheduling the trucks and men, answering the phone, having to address problems. On one occasion I received a call that there was a problem with one of the moves. A couple was going through a divorce, and they were arguing about who got what. My workers would carry something out and the husband would take it back in. At one point he said, "ok everything is 50-50" and he broke a coffee table into two pieces, saying, "There is your half, this is mine."

We also worked for the Montgomery County Sheriff. When they had to seize property, they would call us to come and pick it up. They called one day with a jewelry store. We packed everything and loaded up six display cases and a safe. The Sheriff held an auction at our warehouse. Anything someone bought had to be removed immediately. The sale went well until only the safe and display cases were left. Someone bought the safe, we had to use a forklift to put it in the trunk of his car. He left with the 2 front wheels barely touching the ground. As they had to be removed, I bought the display cases for $3 per case as I could legally keep them in my warehouse. I later sold them for $120.

One morning I was sitting at my desk when I heard a large crashing sound and I saw bricks fly by my window. A worker had been putting steel beams on the walls of a new warehouse next door but had forgotten to lower the derrick on his truck when exiting the new building. When he drove through the door this caught the front of the building which caused the bricks to fall as did many of the steel beams he had installed. It was a big mess. His boss arrived but didn't fire him. He said, "we all make mistakes."

I was happy with my job and Mary Lee, and I were able to date and to get to know each other. It soon became apparent that this was not the woman for me and our relationship soured. I decided that I would be happier playing music again. I contacted Orchestra Inc. in Chicago and found that I would be able to re-join the Russ Carlyle Orchestra. I gave notice to Bayne & Scates, shipped my tuba and belongings to Wyoming, and drove to where Russ was playing with my string bass in the 1955 Ford Convertible I had purchased when dating Mary Lee.

Russ had a series of one-night stands in the Midwest and then enjoyed a two-week engagement at the Roosevelt Hotel in New Orleans. During these two weeks, I explored New Orleans and was fortunate to meet many musicians who were popular at that time. I sat in and played with Al Hirt and Tony Almerico. My best friend was Jack Delaney who played trombone with Pete Fountain.

Playing in the Blue Room of the Roosevelt Hotel allowed me to have many wonderful experiences, The programs featured Dick Shawn, who was a movie star, Gali Gali, a well-known magician, and Walton and O'Rourke, who were respected puppeteers. Every night would feature these acts, I even learned how some of the magic tricks were accomplished. During the day and at night after we finished, I would explore the French Quarter and listen to live music. A real wonderland for a kid from Wyoming.

One night one of the waiters invited me to go crabbing with him. We left New Orleans early in the morning and drove to his camp on the bank of a Bayou. He had a stack of rotten chicken necks we were to use as bait, we went out in a small boat and were ready to go crabbing. It was still dark. One would take a rotten chicken neck, tie it onto a string, and lower it into the water. You feel the crab grab the neck and slowly raise it towards the surface. We had a fishing net to catch the crab in when it was close to the surface. If you broke the water the crab would let go and drop back toward the river bottom. We caught a lot of crabs and when it was getting daylight we went back to camp. A large pot of boiling water was waiting, and the crabs were dropped in the pot. There was melted butter waiting and when the crabs were done, we began to eat. What an experience and a wonderful feast.

1958 Mexico Trip With My Parents

That fall I returned to Wyoming and resumed my studies at the University of Wyoming. In the spring of 1958, I decided to drive to New Orleans via Mexico. I discussed this with my parents, and they decided that they would go with me, and we could explore Mexico together. None of us had been to Mexico before, so we decided to enter Mexico at Ciudad Juarez, visit Chihuahua, find a hotel in Torreon, and then go to Brownsville, Texas. Driving my Ford convertible that I had purchased in Washington DC. We drove south on Highway 87 (there were no interstates) and entered Mexico at Juarez. We were required to purchase Mexican insurance and get a permit to drive the car in Mexico.

Tony Ries in Mexico in 1955 with my Ford Convertible

While growing up we had always spent our holiday in the Snowy Range fishing. Then, when I was in Germany my parents came to visit me there. Now we had the opportunity to explore something new as a family unit. We saw a lot of interesting sights, people living under conditions that we had never before seen. We saw donkeys pulling wagons, and people walking barefooted in dirty ragged clothes. We had our first experience visiting a toilet with only a small hole and no toilet paper available. No way to flush or wash away what you had deposited.

My father was a member of the Lions Club, and he was thrilled to find that there was a Lions Club in Mexico. He asked to have his picture taken with the sign so he could show it when he was back in Cheyenne. There were always children asking for money along the way. There was light traffic on the highways in Mexico. We experienced good weather during our entire visit.

On several occasions, however, there were flash floods on the road. The locals would string a rope or cable from each side of the flooded section of the road. They would then ask for money to go with you, holding onto the rope and cable and your car to keep it from being swept away. This happened twice. We found a hotel in Torreon and looked for a nice restaurant, which was difficult. After dinner, we took a short walk and then went to bed. The next morning, we had a small breakfast and got ready to drive to Monterrey. I was low on film for my camera, so I found a photo shop that sold film. A young girl sold me the film and we exchanged addresses.

I had always wanted to learn Spanish so I thought it would be nice to correspond with someone in Spanish. I would write to her in English, and she would write in Spanish. I had a small dictionary for translation and would sometimes find a Spanish-speaking person to help me. It was something to do as we had a lot of free time during the day. She sent me a picture, in which I saw a beautiful woman. I had

Tony Ries in Mexico with Lions Club sign

only seen her for a few minutes when I bought the film in Torreon. Now I had a beautiful, intelligent woman writing to me.

We continued seeing more sights and taking pictures. We stopped in Monterrey for lunch and drove east towards the USA. Then we had to make several stops along the way to let my father relieve himself on the side of the road. Montezuma's revenge had caught up to him. Terrible stomach pains. Luckily neither I nor my mother had a problem so we could help him. We crossed the border at Brownsville, Texas so we could find some medicine to help him.

We spent the night in Brownsville so my father could rest and recover. The next day, we drove to Houston and spent the night there. The following day we drove to New Orleans. My parents spent a few days there and, when they were feeling better, they returned to Wyoming.

I began looking for a job as a musician, but nothing was available. I ran short of money and wound up sleeping in Jackson Square and living on one birch beer and a White Castle burger per day. I finally found a job as a busboy at Klop's German restaurant as I could speak German. I had to work 12 hours a day at 11 cents an hour. In New Orleans, I had hopes of joining the Tony Almerico band which specialized in Dixieland music and played on Bourbon Street. During this period I also had the opportunity to join the Al Hirt Orchestra and played some gigs with Pete Fountain. Jack Delaney who was a well-known trombone player and I became good friends, and he introduced me to the community of musicians.

Don Glasser Orchestra

Nothing developed in New Orleans, so I joined the Don Glasser Orchestra based in Chicago. We played many one-nighters. One day, I was in the train station in Chicago with Bill Schneider, a saxophone player. We were having a beer when a man came up behind us and said, "You sound like musicians."

We turned and found ourselves talking to Nat King Cole. We sat together and enjoyed a few beers together. Bill took a later train!

Another incident featured Bill. He was nicknamed Oggie. He was skinny and had a long nose. We had just finished playing a two-week location gig in Muncie, Indiana, and were headed to our next gig which was in northern Michigan.

Muncie had been warm, and Bill was wearing a T-shirt and shorts. He went to sleep in the back seat. As we drove north, the weather changed and, in Michigan, we encountered snow. About 7:00 in the morning, we stopped to have breakfast. The restaurant was full of lumberjacks in their winter clothes and boots going to work. We had put on coats when we entered. Bill woke up and with sleepy eyes came walking into the restaurant with his shorts and skinny legs. You can only imagine the reaction of the lumberjacks! There were some funny comments made, and Bill turned a bright red. He fled back to the car, never to be seen again in that restaurant. We all had a big laugh over this incident.

In the fall of 1958, I returned to Wyoming to continue my studies. I had been corresponding with Carmen, and she sent me a picture of herself where she was very glamorous. At one point she wrote that she had moved to California and had sent out wedding announcements. Since she had announced that we were to be married, I felt obligated, and my mother and I drove to California where I married Carmen in December 1958.

Don Glasser Orchestra, Virginia Beach

First Marriage

Upon returning to Wyoming, we first lived in the upstairs area of my parents' house in Cheyenne. We then found a basement apartment at 1910 ½ Thornburgh in Laramie. I resumed my studies at the University of Wyoming, played music, and worked for Cowboy Moving & Storage moving furniture. On February 2nd, 1959, I received a phone call that my father had been entered into the hospital but that I did not need to worry or come to Cheyenne. I was scheduled to deliver a load of furniture in Cheyenne the next day, so I agreed to wait and to see him on Monday.

We arrived in Cheyenne on the morning of February 3rd and began to unload the furniture. We took a break at noon for lunch, so I went to the hospital and had a nice visit with my father. The nurse came in and asked me to leave as he had to go on a bedpan. I went back to work but received a phone call at 1:30 advising me that when my father attempted to rise onto the bedpan a blood clot had been released, entered his brain, and that he had an in-

Carmen Silva de Arellano Ries

stant death. This was a shock to all of us but, in retrospect, it was a blessing for my father. He never realized what had happened and went peacefully.

During the rest of the spring semester, I continued to pursue my studies at the University of Wyoming. To finance my studies, I worked as a helper on moving vans and played music in the evenings. I also received a small check under the GI bill which was designed to assist veterans to better their education.

Christiani Brothers Circus

During the springtime of 1959, the Cristiani Brother Circus appeared in Laramie, and I made friends with the band. When school was out, I continued to work at Cowboy Moving & Storage. I then received a phone call from Ramon Escorcia, the bandleader of the Cristiani Brothers Circus band, asking me to join the circus band playing tuba. I agreed and left for California to join the circus band. We would normally play an afternoon performance and many times again for an evening performance. Sometimes there would be a parade, and then we would ride on a circus vehicle. All of the other band members had extensive experience playing in the circus. They had all played in the Big Top of the Barnum & Baileys three-ring circus. Two trumpets, a baritone horn, trombone, drums, and the tuba. They were

Ralph - trombone. Tom - tuba, Steve - baritone horn. Ramon – bandleader, trumpet. Joe - trumpet, Max - drums

excellent musicians!

It was interesting to travel with a circus. Once, in California, I needed to use the restroom when waking up in the morning. Normally we used the circus restrooms, located in a trailer that was also used to transport our Llamas, so it would have to be cleaned before use. However, we were required to use chemical toilets in California, so that is where I went. As I was doing my business, I heard a little clank but ignored it, as that was usual in setting up the circus. Suddenly, the chemical toilet began to move. I attempted to stand up, but with my pants around my ankles and the bouncing of the toilet, I did not succeed. When the unit finally stopped, I emerged to discover that the chemical toilet had been delivered where the freeway was to be set up and that my toilet had been moved by an elephant. How many people can say they have had a ride in a portable toilet?

The circus would move from place to place. In small towns we would be there for one day. In larger cities such as Los Angeles we would stay for a few days. It was interesting how the circus would move. This was a three-ring circus, so there was a lot to move. After our performance, the tent would be lowered onto the ground and folded into two sections. There were two trucks with spools on them. The two sections would be reeled onto these trucks, which moved the big top. The rest of the equipment—the bleachers, the poles for the tent, and everything needed for a performance, would be transported on trucks, trailers, and other vehicles. The band had a panel truck for the instruments, which also pulled a trailer in which we all slept. I drove this truck.

There was an arrow man who would go ahead and place arrows on light poles or

Elephants being unloaded in New Orleans

other surfaces. These were large arrows. One arrow straight up meant straight ahead. Two arrows pointing down meant slow down, turn ahead. Then there would be two arrows pointing either left or right so we would know where to go. All vehicles would follow these arrows except the one transporting the giraffes, which was too tall to pass through underpasses and telephone lines. He would have to take a special route.

Upon arriving at the next site, everyone with the circus would work to erect the big top, construct the entranceway, and create an animal section for viewing by the public. To raise the tent, which was a very heavy canvas tent, the elephants would be used. The supporting poles would be placed and then the elephants would be used with pullies to raise the tent. The canteen where we all ate would be erected. There was a semi-truck that carried a huge generator that supplied lights for the big top, the midway, and the trailers where everyone lived and slept. The band trailer had six bunk beds and lockers for clothes.

Luckily, the band did not have to work setting up and tearing down the big top because of the musician's union, which protected us from this hard manual labor. All of the performers had to help with the moves.

The band would be located on an 8-foot-high platform built

Ticket office and midway of the circus

under the big top between the entrance and exit of the performers and animals. One day, an elephant came too close, and the platform collapsed. I managed to hold on to my tuba so there was no damage but that was an exciting moment!

Another day, after performing, the circus was on the move to the next location in Texas. The circus had not paid enough to the local sheriff, so all of the vehicles were being stopped for a violation—dirty license plates, burned-out light bulbs, making a wrong turn, etc. Anything to stop the vehicle. The drivers were all arrested and put in the county jail. As I was driving the band's panel truck I was also arrested. The circus came in, paid a fine and we were all free to go. But we refused to leave immediately. The jail had a warm shower and we all wanted to take a shower! This was a luxury for all of us, as we were used to cold water at best.

The circus had no showers and we all had to do our best to keep clean. I used to shave outside our trailer with a pan full of cold water, using the bottom of a tin can for a mirror. We all ate in a central canteen which had wooden tables and benches. One

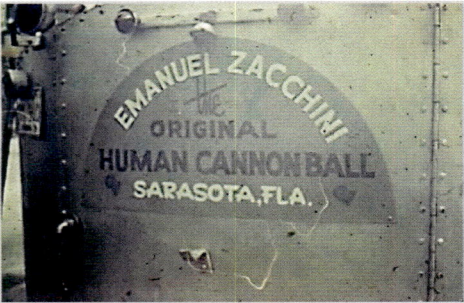

Gun used by the Human Cannonball

day in Texas the hippopotamus died, and the circus paid a farmer to dig a hole on his property and bury the animal. We all swore that we were eating hippo meat for the next week! The clowns were gay, and their trailer used to rock and roll at night!

There were many acts: trapeze artists, a man who would hang by his heels from a high wire, elephants, horses, and the human cannonball, who would be shot out of a cannon and land in a net.

There was always a big bang when the cannon was fired. One day, the big bang failed and there was a whoosh sound as he flew through the air. There was a big spring inside the cannon that would send him flying but, on this day, the big bang failed. The secret was out!

We had a young man who would clean the droppings of the animals using a shovel and a wheelbarrow. He wanted to be a performer, so he would wear a World War I pilot's helmet, sit, and be picked up by an elephant in his mouth and carried around the ring. Then he would go back to his shovel and wheelbarrow.

Carmen wanted to come and join me, so I bought a small car, and we began to travel together. It was very small, a Crosley, so I fixed the passenger seat to fold down, and we could sleep on a mattress with our feet in the trunk. We traveled from California through the southern portion of the US and finished in Tampa, Florida. We then returned to Laramie, and I continued my studies at the University of Wyoming. I played music and worked as a helper and driver for Cowboy Moving and Storage. Working full time and studying kept me very busy.

We rented a small house in the rear of 1417 Kearney. In the fall of 1959, my GI check that I received for education was late and I had to pay my tuition, so I borrowed $100 from The Family Finance. The check arrived a few days later so I went to The Family Finance and settled my debt. In a conversation with the manager, Mr. D.B Holder, we discussed debt collection. I told him I had collected some debts when I was working in Washington D.C. He said, "here are some debts. Would you like to try collecting them?" The first one was a colored man living in the rear of Myrtle's Fried Chicken on First Street. I told him I was there to collect the debt and he handed me $50.00. I didn't have a receipt book, so I used a page of my notebook and wrote him a receipt. I tried another without success. Upon returning to Family Finance Mr. Holder was very surprised, he paid me $16.00 and said it was normal to pay a third of what was collected. He then told me that he had received a phone call from the Laramie Credit Bureau who told him that I had collected money owed to them.

Rocky Mountain Accounting Company

Upon reflection, I thought this was a good way to earn money so I went to the Laramie Credit Bureau, identified myself, and said I would like to work for them. As a result, I was met with some very strong words and told to leave. This made me mad, so I decided what would be necessary was to collect debts on my own. I discovered that I would need to obtain a license from the Secretary of State in Cheyenne. I went to Cheyenne and applied. I needed a $2,000 bond, and my Uncle Lew put this up for me. I returned to Laramie, rented an office at 100 Grand Avenue, and opened the Rocky Mountain Accounting Co. I chose this name thinking that people were accountable for their debts. This brought in revenues, and I was successful in obtaining a lot of customers who were not happy with the service they were receiving from the Laramie Credit Bureau. I had two employees, a secretary who ran the office, and a young man who helped chase debtors and collect debts.

I received a summons to appear in court. A complaint had been filed by Ed Stone, the owner of the Laramie Credit Bureau. He told the court that I was scamming the people of Laramie, and I should be put in jail for operating an illegal collection agency without having a proper license. The judge asked me what I had to say and I replied, "I don't understand what he is talking about, your honor, here is a copy of my license". The case was dismissed, and all charges were dropped. I intended to operate in more locations, which is why I had chosen the name, Rocky Mountain.

I worked hard to build my collection agency. I visited companies doing business in Laramie. I arranged with a local attorney to handle legal issues. I opened an office and hired a secretary, so we were open full time. The credit agency would collect money and hold on to it for a long time. I instigated a system where I told everyone that all monies collected in a month would be remitted on the 10th of the following month. This allowed me to build cash flow. At first, there were objections from the community, but as soon as the checks started to be remitted on the 10th the businesspeople were happy. They could now rely on me and knew that they didn't have to chase me for their money as was the case with the credit bureau. Business grew, and I opened a second office in Rawlins.

My first daughter, Grace, was born in January of 1960, and I continued my studies, running my collection agency, and playing music. Occasionally I would work part-time for Cowboy Moving and Storage. With my other jobs beginning to cover expenses, I concentrated on building my business and earning my degree at the University.

Our family grew. We adopted a Beagle dog we named Mike and a Siamese cat we named Gigi. They fought at first so in the car Gigi would ride in front and Mike would be in the back. One day I said, "Where's Gigi?" We stopped and looked in the rear seat. Gigi was curled up sleeping on Mike's chest. From that day on they were the best of friends.

When Carmen was pregnant again, we bought a house at 1217 Sanders, and we now had our own home with a garage and a yard. Debbie joined us in June of 1961 and life continued forward. I joined a poker club that met every Monday evening and included many local business owners. This helped my standing in the local community and gave me very good contacts with other businesspeople. I felt this was important to build a solid business reputation. This was a friendly game, and we would rotate to various members houses for our games. This gave me some excellent contacts in the community and allowed me to have more business collections from word of mouth.

Grace, Debbie, and Carmen in El Paso

To my surprise, one day Carmen informed me that she was now working in a laundry service. This was not good for my business image, but she refused to understand and said she wanted to do this as she was making friends and was happy there. This did cause some problems with my business image.

Life continued and we were living with a nice home, a nice garden, two wonderful daughters with a Beagle dog and a Siamese cat. We had two cars, a Pontiac and a Willys 4-wheel drive Jeep pickup to use for fishing in the mountains. We would go to Cheyenne to visit relatives, go to the mountains, and I would drive to Rawlins to watch over my collection agency office there. I worked hard on my studies and was looking forward to being able to devote more time to the collection agency when I had completed my studies. We were able to make several trips to Mexico and visit Carmen's family when we were living in Laramie. I felt that we would have a good future.

I received my bachelor's degree in January 1961, and I continued building and running my collection agency. I also played music with several orchestras in both Laramie and Cheyenne. Everything looked good, except the situation at home went off the track. Carmen was insisting that her Godmother should move from Mexico and live with us permanently. I said that she was welcome to come and visit but that I did not want her as a permanent resident in our house. An ultimatum was given by Carmen that either her godmother would come to Laramie and move in with us or she would go to Gomez Palacio and live with her Godmother. I replied if that is what you want, I will drive you to Mexico. Carmen took my children away from me and went to live in Mexico. She never asked to come back.

1217 Sanders, Laramie, Wyoming

Upon returning to Laramie divorce proceedings were filed, I put our house at 1217 Sanders up for sale and I sold my collection agency. During this period, I moved to Woodslanding and lived with my Uncle

Lew who was building a third cabin. This was a pleasant time. It allowed me to put the devastating divorce trauma and loss of my children behind me, and to finalize my affairs in Laramie. I sold our house and also the business I had worked so hard to build. The Rocky Mountain Accounting company was sold to Mr. Bud Clark, who then built it into the Laramie Credit Bureau.

Musician Again

In 1962 Don Glasser contacted me and asked me to come and play with his orchestra. This meant I could go back to what I loved and remake my life. It took a long time to recover from what had happened. So I joined the Don Glasser Orchestra based in Chicago, and started traveling again, playing one-nighters and locations in Chicago, Memphis, Virginia Beach, and New York.

Traveling with Don was an adventure. He had a panel truck which Don, Lois Costello, suitcases, music stands, all the music, instruments, and I used for transportation. There was an easy chair behind the driver's seat in which one person would sleep while another would drive. Don and I would change driving so we could cover long distances between our gigs.

One night we were driving in Illinois when there were a large number of sparks on the highway in front of our van. We stopped to find that there had been an accident. One car was heavily damaged and was on its side. I went to this car to find a young lady on her side, with her foot caught in the foot pedals. One foot was only being held by some skin, as the bones were separated. She said, "My foot hurts." I replied there is a bad cut, but you will be OK. She relaxed and then the emergency services arrived, so we left. I had flashbacks for several months.

When we played at the Roseland in New York City, Don and Lois would always stay in the Bryant Hotel. The rest of us would have to find our own accommodation. I remember one trip when I found a cheap room close to Roseland. There were no curtains on the window, and all the room had was a metal frame bed. The place was full of cockroaches. I put the 4 legs of the bed in coffee cans filled with kerosene to keep them out of the bed. I slept with the light on to keep them off the floor.

As we were always short of money, we saved whenever possible. One trick was to "make the day sheet" in the hotels. In those days, the small hotels would start the day's business at 6:00, 7:00, or 8:00 in the morning. We would play until late, pack up the instruments, and drive to our next location, usually stopping to eat along the way. We would arrive in the next town, where we would be playing that night, and look for a hotel. We would ask the clerk what time he would start that day's sheet? If he said 8 am and it was 7 we would wait until the sheet was started that day. Check in and go to bed. That night we would play and then return to the same hotel and sleep. You slept twice and only paid for one night! Then we would get up and drive to the next location.

We were playing in Ogallala, Nebraska, when the club manager said that I was going to receive a phone call during our next intermission. I had no idea who would be calling and feared that something bad had happened. During intermission, the call was received, and, to my surprise, it was from Clyde McCoy, who asked me to come to Texas and join his band. Clyde was a name band, having achieved fame with his rendition of "Sugar Blues," which was his theme song. I gave my notice to Don Glasser and joined Clyde at the "Six Flags over Texas" for a 2-week location. Then we began a series of one-night stands.

Clyde McCoy Orchestra

While the previous bands I played with all carried written music (called charts), the Clyde McCoy band had no music. We played everything by ear. In other words, the melody line would be established, and everyone would make up their versions. Turns would be taken as the lead instrument and the others would join in and give support. All of the musicians playing with

Clyde were very gifted and talented. I enjoyed playing with these excellent players. The band was highly rated, and we played in some prestigious locations. The Peabody Hotel in Memphis, the Dunes in Las Vegas, the Riverside Hotel in Reno, The Club in Atlanta, Marando's in Milan, Illinois, and many others from coast to coast. I joined Clyde in 1962 and played with this orchestra until 1964.

The Clyde McCoy band I joined was billed as a Dixieland band. We played a lot of famous Dixieland tunes, and also played a lot of dance music, as many of our gigs would be in clubs where people danced. When we appeared in Las Vegas, Reno, and the Six Flags in Texas we were more of a show band. We would feature each of the instruments separately with special numbers. We had one number where a banjo and the tuba would duel with each other.

Clyde played the trumpet and was the band leader. Ed Reed played the clarinet and was an excellent musician. Ed had also made many recordings with his own band which was billed as "The Riverboat Five". The trombone player, Hans Kunzel, was from Ohio and was married to Judy. She traveled with him, as did their daughter, Penny. While driving between gigs Hans would practice. He had arranged a mouthpiece and valve set to be connected to a bell under his seat by a rubber tube. He could then practice as he was driving. He had a beautiful tone when he played; everyone was taken by the velvet sound he made.

Our piano player, Jim Maihack, was very versatile. He could play numerous instruments and was very gifted. He would play the banjo on some numbers and was the banjo player during the tuba/banjo duel. I did not see Jim for more than 50 years but was able to meet him again at his home in Sacramento, California. He still plays and performs at many jazz festivals. He gave me a recording, "Never Mind I'll Do It Myself," where he plays all of the instruments on the track.

The drums were played by Marvin Cox. He had a set of drums called "Flat Jacks," which only had one head. He was featured in all of the company's advertisements. As a drummer, Marvin was one of the best I have ever been privileged to play with! It is difficult to put into words what he could do with a set of drums. I have never seen anyone who was faster with his hands and who was so skilled in using the various tools available to a drummer. Everyone was astonished when he played a drum solo, myself included.

We would play a lot of one-night stands as we traveled around the country. We would also play some location gigs where we would play for two weeks at a single location. In Nevada, we would appear at the Dunes in Las Vegas and the Riverside Hotel in Reno. One night, we were in the Riverside Hotel playing opposite Charles Gould and his Satin Strings. We finished our set and in strolled the Charles Gould musicians. I looked and saw Al Ebat playing the violin. He was my roommate in Wiesbaden, Germany when we were with the 686th Air Force Band. He played drums in the Air Force, and here he was playing a violin. It is a small world. Our trombone player, Hans Kuenzel left and was replaced by Andy Figliolino from Denver.

I always tried to see my parents whenever possible when traveling. On one occasion, Andy was going to spend a day in Denver, and I was going to go to Cheyenne. About 1 am we were on a highway in northern Kansas when I said to Andy, "I think there is a fire burning over there." We turned onto a small road

Jim Maihack, piano, Ed Reed, clarinet, Clyde McCoy, trumpet, Hans Kunzel, trombone, Tom Ries, tuba, Marvin Cox, drums. Six Flags over Texas, 1962.

and headed towards the fire. We entered a small town and there was a bar. We stopped and asked the bartender if he had called the fire department as there was a house on fire. He was surprised and said he would make a call, and I said we would go to the house.

It was a two-story structure in the front, and one story in the back. We broke open a door and entered the back portion which contained the kitchen. We began removing tables and other items. I decided to check the front portion and went upstairs to check the bedrooms. I didn't see anyone, so I went back down to help remove furniture. People began arriving and one asked if the lady was OK. I said that no one was home, and he said that her car was there. I went back upstairs and broke open a locked door. There she was passed out on her bed in her panties and bra. I said, "Lady, wake up, your house is on fire!" She responded, "Save my fur coat!" I grabbed her coat, put it around her, and carried her downstairs. She was drunk.

I went back upstairs to save what was possible as the fire was getting bigger. In the bedroom, I emptied the dresser drawers onto the bed and made a bundle like Santa Claus. Returning to the stairway I found it on fire. I went into the front bedroom, threw the bundle out the window, threw out the mattress, and jumped onto the mattress. By this time there were a lot of people, so we left.

A few months later we were again in the area, so we stopped to get gas in this little town. The attendant said, "aren't you the guys that were here the night of the fire?" I said yes, and he said, "you were lucky, because just after you left the house exploded." There was a gas explosion. Later, I received a letter from the lady thanking me for saving her life and her fur coat.

Between jobs, we would travel together in three cars, sometimes four, depending on if Ed Reed would bring his wife. She was a schoolteacher and would join us when free. Marvin created a fictional character, "Pete Griffin," who was huge. He would use a telephone pole for a toothpick and step over a five-story building. We would make up funny stories about Pete and would envision him doing crazy things like removing a traffic jam so we could proceed or blowing out a raging forest fire with one breath. We had a lot of laughs with some of the ridiculous stories we made up about Pete. Marvin came up with some great comments. Driving through a depressed area, he would say, "I see every kind of empty can, except a paint can," or, "this city is so deserted you could fire a cannon down the main street and not hit a soul." Marvin's sense of humor helped stem the boredom while driving long stretches. It might be interesting to note that this period was before the interstate system was built. Most of our driving was on two-lane roads which went through a lot of small towns. In the fall of 1964, I left the McCoy band in Memphis, Tennessee.

I returned to Wyoming and began searching for a new job. I had always wanted to return to Germany, and I researched what companies had offices there. I had experience working in the Moving & Storage business and had written to the North American Van line office in Mannheim, Germany. I was told that nothing was available, but I sent a second letter and received an answer that there was a three-month temporary sales job, but I would have to pay my way to Mannheim. I accepted these conditions and prepared to fly to Frankfurt. I booked a one-way flight and packed a suitcase.

The day before I was to leave, I received a phone call from Leon Kellner. He had the house band at the Roosevelt Hotel in New Orleans. Leon wanted me to come to New Orleans and join his band, which played 6 nights a week in the Roosevelt. I turned him down as I was excited about returning to Europe. If I hadn't obligated myself to North American, I might have spent the rest of my life as a musician in New Orleans.

Businessman 1964-1990

North American Van Lines

I arrived in Frankfurt and was met by Tom Yates, who was in charge of the North American activities in Europe. They owned Feldner Moving in Munich. They had a French moving company in Ermont, France, and a NAVL container service in Hamburg. In Mannheim, the head office, everything was reported to Tom Yates. My job was to find people who were planning to move, and book them with North American Van Lines.

We drove from Frankfurt to Mannheim. Tom checked me into the Steigenberger Hotel, and we had dinner. I was to report for work the next morning. Thrilled to be back in Germany I went for a walk to explore Mannheim. The hotel faced the Wasser Turn which was a park, so off I went. To my surprise, I met a young lady, Rosa Nagel, as my first new friend in Germany. Little did I know that this was my future wife.

Tom Yates met me the next morning and explained what he wanted me to do. He gave me a used Opel as a company car to use as I would be traveling. I decided to start in Frankfurt as there were many American companies based there. I obtained a list from the American Chamber of Commerce in Frankfurt and began knocking on doors. I would write a brief report on each call and a copy would be given to Tom Yates. In Mannheim, there were separate departments for military moves, civilian moves, and claims. I was given responsibility for all of the civilian moves. George Young was in charge of the military moves and Paul Froelich handled all of the claims.

I could not stay in the hotel forever, so I began searching for someplace to stay. My first attempt was a rented room in a private home. As I would come in late many times due to entertaining clients in Frankfurt and then driving back to Mannheim, the landlord became unhappy. I needed to find something more permanent. Rosa lived in Frankenthal, Morsch and worked for Chio

Chips, which had a factory close to her home. She found an apartment for me in Oggersheim, which was convenient to where she lived. This allowed us more flexibility for dating. As this apartment was in a larger building there was no problem in coming home late.

I began by visiting Frankfurt and calling on American companies. I would write a report about what I found and if they had any impending household goods moves scheduled. I handed these reports to Tom Yates on a daily basis so he would know what I was doing. I was successful in obtaining some moves for North American. I also worked with the North American agents who were handling household shipments for the US military. This also resulted in some moves being booked. Then I was given the responsibility for all of the North American civilian moves in all of Europe. This allowed me to travel to many countries and to visit North American agents throughout Europe.

I continued calling on various business locations with limited success. I visited the North American agents around Europe, and this yielded some further moves. I concentrated on the agents who were handling US military moves and then began visiting agents in more distant locations. On one occasion I was in Sweden with my next stop being in Belfast, Northern Ireland. My flight was delayed so I called Thomas Johnson in Belfast. I was told, don't worry, we will meet you at the airport.

Upon arriving in Belfast, I was met by a gentleman who insisted on carrying my suitcase. As we went to the parking lot there were many small cars and one big black monster. We went to the Rolls Royce and the man who met me placed my suitcase in the trunk, opened the door for me and then entered the driver's compartment and put on a chauffeur's cap. I had a large compartment in the rear and was told there was champagne, wine, and beer in the refrigerator and cigars in a box. I did not use any of these items. We went to the hotel, was met by a doorman and I asked my driver when I would meet Mr. Johnson. He replied, "I don't know. I was only told to meet you at the airport," and he left. I checked in and decided to visit their office which was close to the hotel.

When I found the office, it read "Thomas Johnson & Sons

Undertakers." Upon entering I asked for Mr. Johnson and was told that he was busy, but he would see me in an hour. I left, had some lunch, and walked around Belfast, which was very depressing and still showed signs of the bombings and problems they had been having. Later I met Mr. Johnson, and we had a good discussion. He promised to keep us in mind when he had any moves to the USA. I guess it makes sense, they use wooden boxes in their business, and we move household goods in wooden boxes. He asked me if I needed a car to the airport in the morning and I said that was not necessary. In checking out the hotel clerk said my bill was covered, I said that I would pay my bill which I did.

About a week later I received a letter from Thomas Johnson & Sons. It was a bill for my hotel room and a large bill for car hire. I wrote back and said that I had paid my hotel bill and that they had offered to pick me up at the airport. They responded OK forget the hotel, just pay the car hire. I never paid their invoice, and we never received any moves from Northern Ireland to the USA.

Tom also asked me to visit the North American companies in Munich, Germany, Ermont, France, and the NAVTRANS container division in Hamburg, Germany. The person in charge of our container operation in Hamburg had a reputation for heavy drinking. One day he was out of the office after lunch when the head office in Fort Wayne, Indiana called and asked for him. They said he was out to lunch and the Vice President asked to have him call back when he returned. It was late when he returned, and he called Fort Wayne. He had been drinking and was incoherent during the call and said a lot of things that were out of line, the result was that he was fired. Tom Yates and I would make numerous visits to Hamburg after that incident.

Bronnbach

When I was dating Rosa, we decided to visit the Christmas

Market in Nurnberg. Her sister Karola and her boyfriend, Rudy, went with us. We were driving on the autobahn from Frankfurt to Nurnberg to visit the 1964 Christmas market. It was time for lunch, and

Klosterhof Bronnbach

I knew that I had stayed in the Klosterhof in Bronnbach with my parents. Ernst Lang, the innkeeper, had treated us as relatives and had always treated me to free beer when I visited after my parents returned to the USA. I exited the autobahn and drove to the Klosterhof, intending to give everyone a nice experience and renew this family connection. We arrived and Rosa refused to get out of the car and go into this place, it did not meet her standards. So we drove to Wertheim and had a beer and bratwurst at a bratwurst stand.

Rosa's sister Karola married Rudy Mueller and they had a horse stable not too far from Mannheim. This meant that our family travels were simply visits to Frankenthal where Rosa's mother lived and to her sister's stable. I traveled a lot due to my job but, as a family unit, we were restricted. I did travel a lot visiting the US bases around Germany. In May 1965 I was again close to Bronnbach, so I decided to stop and renew our family ties that my mother had found. When I arrived at the Klosterhof I learned that Ernst Lang had died. two months earlier This ended my connection to my father's family in Germany.

I continued making trips to various companies to find civilian moves for North American as well as monitoring incoming moves. There was one inbound move held by customs. The wife had heard that the German toilet paper was rough so she had included enough to stock a store in their household goods shipment. German customs were demanding that they pay duty. I had to go to Dusseldorf to solve that issue.

Second Marriage

In 1966 Rosa and I visited Wyoming. Together with my mother and my niece Kym, Rosa and I made a trip to Torreon, Mexico so she could meet Grace and Debbie, the children I had with Carmen. The trip went well, and we agreed that Rosa would be happy to have my two children included in our family.

Upon returning to Wyoming, I asked Rosa if she would marry me. She said, after she spoke to her mother, so we called Germany, she spoke to her mother, and we got married with my mother present and my Uncle Lew as my best man.

Returning to Germany, I continued working with North American. Rosa and I rented an apartment in Käfertal and Rosa moved from Frankfurt. I continued my efforts to book civilian moves and the office in Mannheim, which contained Tom Yates at the Central control office, George Young handling military moves and Paul Froelish handling claims. Those were happy days, and everything looked bright.

One day at the close of work, one of the girls working for George Young asked me for a ride home. I was living in Käfertal, and she said I went by her home on my way, so I agreed. I called Rosa and told her I was on my way home and she asked me to pick up a loaf of bread on my way. The next day I received a phone call from Fort Wayne from Bob Stout, the vice president of North American Van Lines, and he said he was coming to see

Rosa, Kym, Grace Ries, children Debbie and Grace in Torreon, Mexico

me. He said that there was a problem in the office, and I should not say anything to anyone that he was coming.

The next day I met Bob at the Frankfurt airport, and he informed me that I was accused of a sexual assault by one of the girls in the office. Evidently the girl I had given a ride to had filed a complaint.

We arrived at the office, and I was told to go into my office and stay there. I received a phone call from Rosa, who said that George Young's landlady had called her to say that he was talking about Tom being fired because of a situation he had created. He was laughing and telling her what they had done.

Bob talked to everyone. George and the girl were fired, and I was put in charge of military moves.

Now I had the responsibility to visit all of the U.S. bases and work with the agents servicing those bases. This required a lot of traveling but was rewarding. Rosa and I found an apartment on the Stephaniennufer, overlooking the Rhine River, and moved from Käfertal. This apartment had a balcony where we could sit and watch the boat traffic on the Rhine. On the opposite bank was the beach of Ludwigshafen.

North American Vans lines was based in Fort Wayne,

Tom Ries, Rosa Nagel, Grace Ries, and Lew Thomas on Tom and Rosa's wedding day

Indiana. I was invited to visit the headquarters and spend time with the President, James Edgett. I flew to the US and spent a week learning about how the system worked and many of the fine details. Before I returned to Europe I booked a flight to El Paso, Texas. Carmen brought Grace and Debbie to see their father. I was able to see them for a day before I had to fly back to Germany. It was a wonderful experience for me and also very emotional. This was the last time I saw my daughters before divorcing Rosa.

One day, Rosa said that she was pregnant, so we began preparing for the new arrival. When it was time, I drove Rosa to the hospital. She was admitted and I sat down waiting for the birth to take place. One of the nurses came out and said it will be a long time before the birth, and that I should go and have lunch.

Upon my return I was informed that I was the father of a baby girl. Rosa had told the nurses to get me out of the hospital while she was giving birth. I was upset. Tonia arrived on July 25, 1967.

Life continued and we hired a new man to solicit civilian moves and I concentrated on the military moves.

I made trips to our French subsidiary as well as the Hamburg office. Tom Yates left in 1958, so Jim Edgett came to Mannheim to name his replacement. There were two possibilities: myself, and Gunther Pressure, who was in charge of Feldner Transport, our German subsidiary. We both interviewed and Mr. Edgett decided to put Gunther in charge of Europe. Evidently, I was a threat to Gunther, so discussions were made to move me to Nairobi and to open an African office reporting to Gunther. I began a job search.

I was contacted by Doug Burrell from Home Pack Transport, and it was arranged that I go to Paris for an interview in their Paris office. I flew to Paris and met Doug and Mr. Santini from New York. We had a long conversation, and I was asked if I would be willing to move to Paris where they had their European office. I agreed and was hired. I returned to Mannheim and told Rosa that we would be moving to Paris.

Home Pack

As a result, I gave my notice to North American Van Lines and flew to New York City to be oriented in the Santini operations. The Home Pack headquarters was located in Maspeth, New York where they also had a huge freight forwarding and packing operation. This facility used a minimum of 4 railcars of lumber on a daily basis, building crates and boxes for their shipments. There were more than 100 employees working in this plant. The building was large. I spent several days in Maspeth and got acquainted with all of the people I would be working with in the future. Marty would treat all of us to a three-martini lunch at Mamma Leone's. I later learned that this was a favorite hangout for some of the mafia bosses in New York.

I returned to Europe and began to prepare for my new position. While I was in New York, Guenther came to our apartment and demanded the keys to the North American company car, so we were without any transportation. We then bought a Ford Escort and licensed it with a Zoll (customs) plate. I drove to Paris and began a search for a residence. The office in Paris was located at 115 Av. des Champs-Élysées. You entered this building and took an elevator to the third floor. There you walked almost a block to the rear of the building. The office had two rooms and was very small. I had three employees, a Dutch secretary, Yoke, and two French employees, Jacques and Bernie. Yoke had a small office, and the three men shared a small room with 2 desks being placed against the front of the third desk. It was very crowded.

Both Jacques and Bernie smoked French cigarettes and there was a terrible odor in this small space. Even with the small window open, it was filled with smoke. One day I decided enough was enough, I bought a big cigar and began to fill the room with cigar smoke. Both of the cigarette smokers asked me not to fill the room with cigar smoke and I said, fine, as long as the cigarette smoke disappeared. We reached an agreement, and they would then go outside to smoke. Bernie and Yoke were good employees and we got along fine. Jacques was not happy as he wanted to run the office and I had been hired over him. He purposely did things to upset me and tried to show that he was better and more equipped to run the Paris office. This caused problems in the office.

We found a small house in Enghien-les-Bains in the north of Paris. This was a small town and had a casino. There were two rooms and a kitchen on the main floor. Tonia slept in the bedroom, and Rosa and I slept on a couch in the living room. There was a small room upstairs with closets on both sides. The basement had a low ceiling, and I bumped my head many times. Rosa could walk without problem as she was shorter. There was a morning train via St. Denis that would arrive in the Gard de Nord where I would change for the subway. The train was always crowded, so I quickly learned to wait until the last minute and then to jump onto the train to have the lead when changing to the subway. There was a Frenchman who was doing the same thing, and we would both try to outlast each other. One morning I waited a very long time and was able to wave to him, standing at the station as I left for Paris. I outlasted him! The subway to the office would make one change along the way.

I usually went to Paris by train but occasionally would drive in. There was always a parking problem, and you used a disc to show what time you parked. We would take turns going to each other's cars to change the disc so we wouldn't get parking tickets. I installed yellow light bulbs in the Escort, which was required on French automobiles. I had an international customs plate on the car, so I applied for a French license plate which required a car inspection.

One day I was driving into Paris and was stopped by the French police who were checking license plates. As I had a customs plate, they stopped me but, since I had paperwork showing that I was scheduled to have my car inspected, I was free to go. Many people try to drive for years on a customs plate. I drove to have my car inspected at an address sent to me, to discover it was a parking area in front of a cemetery. I was flagged down by a gentleman who said he was the inspector. He asked me to turn on my headlights and saw they were yellow, so I passed the inspection! Now I would receive my French license plates.

I settled in to work. Bernie Poisson, the secretary, and I

concentrated on developing a system to control the shipments being handled by Home Pack, while Jacques was in and out showing that he could book moves for Home Pack. He did bring in a lot of business but was not pleasant to work with. He was always causing trouble and creating problems. It was not a pleasant atmosphere in which to work. Doug Burrell would visit from New York and Jacques would always complain about everything. He wanted to be the boss in Paris. In spite of this, we were getting a good system for monitoring the Home Pack moves. A lot of the moves were for US military families throughout Europe, with most in Germany.

One day when I was returning to Paris from a trip to Germany, I was following a couple of slow drivers on the two-lane highway. This continued for several miles as they were taking their time and staying close to each other. Finally at the top of a hill with a clear road to pass, I sped up and started to pass them when a car pulled onto my lane in front of me. There were cars on my right, trees on my left, no time to brake, so I hit him. I was wearing my seat belt, but I remember my glasses flying off and hitting the windshield with a lot of force. The driver had been stopped in a field to walk his dog and pulled out on the highway without looking. I hit his left front fender and there was major damage. A friend drove out from Paris to pick me up, and my car was towed to a French garage for repairs. I told them to fix it so it would run, and not to do the body work. I later took the car to Germany for repairs, and it took the insurance companies 10 months to settle the claims. I was given 4% fault and the other driver 96%.

The friction in the Paris office continued. Business was increasing in Germany, a lot of it due to the visits I had been making to military bases. It was putting a strain on the Paris office to cope with everything and there was no room for expansion to hire an additional person. I flew to New York, and we had some in-depth discussions about what to do. It was decided Home Pack had a lot of civilian moves in the Paris area, and we also supervised the military shipments which were mainly in Germany. Both Jacques and Bernie were working to find moves in the Paris area. Yoke kept all of the records, and I was in charge of coordinating all of the moves and watching over the military shipments which were in Germany, some in the UK and some in France. One day, Doug Burell visited from New York and, because the number of shipments in Germany exceeded those in France, it was decided to create an office in Germany.

Frankfurt, Germany

Doug and I flew to Frankfurt and began making plans for this new office. He was having problems and was not feeling well. He returned to New York, and I continued looking for a good location. I found an available office in the Kroegerstrasse, close to the Eischeimer Turm. We created a German company (Gmbh). I was the *Geschäftsführer* and as such could open bank accounts and do business in Germany. I then created forms for the control of shipments in Europe. This was a three-part form, one for operations, one for finance, and one for the control of the operations. The first section was used to record the shipment and to follow its progress, the bottom right-hand side of this form was blank and could be used for notations. The left-hand side of the second form was blank and this form recorded all of the financial transactions for the shipment. The third form had all sections and was used for management control.

The form had labels and numbers: i.e. DE 1 meant Germany export 1, DI 1 meant Germany import, FE meant France export, FI 1 meant France import. The country codes were used for other countries, NL Netherlands, SF Finland, DK Denmark, etc. When a shipment was created by operations, they would fill out the general information. Carbon paper copies were made for finance and management. I would have the management copies and place them numerically in a folder. As a shipment was completed, I could review it and see if we had a profit or loss and make necessary adjustments. This also allowed me to monitor how the various agents were performing.

As the shipments progressed, I would finalize my copy and place it in a completed file. As time went on, if there was an outstanding shipment with a low number I could zero in on that shipment and take whatever action was required. This identified problem shipments. If DE 36 was still open and we were processing DE 103 and higher, I could see what there was a problem with DE 36 and follow up where necessary. It might be in storage, or there might be a problem with paperwork, or a missing invoice etc. New York was amazed as to how efficient the Frankfurt office was performing.

We found an apartment in Offenbach and had our furniture moved from Enghien-les-Bains. As I would now be traveling more, visiting the military bases, we traded the Ford for an Opel Record. I was able to hire some employees and started to set up the office. I developed a system for controlling the shipments, and we were open for business. In addition to the military business, we also wanted civilian moves, so I began visiting local businesses and advertising. All of the military moves were transferred from Paris, and I contacted all of our agents to let them know about our new office. They were pleased to have an office in Germany. I began visiting the military bases and the agents serving them. Business increased quickly, and I hired additional employees, including a full-time bookkeeper.

Higa Fast Pac, another military household goods shipper, asked if we would be interested in being the general agent for their shipments. I was visited by Tom Higa from Hawaii who owned this company, and an agreement was signed. Now, in addition to Home Pack, I was also a general agent. In addition to Higa Fast Pac, I also signed agreements with Wheaton Van Lines and Allied Van Lines. Business increased and I hired additional staff. I worked with local agents on civilian moves and made useful contacts at the airport cargo area for air shipments. I was able to expedite shipments using these contacts to ensure my shipments were loaded on the first available aircraft. I was first in line where others had delays.

The University of Utah had a program at the Rhein Main military base in Frankfurt. The professors from Salt Lake would come to Frankfurt and teach a semester on the base, the same class they taught on the home campus. I enrolled in their MBA program and began taking classes. I would attend classes twice a week and then do my homework on the weekends, using the base library and other facilities. In addition to calling on the US bases, visiting my agents, monitoring local shipments, running a full-time office, and attending classes, I would also have to entertain visitors. This kept me very busy, and I had very little free time.

At home, my family was growing, as my daughter, Alexandra Nicole, joined us on April 7, 1970.

I had developed a friendship with the manager of the Global Van Lines office in Frankfurt. We were friendly competitors attempting to book civilian moves to the USA. I was proud of my office as it was self-sufficient, meaning I was free to travel as my staff could handle all affairs without my being present. The global office required the boss to be there to make decisions. This gave me an advantage in booking local moves. We all required the use of a port agent for booking our shipments on vessels sailing to the USA.

These companies began calling on us to get our business and I developed good relationships with many of them. I had a good relationship with Waterman Lines and would visit them often in Bremen. I also had a close relationship with Sea Land whose representative would visit me often in Frankfurt.

I had a staff of seven people working in the Frankfurt office. We were also successful in booking many civilian moves in the Frankfurt area. One day I found a Fiat 500 for sale for 50 DM. I called and was told it needed work but would run. We bought this well-used Fiat and got it back to Offenbach. Then I and another man took it apart, made repairs, installed new parts and got it running. The body was bad, so I repaired the rust spots using some webbing which I covered with plastic. I then painted the car using spray paint. I took it to the German car inspection, and it passed!

A large expense in moving shipments was the port charges in Bremerhaven. Everyone used an agent in the port area. We used Rosebrock in Bremen. I had many discussions with this company and negotiated many rates and charges. This company handled the bulk of the US military shipments. It was also used by North American Van Lines and many others. Because of the friendship I had with Peter, the manager of Global Van lines in Germany, I suggested that we create our own port agency.

HHG Shipping and Spedition

We decided to open a port agency in Bremerhaven to be jointly operated by Home Pack and Global. We named this company HHG Shipping and Spedition GmbH. The first H stood for Home Pack, the second one for Higa and the G was for Global Van Lines. Both Peter and I were the Managing Directors for this new company. We hired a local man who was very familiar with port operations, Lother Welker, and we were in the port business. We were now able to negotiate our own rates with the ocean shipping lines and consolidate our cargo for good rates. This was profitable and added to the profit in our Frankfurt office. I would visit this office on a regular basis, taking an overnight train from Frankfurt to Bremen.

There were a lot of contacts with the business world from the Frankfurt office. Many times, I would have to entertain business clients, agents visiting from other cities, vendors, shipping line representatives, and the people visiting from the various companies we were representing, such as Wheaton Van Lines, Higa Fast Pack, Allied Van lines etc. There would be many dinners and late nights, visiting the many sights offered in Frankfurt. I would be in the office at 7:30 am and work until 7 or 8 pm keeping up with the various activities. If we had some outgoing air shipments, I would go to the airport in the late evening to ensure that our shipments were loaded. A lot of our competitors' shipments would be left behind as I insisted that mine be loaded first. We had a better on-time record due to this monitoring and this gave us an edge over the competition.

One day we had a visit from a custom official. They were inquiring why we were always receiving a refund on our Mehrwertsteuer (turnover tax) as almost all companies would pay this tax each month. We were being audited! As the Managing Director, I had to deal with this issue. Simply, our local agents would send shipments from their German locations to the port of Bremerhaven. When they billed us for their services, they would add the Mehrwertsteuer on their invoices. We then shipped these shipments to the USA, meaning that they had left Germany, and we could claim a refund for this tax as the cargo had been exported from Germany. This took almost a week of discussions before the tax officials would agree that this was indeed a legal transaction.

Now corrective action was required. I was to inform all of my agents not to add this tax on their invoices to us. The tax representative was to inform all of the tax authorities in the various German states that this was to be the new rule for these shipments. As you can imagine there were a lot of different opinions from both the agents and the state tax authorities. I needed to placate all of my agents, and the tax representative had to convince the various tax authorities that this was the correct procedure to follow. For a period of three months, the tax representative and I were making visits and dealing with a lot of very upset individuals. I met a lot of German tax enforcers and spent a lot of time before this issue was settled. The only holdout was the tax office in Stuttgart. They insisted that our Stuttgart agent should continue to add the Mehrwertsteuer to his invoices. The federal tax representative that I had been dealing with agreed, and now I could get back to work on the many issues put aside because of this situation.

In addition to all of the business activities I also enrolled in the University of Utah's MBA program. I started this when we were living in Mannheim but had to drop out when we moved to Paris. The University offered the same program at the American military base at Rhein Main airbase as they offered at the campus in Salt Lake City. The professors who taught at the main campus would come to Germany and teach the same class as was offered in Utah. These were evening classes, or some were offered on Saturday. This meant that I needed study time, which was usually on Sunday. My days were full from morning to night which did not sit well at home. My activities did not receive any support and further demands on my time were forthcoming.

Doug continued to visit Europe however, he was having

major health problems. He developed a bad infection in his kidneys and was required to go on dialysis every two days for treatment. I made arrangements for him to receive treatments at a medical center in Frankfurt. Each treatment would require six to eight hours, so we had a lot of business discussions while he was receiving treatment. I remember a young German boy who had a shunt placed in his arm. He would come in and hook himself up to the dialysis machine for his treatments.

On one trip Doug also planned to visit the US airbase in Tripoli, Libya. He would fly down one day and return the next for his treatment. On this trip, his return flight to Frankfurt was delayed by a day. When he returned, his ankles were badly swollen, and he had trouble putting his shoes on. After treatment, he was back to normal. He exhausted his medical insurance, so he bought a dialysis machine which he kept in his home in Larchmont, New York. He would work all day and then hook himself up to the machine at night. Doug eventually had three kidney transplants. After I left Home Pack he passed away because of this illness.

Shortly after completing my MBA studies and receiving my degree in 1973, I received a phone call from Dick Sweeney who was the Sea Land representative who had been calling on me trying to obtain my cargo for Sea Land. This was on a Friday afternoon, and he said, "I want you to come to Brussels and meet Ed King." I asked who he was, and Dick responded that Ed King was the Executive Director of the Massachusetts Port Authority in Boston. Dick said that they would send me a round-trip first-class ticket and that I would be placed in a room in the Brussels Hilton hotel. I agreed, went home, told Rosa where I was going, and packed a bag.

I met Dick at the Frankfurt airport, and we flew to Brussels. Dick gave me a lot of information about what my position would be if accepted. We arrived at the Hilton, and I had a short time alone before we met Ed King for dinner. During dinner, I shared some thoughts I had about how to increase traffic through the Boston airport and shared some other ideas about the cargo moving via the Sea Port of Boston. We enjoyed a wonderful dinner in a first-class restaurant and then returned to the hotel. We agreed to meet for breakfast the next morning in Ed King's suite. In my mind, I went over what had been discussed and formulated some additional thoughts about future activities.

Massport

The next morning, we had a delicious breakfast and then Ed King said, "I want to have you join my team, what is your salary expectation?" I was earning $24,000 annually at Home Pack, so I said $28,000. Ed responded that the authority has only budgeted $26,000 for this position. I will make you this offer: "Take the position at $26,000 and I will give you a letter raising your salary to $28,000 in one year. That way you will have an average of $ 27,000 over the two years" I agreed and was hired with the title and responsibility of Director General for Europe, Africa, and the Middle East. I flew back to Frankfurt and informed Rosa that we would be moving to Brussels, Belgium. I found a replacement for my position with Home Pack and spent the next two weeks orienting him in the Frankfurt office. We began preparing our personal belongings for the move to Brussels. The big question was where we were going to live.

I flew to Brussels to see my new office and meet the employees. The office was located in the Martini Center on the Place Rogiers. This was a 24-story building; we were on the 8th floor. I was now the Director General for Europe and the Middle East, in charge of the Massachusetts state office in Brussels. I had three employees: Patrick Oconner, Aviation division, Gustave Morris, Maritime division, and Roberta Coen, secretary. We got to know each other and there was a positive working attitude among this group. Patrick dealt with all of the airlines and Gustave dealt with the shippers and shipping lines serving Boston. Another huge source of business were the travel agents booking their passengers via Boston. I had the oversight responsibilities for all of these activities.

I was staying in a hotel and began looking for accommodations. Rosa came to Brussels, and we decided to purchase a home. We looked in both the Flemish speaking area and also in the French speaking area. Rosa had some money to invest, so we decided to buy a house. We decided on a house in Waterloo, and this was to be our family home. MASSPORT shipped a new Chevrolet Impala to Brussels which was to be my company car. We sold the cars we had in Offenbach, and I bought Rosa a new Fiat 500, which we drove while waiting for the Chevrolet. I remember driving this Fiat from Brussels to Frankenthal to visit Rosa's mother. This was an adventure on the German Autobahn!

Tonia was enrolled in the German school in Brussels, and Alexandra was enrolled in kindergarten in Waterloo, which was French speaking. Her first day was traumatic as the nuns thought she was speaking Dutch and did not realize that she was speaking German. They locked her in a bathroom and told her she could only come out when she stopped speaking Flemish and would speak French. This was clarified and she began learning French.

In my position, I also worked with the US Embassies in Europe, representing Massachusetts at official functions Europe, and met many of the US Ambassadors in various countries, such as John Volpe in Rome and Leonard Firestone in Brussels.

All of the arrangements had been made, so one of my first duties was to host the international freight forwarders convention, which was being held in Cannes, France. MASSPORT was hosting and paying the bill for this event.

Gustave and I drove the new Chevrolet to Cannes. The meet-

ings were to be held in the Carlton Hotel and I, as the host of the convention, was given a suite on the top floor. I enjoyed hosting this event and met a lot of high-level individuals from numerous countries. Upon arriving at the Carlton Hotel, I was given a suite as I was in charge of this con-

The house Waterloo, Belgium   vention. Gustave was there

to assist me as he had been involved in making the arrangements. Everyone wanted to meet me, and I was kept busy from morning to night. It was a three-day convention and was a big wake-up call for what responsibilities my new position would command in the future. The chef from the restaurant invited me into the kitchen, and I was treated to a special bottle of champagne and met everyone who prepared and served the meals to the thousand participants at this convention. The convention lasted 3 days and was a breathtaking, wonderful experience.

The MASSPORT experience was very rewarding. We were mandated to fly first class full fare when we traveled. This was to avoid any of the airlines upgrading us and then asking for preferential treatment at Boston Logan Airport, which was owned and operated by MASSPORT The seaport of Boston, Hanscom Field, and the Tobin Memorial Bridge were also owned by MASSPORT

The Massachusetts Port Authority also had leased private property, and some of these were famous restaurants. We would receive VIP treatment when we dined there. On one occasion I was with Ed King at Dan's Pier Four when we were joined by Tip O'Neil, the speaker of the House of Representatives in Washington, D.C. I met a lot of politicians during my time at MASSPORT

Every year MASSPORT would host a trade mission around Europe. We would host dinners at six to eight various locations such as Paris, Brussels, Rome, Stuttgart, and London, and would normally hold the last dinner in Dublin, Ireland. Ed King, the Executive Director of MASSPORT members of the MASSPORT Board of Directors, and leading businessmen from Massachusetts would come to Europe for these events. All of the preparations for these dinners, the venues, the invitees, the ar-rangements, and the dinners would be made by our office in Brussels. Gustav and Patrick would submit a list of names to be invited, we would invite travel agents, shipping agents, airlines, and VIPs.

We would include Directors and Senior Managers as well as US Ambassadors and other top government officials from each country we would visit. The hotel arrangements were made by

Roberta in the Brussels office. Then either Gustave or Patrick would visit the hotel to make plans for which room to use and the catering service for both the reception and the meals that would be served after the presentations.

The events would start with Ed King, Patrick, Gustav, and myself greeting everyone as they entered. Then cocktails and treats would be served. Then we would ask everyone to be seated and I would welcome them and give a speech about the benefits of using Boston as a major center for ocean cargo and using Boston Logan airport for air transportation. Then I would introduce Ed King who would then give a speech. Many times, we would also include some short visual displays about both the harbor and the airport. Then we would invite everyone to enjoy their dinner. Ed and I would leave, and we would have dinner at a first-class restaurant. The last stop would always be Dublin, Ireland before the Massachusetts attendees would return to Boston.

Gustav and Patrick were excellent in their positions; however, things were to change. Gustav received an offer from the Port of Maryland for Director and left MASSPORT. Then Patrick, an Irishman, was asked to be the director of the Irish Tourist Office based in Brussels, which he accepted. Frank Rovers was hired to replace Gustav, and Willie van Sittert was hired to replace Patrick. These two individuals were not as supportive, and both attempted to be the boss in their areas. Both of them tried to report to Directors in Boston and bypass the Brussels office which caused numerous problems.

Tom Ries, Gustav Morris, Ed King, Patrick O'Conner host a trade mission

I was a Vice President of the NDTA (National Defense Transportation Association). This is a group where top industry leaders met so they could get to know the top military officers who handle military logistics. This would allow top officials to work together in case of a war or other military emergency. The group is headquartered in Washington D.C. with branches around the world. I was a member of the European branch based in Frankfurt, Germany.

One year, a two-day conference was arranged to be held in Amsterdam. I was chosen to be the moderator for this conference. I was asked to arrive one day before the conference to ensure everything was ready and in place. The conference was to be in the Hilton Hotel, and I was given an executive suite. We would have Prince Bernard of the Netherlands present to open the conference. I looked over the program and what was in place and approved everything to proceed.

The day of the conference I met Prince Bernard and we discussed how he wanted to be introduced. We had breakfast together in my suite. We went to the conference room. I made a few short remarks and Prince Bernard officially opened the conference. He made a presentation of his country, the Netherlands, and spoke about the royal family, He then left the stage, and I introduced the panel. This day was to feature ports, railroads, trucking, and other surface transportation modes. The panel

Ed King, Roberta Coen, Frank Rovers, unknown, Willie Van Sittert, and Tom Ries in 1975

consisted of presidents of several large European freight forwards, executives from Dutch and German railroads, and the directors of the ports of Rotterdam and Hamburg. I would introduce each person; they would give a short presentation of their organization and then there was an open question and answer session which I would monitor.

The second day focused on air transport. Again, I was to monitor the session. The panel was to have two four-star generals, General Patch from the Pacific fleet, and General Klingenhagen from the European theater, the presidents of KLM, Sabena, and Seabord Airlines, and a vice president from United Air Lines. There was an executive from the New York Port Authority which was in charge of JFK and other New York airports. The top member was Knut Hammarskjold, the secretary general of IATA (International Air Traffic Association).

I met Knut at Amsterdam airport, and we had breakfast together. He was a very intelligent man who was fluent in 7 languages, including Dutch. We drove to the conference site, and I introduced the panel. Again, each member gave a short presentation and then there was a question-and-answer session which I would monitor. I met a lot of important people at this conference.

Russia

One day we were asked to investigate possibilities for developing a relationship with transportation between Soviet agencies and the Port of Boston. Dick Sweeney from Boston and I were to visit the Soviet Union. We obtained first-class tickets from Brussels to Moscow and Leningrad. Appointments were made with Aeroflot for aviation and with Sovietflot for ocean transportation. On arrival in Moscow, we booked into a four-star hotel located in the Red Square. We had a free evening, so we asked for a good restaurant and were directed to the hotel next door which had a fancy restaurant.

We ordered some Russian champagne and some steaks. When asked if we wanted a salad, I ordered a cucumber salad and Dick passed. In the first hour, we finished our bottle of champagne and then my cucumber salad arrived. We ordered another bottle of champagne which we then finished in the next two hours. We kept asking about our dinner and were always told it would be coming shortly. After 3 hours we asked again, were told it was almost ready, so we ordered another bottle of champagne which we finished in the next thirty minutes. We decided to ask for our bill and were told to wait a minute. We waited another thirty minutes, nobody came, we could not find our waiter, and there was no cashier. We walked out, no one said anything, and we went back to our hotel.

The next day we met with some officials from Sovietflot which seemed to be productive. We then met the top officials from Aeroflot and discussed the possibility of scheduling flights between the USSR and Boston Logan airport. In Russia there are always the same number of hosts as members in your party. Vodka is always served in abundance on a small tray in small glasses. We learned to switch the glasses on the tray as the ones served to the guests always had a higher alcohol content than those of the hosts. When they realized that we knew the trick, the vodka bottle would be placed on the tray, and everyone would be equal. The next day we flew to Leningrad and enjoyed the white nights. Shortly before midnight there would be a small dusk and 15 minutes later bright daylight would be back.

We were scheduled to meet with some dignitaries the next day for lunch. Before leaving the hotel, I stopped in the travel agency to reconfirm our flight the next day. I was told that we would be on an afternoon flight back to Moscow. I objected and said we had a meeting in Moscow the next afternoon. I was told in no uncertain terms that we would be on the afternoon flight, not the one we had scheduled in the morning. We went to our meeting at which we both had a red soviet star pinned on our jackets. When we returned to the hotel, I again went to the travel agent we had spoken to before. She was very rude but then saw the red star and immediately became very helpful. We were now placed back on our original morning flight.

That evening we took a dinner cruise on the Nevsky river and had a quiet evening. During our river cruise, we were lectured about the accomplishments of the different businesses and factories along the river. There was no historical content in any of these lectures. We were also able to visit the Hermitage Museum and explore the city park.

The next day we returned to Moscow, had a follow up meeting with Aeroflot, and then boarded our flight back to western Europe. When boarding a flight in Russia you have a boarding card with three sections. The first section gets you to the gate area that has military guards around the room. The second section gets you on the bus from the terminal to the aircraft. There you pass between a row of armed guards with machine guns. The last section is taken at the bottom of the stairs before you enter the aircraft. You have nothing left to show that you were on this flight.

Trade Mission to Rome

The final trade mission I organized for MASSPORT included a presentation in Rome. I always tried to say something in my introduction in the language of the country and this was also the case in Rome. Our honored guest at this function was The Honorable John Volpe, the US ambassador to Italy. Ed King was not able to join this Trade Mission, so Boston was being represented by Ed Hanley who was number two at MASSPORT and who did not like me. He was always creating problems.

One of the young ladies working in the Italian Embassy office offered to help me prepare my remarks. I have to say that she was a very attractive young lady. We were sitting in a quiet corner of the hotel where the function was to be held and were working on the remarks I would be making when Ed Hanley approached and in a very rude voice and a very mean manner demanded, "Who is this woman?" I explained that she was Ambassador Volpe's secretary and he walked away.

A few weeks later, we received the news that Ed King had been fired by the Board of Directors after serving eleven years. The Board of Directors is appointed by the Governor of

Massachusetts and serves a seven-year term. The governor appointed a new board member, and the first meeting of the new board was held. The new appointee passed a motion that Ed King be replaced, a vote was taken, and the new member cast the deciding vote to fire Ed King. Ed Hanley was appointed as the intern director until a new Director could be installed. I don't know why, but Ed Hanley never liked or supported me. I had a trip planned to the port of Hamburg, so I flew there and checked into my hotel. The next morning Roberta called me from the Brussels office and told me that there was a message for me to call Ed Hanley immediately. I assume that was to terminate me or make an immediate change to the Brussels office. I told her that she couldn't get in touch with me.

Ed Hanley was only the acting director for two days before he was replaced by Dave Davis, who was appointed as the new permanent director. One of the first actions of the new board was to change the termination package for people leaving MASSPORT. The new rule was they would receive two weeks' pay plus one day for each year they had been with MASSPORT. Shortly thereafter a decision was made to close the Brussels office. Tom Foley, the port director in Boston, was sent to Brussels to arrange the closing. He said that I would receive two weeks' salary. I said, "I'm hired under Belgium law. MASSPORT owes me a year's salary." I gave Tom contacts for the Chamber of Commerce, a lawyer, and a contact in the Belgium government employment office.

Tom returned and said that I was correct. He and I were friends and had worked well together in the past. We were able to agree on a settlement that included my being given title to the Chevrolet Impala plus six months' salary. The office was to be closed at the end of the month. I still had an obligation to fill before leaving. I was the vice president of NDTA (National Defense Transportation Association). The annual meeting was to be held in the Park Hotel in Bremen, Germany April 20-23, 1976.

Rosa accompanied me, and we were seated at the head table with Jerry Collins, the NDTA president in Washington DC, Dr. Fastenau, the Hamburg Port Director, and General Alexander

Haig, a previous US Secretary of State. It was all formal wear, the men in tuxedos and the women in evening dresses. It was a gala occasion: dinner and dancing along with the speeches. I believed it was a total success but was told by Rosa that I had not properly pulled her chair out for her and that was seen by everyone. I received a twenty-minute lecture on how to act at a formal dinner. A disappointing end to an important event.

The next day I read an ad in the Wall Street Journal advertising for a logistics person with certain skills. I read it and said, "They are describing me!" When we returned to Brussels, I prepared a resume and mailed it to the address given in the ad. I also began using other channels to look for a new job. I looked for possibilities in Europe and also considered returning to the USA. Then I received an answer to the resume I had sent. I was asked to visit the Human Resource office of the ITT Corporation in Brussels! I called and made an appointment. This was in June of 1976.

I had written in my application that I spoke German so when I arrived for my interview, I was met by Dr. Ewald. He greeted me in German, and we sat down and began to converse. It was all in German for the first 10 to 15 minutes and then he said in perfect English, "Well, you do speak German." Dr Ewald was from Austria. The interview went well and then I was asked to meet Jim Reddy and Danny Weadock. I spent about an hour with these two gentlemen. When I returned to the Human Resources office, I was told that they would schedule an appointment with a psychiatrist for a review. This I did and then a few days later was asked to return to the Human Resources office. At this point, I was told that that was all that was required and that they would let me know the outcome.

ITT Corporation

Two weeks went by, and I received no news. I then decided to return to Wyoming and begin a job search in the USA. I began looking for possibilities and preparing a resume for use in the

USA. I was in Cheyenne when four or five days later I received a message from ITT that I had been hired and should report as soon as possible. I flew back to Brussels and was told to report to Danny Weadock. I met Dan, and he handed me a stack of papers at least eighteen inches in height and said, "These are the logistic problems I am having, read these and tell me what needs to be done." It took several days to understand the problems, then I went to Dan and said, "I need to go to Nigeria to fully understand and solve these issues." He responded, "go to Nigeria, stay as long as necessary, and come back with the answers."

I submitted my passport to the Nigerian Embassy for a visa and while waiting I organized my personal affairs. MASSPORT had agreed to pay for a household goods shipment from Brussels to the USA. To maintain my status as an expat working in Belgium, I had to officially leave Belgium. We shipped some items to Wyoming, giving documentation that I had left Belgium. Another control was to turn in your registered garbage cans to the Commune where you were living. We did this and had officially moved from Belgium to the USA. Then I was rehired, and ITT paid for a household goods shipment from Wyoming to Belgium so I could officially move back to Belgium. We went to the Commune, applied for and got new garbage cans, so now I had officially moved back into Belgium and could again have an expat status for taxes.

Upon receiving my visa to visit Nigeria a first-class ticket was booked and off I went to identify the logistics problems ITT was experiencing. ITT had a 2-billion-dollar contract to install a telephone system in 307 locations in Nigeria. My responsibility was to arrange everything for shipping materials to Nigeria, storage when needed, transportation to all 307 sites, housing for ITT employees, identifying medical support, and building support systems for the total project. There were numerous problems to be solved. This would prove to be a very complex assignment.

When I joined ITT there were eight telephone lines connecting Nigeria to the rest of the world. Of these eight connections, five were assigned to the government, leaving only three lines to serve the 125 million people living in Nigeria. To obtain a connection was extremely difficult. The office in Brussels was able to make a connection, they spoke with our staff in Lagos, and it was arranged for me to be met when I arrived in Lagos. There was to be a car and driver waiting for me. It felt good to know I would be taken care of in Nigeria.

My flight arrived in Lagos in the evening, and it was raining heavily. We went down the stairs from the plane and ran to a waiting bus. The bus had a roof but no sides, it was wet. The bus drove a short distance to the terminal and again we ran through the rain. There was no power, so everything was dark.

I had been briefed on the entry system. First, you had to have your passport stamped by the medical officer. Everyone was pushing to get to this official and it was extremely crowded. You pushed your way in through the mob, got your stamp, and then pushing back out was even more challenging than pushing in! Next, you had to receive an entry stamp, which again was pushing to get to an immigration officer. All of these officials were sitting in the dark, working with a candle that gave very little light. This process took almost an hour. Next, retrieve your checked luggage. Again, no lights so people were searching through a huge pile of luggage using cigarette lighters. There were no luggage carriers, no organization, and just luck to find your suitcase.

Finally, almost two hours after landing, I was able to exit the terminal to find my driver. There was minimal cover from the rain and there were a lot of very wet people. There was a large number of taxis attempting to get customers. I was continually set upon by these drivers, many of whom tried to grab my suitcase so I would go with them. I kept saying that a driver was coming to meet me. This lasted for more than an hour. I finally gave up and selected a taxi to take me to Lagos. All I had was the office address, so this is where I told the driver to take me. The floor of the taxi was flooded with water, so I sat with my legs on the seat holding my suitcase beside me. It was a 45-minute drive.

Arriving at the office I found a locked gate with a security guard who did not speak English. Using the driver, we discovered that the guard knew nothing and that I would have to come back the next day when the office was open. I knew that some of the ITT staff were staying at the Federal Palace Suites hotel, so that was my next destination. The rain continued pouring and driving was difficult. Arriving at the hotel I had the taxi wait while I checked for ITT people. The front desk knew nothing about anyone from ITT, so I decided to book a room. Nothing was available, and some people had been waiting for 24 hours for a room. What to do? Flight from Brussels and now almost 6 hours of frustration.

I told the driver to drive me to a hotel where I could get a room. We drove to at least 10 hotels, all getting lower in standards—nothing available anywhere. Finally, the driver said that he knew of a small hotel where we might be lucky. He drove through some of the worst streets I have ever seen in deep mud with the tires spinning from time to time. We arrived at the Hilton hotel (not of the chain). The driver went in, came back out, and said he had a room. With no other choice, I entered and booked a room. The driver said he would come back in the morning and drive me to the ITT office. I walked up to my room. It had clean sheets and a window air conditioner. The door lock was broken but there was a dresser I could use to block the door. I went downstairs and asked if he had a beer, and he said yes! He walked to a large old floor Coca-Cola container with a padlock, opened it, and there on a large block of ice were bottles of beer! I was happy, I had an air-conditioned room and a cold beer. Life was good....

The next morning, the driver arrived. The rain was still coming down but not as bad, and off we went to the ITT office. The first question asked was, "where were you last night? We had a welcoming party planned, but you did not show up." I explained what had happened. Apparently, the assigned driver had dropped off another ITT person and was supposed to wait for me. Instead, he dropped the other person and went home. I quickly learned that you could only give one instruction at a time. With two at a time, the second one would be forgotten.

There were apologies, and we began discussions concerning the logistical problems that were being experienced. I said that I would need to look at the various sites, so I was given a Volkswagen minibus and a driver. I would visit the major cities.

Nigeria

In 1976 the roads were in bad shape in the country. The VW was not air conditioned, so we drove with open windows, would sweat a lot, and by the end of the day we would be covered in red dust from the dirt roads. Accommodations were difficult and I will not comment on some of the places that I was forced to sleep in. There was one "highway" between Lagos and Enugu. It had been paved, but most of the pavement was missing and there were a lot of muddy areas. Bridges were one-lane concrete sections with no side rails. Drivers would race to be first on the bridge so oncoming traffic would be forced to stop. Mistakes were made, and there were a lot of wrecked vehicles by the bridges. Driving was very dangerous, but we survived.

I was able to visit Benin City, Enugu, Port Harcourt, and Calabar on one trip. A second trip allowed me to visit Kaduna, Jos, and Kano. I also visited the ports and airports in these cities to see what the problems were that we were experiencing.

In Lagos, I reviewed all of the warehouses the various companies were using. At ITT, these companies were called "system houses." There were seventeen system houses working on the Nigerian project. They were based in Italy, Germany, Belgium, the Netherlands, the UK, and France, and there was one from the USA. It was my responsibility to coordinate all of the materials and manpower between these companies and the 307 sites in the contract.

I spent three weeks in Nigeria before returning to Brussels. I submitted a 17-page report on my findings, and there were many discussions about what to do next. That was my call. I said that I would need to visit the various system houses to see the problems from their perspective. It was interesting work, and there was a lot to digest and consider. Any problems with logistics came to my desk. Dan Weadock would simply write in green ink on any problem: "Please handle." I was left with full responsibility to ensure that everything went smoothly and to take care of any problems that were encountered.

I began to visit the home offices and factories of the various system house units that were operating in Nigeria. The major ones were FACE Battipaglia, Italy, CET Milan, Italy, SIETTE Florence, Italy, TEVES Frankfurt, Germany, SEL Stuttgart, Germany, BTM Antwerp, Belgium, and STC Cardiff, Wales. There were others that supplied some materials, but these companies all needed to have shipments, warehousing, customs clearance, support for in-country installers, and in-country trucking. Coordinating these was my responsibility.

Italian Nigeria Shipping Line

The largest movement of materials was from Italy to Nigeria. There were major problems finding ships to take this cargo. I spent time in Genoa, speaking with various shipping lines, and was able to find a company willing to work with us. They agreed to set up a new service to sail between Genoa, Italy, and Lagos, Nigeria. They would use the ITT cargo as their base cargo, allowing us to have a reduced price, and would sell their services to other shippers at a normal price. This proved to be a good match and allowed us to have the ITT shipments delivered on schedule. This new service was listed as Italian Nigerian Line and was incorporated under this name. Problem solved.

Two other companies had major shipments going to Nigeria. BTM in Antwerp was sending communication materials to be installed in the Nigerian telephone exchanges. STC in Cardiff, Wales was shipping large drums of cable for the outside cables to be installed between the numerous locations in Nigeria. Because of the volume, the Italian Nigerian shipping line also agreed to call at both Antwerp and Cardiff on an as-needed basis. The problems that everyone had been having getting materials to Nigeria had a new solution.

I continued making trips between Europe and Nigeria regularly. As soon as I returned from Nigeria, I would immediately submit my passport to the Nigerian Embassy in Brussels for a new visa. Any problems arising in Europe would be brought to my attention, and I would travel as necessary to solve the problem. It was necessary to visit many ports and airports throughout

Europe and Nigeria.

In Nigeria, access to the port areas was very restricted. I needed to find a way to enter the areas where our cargo was being handled. We had a lot of shipments by air, so I needed to enter the airport, which was guarded by the Nigerian military. I found a simple solution. I had some good contacts with Sabena Airlines, so I was able to obtain a shirt for the Sabena crews. When I wanted to enter the Lagos, Kano, or Port Harcourt airport, I would wear this shirt and the guards would allow me to pass. Another problem solved!

The sea ports were also guarded by the military and also had their police force. I went to the head port office of the Nigerian Port Authority in Lagos. At least 50 people were sitting in the waiting room, and I was told to take a seat and wait. I objected and, as I had been with the port of Boston, MASSPORT, I was able to gain access to see Dr. Tukar, the executive in charge of the Nigerian Port Authority. We had a good conversation and as a result, I was given a pass signed by Dr. Tukar. This badge gave me access to all ports as I was viewed as a member of the Nigerian Port Authority. It also allowed me to solve some problems being caused by port and customs individuals who would deliberately cause an issue to make our people pay to have their materials released. That badge carried a lot of authority.

ITT Mailbag

We had another major problem. Getting mail in and out of Nigeria was a nightmare. The Nigerian mail service was poor, messages would get delayed or lost. Telephone communications were also extremely difficult with only 3 lines being available for public use in the country. People were very frustrated and would even send employees back and forth by air to get messages through. I approached the president of Sabena Airlines who I knew on a personal basis. We had worked together when I was with MASSPORT I explored the possibility of having a mail bag dedicated to ITT to be carried on the Sabena flight to and from Nigeria. He agreed with this idea but said it would also have to be cleared by the postal authorities in Belgium.

After about three weeks I again met with Sabena, and we were approved to send a mail bag as Sabena company mail on each flight. I arranged to have a Sabena mail bag placed in the ITT mail room in Brussels. Now we could have direct communications with our people in Nigeria. The tag on our mailbag would have a blue rim so everyone would know which mailbag was for ITT. I arranged for a mail employee in Brussels to deliver our bag to Sabena in Brussels and then I arranged for one of our warehouse employees in Lagos to meet each flight and then to deliver our bag to the ITT head office in Lagos. We had better communication than any of our competitors doing business in Nigeria. I received a lot of praise for this accomplishment!

The word got around in the ITT systems houses, and soon everyone wanted to use this service. I allowed this but on a limited basis. At one point one of the Italian companies attempted to send a huge number of instruction manuals which were bulky and heavy. The mail room called me, and I stopped this shipment. The manuals were sent back to Italy, and they had to find another way to send their materials. I advised them to load their manuals in a sea shipment that was running between Genoa and Lagos. We also had cargo moving via the seaports of Port Harcourt and Genoa.

Our contract with Nigeria was to install the telecommunications systems, and the PT (Post and Telegraph of Nigeria) was to construct the buildings. There were major delays at many sites including Lagos. A new contract was signed for 6 sites where ITT would be responsible for the buildings. To expedite this, ITT would supply prefab buildings made in the Netherlands. A company called Vulsteker would make the buildings. My job was to get these buildings from the Netherlands to Nigeria. I was able to charter an entire ship that could carry this cargo in a single shipment. Then arrangements had to be made to move the materials inland in Nigeria to the various sites. I flew to Nigeria and made arrangements with trucking companies in Nigeria. We now had prefab buildings at six sites in Nigeria, three of which were in the Lagos area.

The ITT Corporation took good care of its employees. We were paid in dollars but, because we were living in Belgium, the dollar was pegged to the Belgian franc. That meant that we were protected if the value of the franc were to rise, making life in Belgium more expensive. If the franc increased in value, we would receive an additional dollar amount. We could make an annual visit to the USA; this was to keep employees from getting homesick. Additionally, they paid for the education of the children in the International School in Brussels. The executives were to fly First Class on any flight of eight hours or longer but were then expected to go to work immediately when arriving at their destination. Nigeria was a 6-hour flight from Europe but, because of the terrible conditions at the Nigerian airports, we all flew first class when going to Nigeria.

Travel in Nigeria was dangerous and not reliable. Nigerian Airways had inland flights which we would use between the major cities. These flights were always overbooked and there were no seat assignments. When a flight was to depart there would be a mob at the gate waiting for it to open. The gate would open, and everyone would run to the airplane. There would be a lot of pushing and shoving to get up the stairs into the plane and then you would grab a seat and sit down. As the flights were overbooked, late arrivals were not allowed on the plane. Those left standing were taken off the plane.

Occasionally there would be someone of importance who would bribe the airport personnel with a sum of money who would demand a seat. Then the staff would enter the plane and begin asking people if they had any checked luggage. If a passenger said no, they would be asked to leave the plane and the other party would get their seat. I always said I had checked luggage so I would be left alone.

There were also many problems with boarding passes as there would be more passes than there were seats. Again, for a sum of money, a person could buy a boarding pass. In Enugu, for example, boarding passes were sold in the men's room in the airport, and these had more value than those that people received at the counter. They were placed at the front of the mob when the doors were opened.

Port Harcourt

Port Harcourt was very difficult. First, you had to have a confirmed booking made with the airline. This, however, did not guarantee that you would be on the flight. Here you had to go to the town office of Nigerian Airways, confirm your booking, and then have your name entered on the confirmed list that was made in the downtown office, not at the airport. This list would be made the day before for early flights and in the morning for flights leaving in the afternoon. Even with a confirmed booking, if your name was not on the list prepared in the town office you would not receive a boarding pass. Then, at the airport, there would be a huge mob pushing and shoving to get a boarding pass. It was difficult and time-consuming to fly out of Port Harcourt.

Hotel rooms were another huge problem. No credit cards, everything was cash. You had to pay in advance, plus an additional day's room rate. This was because people would make charges in the hotel for food and drink. When you check out, any excess money would be returned to you. In Port Harcourt, I entered the Presidential Hotel and asked for a room. There was one available, so I thanked the clerk and gave him a 10 Naira tip. He was surprised and said, "That isn't necessary." I replied, my friend whenever I arrive you will always receive a 10 Naira note for taking care of me. He smiled and said thank you.

I always got a room. One day when I arrived, he looked at me and said the hotel had been taken over by the military—go sit down and wait. This I did. About 30 minutes later he said to follow him to the restroom. He said there is a key to a room in the annex, this is the best I can do. I thanked him and gave him his 10 Naira note. I was the only non-military person to get a room that night. All others were turned away.

One evening I was sitting in the hotel lobby enjoying a beer when I saw one of the staff from the airport enter and sit down. I told the waiter that his drinks were on me. The staff member came to where I was sitting and sat down. Then more of the airport personnel began arriving, I bought drinks for all of them. We had a nice evening and it cost me the sum of 90 US dollars. But it paid great dividends. When I would arrive at the airport, the staff would tell me to wait at the bar. No more jostling in the counter lines. At the bar, the bartender would give me free beer (he was one of those I had hosted) then someone would arrive with my boarding pass and escort me through the terminal. When they were ready to open the door, I would already be outside, so I was at the front of the line going up the stairs into the aircraft. I always got on my flight where many of my colleagues would get stranded. That $90 was a great investment!

Traveling by road was also dangerous and difficult. I previously mentioned the one-lane bridges. These were slabs of concrete and there was one that had a 45-degree turn in the middle of the river. There were many hills on both sides of the bridges. Drivers would race down these hills to be the first on the bridge so the oncoming traffic would have to stop until they crossed. There were numerous wrecks by these bridges from this game of chicken. There were also a lot of overturned tanker trucks on the roads. These trucks did not have baffles inside so when a driver was speeding the contents of the tank would go back and forth, overturning the tanker. Wrecks were just left where they happened. There were no towing companies to clean the roads.

One time, the road between Lagos and Onitsha was being redone. The current highways, which had been built by the British in the 1950s, were in bad shape. Most of the pavement was missing, and the remaining stretches had major potholes. Where there was no pavement, there was red clay dirt. In the dry season, the roads would be covered by red dust and visibility would be limited. In the rainy season there were huge mud puddles and a lot of slippery places where cars would get stuck. The Nigerian drivers were very aggressive and rude. Any trip by car was an adventure. There were contracts given to various foreign companies to build a new highway from Lagos to Onitsha. This was to be a four-lane highway. The companies selected were from

Germany, Switzerland, France, the UK, and others.

This drive took on a whole new experience! The Nigerians would discover where a new section was completed. The locals would put up oil drums with a pole across them and charge a fee to allow vehicles to pass. A white face in the car would increase the amount of the fee that was required. Everyone wanted to use the completed sections, so this became a thriving business for the locals, most of whom were rural farmers. When traveling, we would approach these "toll booths," and I knew which company was building that section. I would roll down my window and in French or German would say, "What do you think you are doing? Open this gate immediately!" This worked and we would be given free passage. It was a fun game to outsmart these locals.

One day when I was in a car driving north from Lagos, our car hit a sheep that was being herded across the highway. The driver asked, "What should I do?" I said, keep driving. If you stop, then there would be a huge discussion, and you would be set upon by locals who would demand a huge sum of money to replace the sheep. One time, one of our shipments of PVC duct was being transported in southern Nigeria when a local drove in front of the truck and was hit. A mob gathered, pulled the driver from the truck, killed him, and set the truck on fire. The other driver escaped by running for his life through the jungle. It should also be said that signage for highways was limited, and your driver had to know the area, especially on local roads. Every road trip was an adventure as you could never know what the day would bring.

Another incident took place one evening in Lagos when we were going back to our living quarters from work. There were four of us plus a driver in a Peugeot four-door sedan. At an intersection, a man on a motor scooter ran into our car and landed on the street. Immediately a mob gathered and surrounded our car. The driver had to deal with this huge crowd, and they were calling us white monkeys and began hitting the car with their fists and umbrellas. The car was being shaken by the mob and we were being thrown back and forth inside the car. The mob demanded money to help this poor man who had run into our car. We took a collection; the driver paid the man, and we were allowed to continue our journey. There were a lot of dents in the car when we finally got to our apartment.

Living arrangements in Lagos were scarce. In the beginning, we rented a suite in the Federal Palace Suites Hotel for $750 per night. It could accommodate up to six people and had one bathroom. Electricity in Lagos was supplied by a turbine. The city had three turbines but normally only one would be operational. What grid would be supplied by this turbine would depend on which chief had given the NEPA (Nigerian Electricity Power Administration) the largest bribe. The locals would say that NEPA stood for never power again! One day, I had been staying in the hotel for a week and we had not had any water in the bathroom. I entered the room late afternoon and a miracle! I tried the shower and there was water. WOW. I got undressed, got under the cold water, covered myself with soap—and the water quit! I dried off with a towel but itched for the next few days.

Later, the company was able to find a block of flats. One apartment was dedicated for headquarters staff to use when in Nigeria. There were three bedrooms, each with two single army-type cots for sleeping. There was a single bathroom that was shared by everyone. The sleeping area was behind a steel door that we could lock at night. There were iron bars on all of the windows for security. There was also a common living room, a dining table, and a kitchen. We had a dedicated cook who would prepare the meals. Water had to be boiled and filtered three times, and care had to be taken with what was served. Many bugs in Nigeria would give us severe stomach cramps and dysentery. I spent many days in a fetal position on a bed with severe stomach cramps. We all carried a medical kit and took medicine against mosquitos and malaria.

The other apartments were occupied by expats who were living and working in Nigeria. Finding edible food was always a challenge. If a store imported some frozen chickens, everyone would rush to the store and buy as many chickens as possible. These would be placed in freezers. Problems arose as the power would be turned off, sometimes for a week or more, and the frozen food would be spoiled. To solve this problem ITT imported power generators for the apartments and houses being used by

ITT. Then the challenge was to keep them properly maintained and find fuel to run them. We still had to find hotel rooms in many of the locations we had to visit, monitor, and inspect.

We also used helicopters to visit the various sites. These would find a landing place close to the site where the local crew would have a car waiting to drive us around. Many times, this would be a schoolyard or a sports area that had been cleared of trees. Many sites had dense jungles around them. There would be a huge crowd waiting to watch the helicopter, as this was a huge event for the locals. We would have to wait and hover while space for us to land was cleared. We would then visit the site and make our reports. The pilots would stay behind to protect the helicopter. Upon returning we would always find a huge crowd around the helicopter, many of them touching the helicopter.

We would ask the crowd to move back with limited success. Then the pilot would start the engine and they would all run screaming away from the plane. The blades would begin turning and we would lift off. Once in the air we would look down and see the mob back on the field smiling and waving to us. This was a big event in their lives as they had always lived in a rural area and had never seen anything but beat up muddy cars and trucks. Each landing was a new adventure.

ITT received a new contract to supply all of the cables that were to be used for this huge project. There were to be big shipments from our facility in Cardiff, Wales to the port of Lagos. Contract Administration had designated the destination for these shipments as the P & T stores in Apapa. I knew this port area and said that I needed to check this facility. The P & T destination warehouse turned out to be a double-car garage. Unacceptable. I gave instructions to the ITT staff in Lagos that they would have to find a place to store these large reels of cable, some weighing five to six tons and standing six feet tall. I went back to Brussels.

The shipments began, and Contract Administration said that ITT Nigeria had solved the problem by hiring a local company that agreed to store the cable for only three percent of the shipment value. A sum exceeding $300,000.000! I said NO and booked a flight to Lagos. The company in question was called Freight Agencies. I immediately met with the Managing Director of this company and said that we would not agree to this arrangement. We had some very long heated discussions but at the end of the day, we became friends and agreed to a normal rate for transport from the arrival pier to the storage area, which had one large warehouse in which the smaller drums could be stored, and a smaller one to be used for the boxes of other supplies needed for this project. The large drums were to be stored in an outside area which was fenced and secured. We agreed on a proper rate for storage. Now, everyone was happy.

I continued to make regular trips to Nigeria and became very familiar with the country, the weather, and the conditions. I developed a very close working relationship with everyone involved, both in Nigeria and also in the system houses working on these projects. There were always problems to be solved and I was kept very busy. I spent a lot of time monitoring the movement and storage of materials and conditions for those working in Nigeria.

Those who were living in Nigeria found some houses and some apartment complexes. We had one American company that erected some buildings in their compound. They drilled a well, so they had their water and installed generators for electricity. They were self-sufficient. The British shipped in some modular units that were used as offices and living quarters. The Germans also used modular units but on a lesser scale. The Italians all rented houses and apartments for their sites.

We had people scattered all over Nigeria. I traveled to all of the sites to keep tabs on what the various system houses were doing at a local level. Company meetings were held in both Brussels and Lagos for the overall control and monitoring of progress. Goals would be set, and we had to follow through to be sure that we were on target with budget and meeting deadlines. I was in charge of all logistics and had a close working relationship with all of our system house transportation units as well as being in charge of our logistics staff in Nigeria.

Containerized Exchanges

ITT received a contract to build 39 mobile containers that could be transported to a location in Nigeria to be used as a telephone exchange for the area. These were valued at $1.3 million each. These were to be stored at our warehouse complex in Lagos, and then transported to the various sites for installation. Other telecommunication companies also received contracts for containerized telephone exchanges. The exchanges would be installed in 40-foot shipping containers. The ITT containers would be manufactured by our subsidiary BTM, located in Antwerp.

The first of these containers arrived in Lagos, and there were immediate problems. When loaded on a truck to be taken to our warehouse, they were too high to transport without tearing down power lines along the roads. I was called and learned that the engineers at BTM had increased the height of the shipping containers to accommodate their equipment. Our containers were too high to be loaded onto a normal truck. All 39 containers had been built and were waiting for shipment to Lagos. The solution was to ship two lowboy trailers to Nigeria which could be used and would allow these high containers to be transported in Nigeria. Another problem was solved.

Our warehouse complex was located in the Northern part of Lagos and consisted of six separate warehouses connected by a walkway that ran between them. There was an office area where I would work when in Lagos. Each warehouse was 1200 by 600 feet, so there was a lot of space. It filled up. The various warehouses were allocated to the system houses, which were responsible for maintaining the movement, storage and care of their materials. I would inspect these when I visited and usually found a lot of things that needed to be fixed or cleaned up. The man in charge of this complex was Mr. Ade Sogbamu, and he would report to me on a regular basis. He was very capable, and I enjoyed working with him. Ade had a staff of 40 warehousemen that reported to him. Locally, Ade reported to the ITT headquarters in Lagos. In reality, he reported directly to me for most logistical operations.

ITT Nigeria had a main office located on a 12-lane highway.

There were several buildings in this complex. The main building was used by Chief Abiola and his team. The second building was occupied by the various system house managers in Nigeria. This is where we would hold the meetings for updates and overall control of all of the ITT contracts and projects the company had in Nigeria. There were a lot, and they spanned 307 different

Oversize containerized exchange on a lowboy

Walkway between Lagos warehouses

locations.

Ade would be advised when I was to visit, and this would be the excuse for him to motivate all of the workers to prepare for my visit. In Lagos, Ade would come to the ITT headquarters and pick me up for my visit. We worked out a plan which would give Ade the ability to get some things done that were being ignored or delayed. During my inspection, I would get very upset and scream at Ade, telling him that he was not a good manager and that he should be doing a better job. The workers would see this and try to defend Ade. I would continue to find fault and demand that things be corrected. Then I would go to the office and do other work. All of the workers would then get busy correcting everything so Ade wouldn't be in trouble. This ploy worked, and a lot got done that had been put off.

The prefab buildings had been constructed, but another problem developed. The floors were metal, and the installers discovered that this was causing equipment malfunctions. The exchanges which were being shipped to Nigeria were all electro-mechanical switch bar frames. These could not be installed on metal floors. To solve this problem, there was a product manufactured in the UK called screed. This could be applied to the metal floors and, when dry, would enable the switching equipment to be installed in the prefabs. This was a rubber substance which would prevent the metal frames from shorting out when attached to the metal floors. Now I needed to arrange shipments of these 55-gallon drums from the UK to the six sites in Nigeria. This was accomplished and life was back to normal.

Coaxial Cable Problem

One morning at 6:30am there was an urgent pounding on my door in Lagos. There was a major problem with the area where the ITT cable shipments were being stored. When I arrived on the scene, we were blocked from entering the storage area by the Nigerian Army. They were using a bulldozer and knocking down the walls of the warehouses. I spoke to the officer in charge and was told that this was illegal storage and that everything needed to be removed. This area was property of the federal government, and a new highway would be built where our cable was being stored. I explained that we had a contract with Freight Agencies and were paying them for this storage. They said they didn't care and continued to block us from entering the area until they finished destroying the walls of the warehouses.

We had a long discussion. The manager of Freight Agencies arrived and there were some heated words exchanged. It took several hours, but finally we reached an agreement. ITT would vacate the area and remove all of the cable drums and other freight stored inside the buildings. We were given 30 days to accomplish this task. I put Freight Agencies on notice that they would be responsible for the removal of our materials. The large warehouse had a steel frame, so the roof remained but the s ide walls were destroyed. The smaller warehouse only had cinder block walls, so here the roof was supported by the boxes containing the ITT materials. It was up to me to solve this problem.

I had security guards posted around the area and went to the ITT headquarters in Lagos. I requested that the traffic manager from STC in Cardiff, Wales be sent to Lagos. Then there were a series of discussions involving the Nigerian P&T officials, the

Warehouse with walls removed by the Nigerian military

top managers of ITT Nigeria, myself, and the ITT Contract Administrators who had originally designated the PT warehouse as the destination. (This was the two-car garage in Apapa.) After two days of meetings, the decision was made to store these shipments at the various PT exchanges located around the country. Some of the drums stood six feet tall and would weigh three to five tons. There were several hundred large cable drums, and many smaller ones that could be handled without the need for heavy equipment. I applied pressure on Freight Agencies to arrange transportation to more than 50 exchanges.

The traffic manager from STC Cardiff arrived, and Fred and I spent the next two weeks sorting the shipments and getting them loaded on trucks. There were hundreds of shipments to be arranged, and local trucking companies from all over Nigeria were hired for the movement from Lagos to the PT exchanges. We set up a small tent with a wooden table on the side of the road to monitor these shipments. We would authorize each load, and then require a receipt showing the delivery of each shipment to the proper location. Fred and I would work from 7 am until 7 pm each day, including weekends. It was hot, dusty, and in an area that most people would not want to visit. We had to bring our own food and water as nothing was available in this area. This was a hot, dirty, nasty job, but we managed to clear the area and safeguard all of the materials.

This movement of cable took place during the dry season. This means that the heavy drums were stored outside of the various PT exchanges. At the PT telephone exchange in Calabar, three large drums had been stored in the yard next to the telephone exchange. During the dry season these were above ground. Then came the wet season with heavy rains. The ground became muddy, and these four- and five-ton drums sank deeply into the mud. The dry season returned and the ground hardened. There were only 10 to 15 percent of the drums above the ground. The rest was encased in dirt that was hard as cement. I would be surprised if the cable could be saved and used. I am thankful that I didn't have to handle that problem.

We had one of our Italian companies working in Port Harcourt. To prepare for the materials that would be coming, they rented a piece of ground and a building to be used for the storage of their supplies. They erected some telephone poles and placed security lights on them connected by copper cables. The next morning, when they arrived on site, both the lights and cables were gone. They had been stolen during the night. They replaced everything and left two security guards. The next morning, everything was gone, and the guards were missing. I was asked to come and help. I found a solution. We brought four guards from Kano in the north who were from a different tribe. These guards used bows and arrows. In their tribe, the tips of the arrows would be dipped in poison and used for hunting. They stationed themselves in the jungle surrounding the storage area. When there was an intruder, an arrow would come out of the jungle, scaring the culprit away. Some locals became bold and tried again. Then arrows with poisoned tips were used; those that were hit by these arrows had major medical problems. Now we had a secure area in which to store our materials.

To guard our warehouse complex in Lagos, we hired guards with dogs. The complex had a wall around the perimeter, and there were two entry gates on the street leading into the complex. The complex was 700 feet wide at the street and extended back for 2,800 feet. An area exceeding one million square feet with six large warehouses, and an office area with a lot of outside storage. The 39 mobile exchanges were stored at the rear of the complex on four-foot-high cinder blocks and timbers. The dogs were let loose in this complex at night. You would not want to be around these dogs. They were very vicious and dirty. Only their handlers could be in that area. Any stranger would be attacked and bitten. We never had a problem with theft from this complex. I would never enter this complex if the dogs were present.

One day during the rainy season we drove into the compound to find at least a foot of water with monsoon rain falling. I had my driver take me around the complex to discover even deeper water where the mobile exchanges were stored on cinder blocks. There was one large open sewer in the right rear corner of the complex. Everything was contained inside this cinder block wall surrounding the complex and the water was rising.

The one sewer was overflowing and there was no place for the water to go but up. Something had to be done. All of the warehousemen were inside, staying out of the rain. I was told that the people in the complex behind ours had cemented all of the drains from our complex shut. Their complex was at a much lower level and water had been flowing from our yard into theirs.

I was wearing a safari suit which I removed, grabbed an iron bar and waded out into waist-deep water. The water was almost reaching the mobile exchanges by this time. I began punching holes through the cinder block fence next to the open sewer. Some of the warehousemen came out and began to help. The water level began to fall, and our materials were not damaged. I was the only white person in the complex that day and I was regarded as a hero. It actually worked out well, as all of the warehousemen gained respect for me as they saw that I was not afraid to get my hands dirty when there was work to be done. They would follow my instructions and things would get done much more quickly and to a better degree than was previously the case. We developed a team spirit and people began working together as never before.

We had no running water in our complex. Electricity was supplied by generators. There were two restrooms in the compound. We had a dedicated "executive restroom," and everyone else had to use the larger restroom. Ade placed a 55-gallon drum in the restroom which we had filled with water by a water truck. This we could use to wash dirty hands or flush a toilet. We kept this facility locked. No one else had access to water. Life was good as an executive. There were only four of us who had a key to our retreat.

Each Friday there would be a line of people waiting to see Ade. This was part of the system which allowed contact from the tribal elders to everyone in their tribe. In Nigeria, everyone in a tribe would be recognized with a gift from the chief and Oba of their tribe. The Oba would hand the respective chiefs the weekly gift. Then the chiefs would pass the gifts down to the next level, who would then hand the gifts down to the next level. Ade was at a higher level than most, so he would be handing out the gifts to a certain group. The gifts were usually money, so everyone received something from their chief. This gave loyalty to the chief and tribe. Even a janitor or cleaning woman would receive something from the chief. There were four major tribes in Nigeria, the Yoruba in the South, The Hausa and Fulani in the north, and the Ibo in the east of the country. Ade was fluent in English, Yoruba, and Hausa. Chief Abiola, the head of ITT Nigeria, was Yoruba. It is said that there are more than 160 tribes in Nigeria, and most have their own special language. The official language of Nigeria is English. It was previously an English colony.

We faced major obstacles and unforeseen problems working on these Nigerian projects. One of our Italian companies was laying some underground cable to connect some villages with their telephone exchange. They were using a Ditch Witch, a machine that digs a trench with the front of the machine. There is a reel of cable on the machine which unrolls and lays cable in the trench, then the rear of the machine will push the dirt back into the trench covering the cable. They were using this machine alongside a road when a mound of rocks was in the way. They pushed the machine through this mound and continued along the road, laying the cable.

About two weeks later, a letter was received by ITT stating that we had destroyed a sacred shrine that was protecting their village from evil. They demanded that this shrine be replaced, or we would be responsible for the health and safety of their village. The people in Brussels laughed and said it was a joke. I said this was no joke and that these people are deadly serious. Further investigation found that this was a serious matter and that something needed to be done. I met with the village elders, and I said that we would replace their shrine. A ceremony was held, the rocks were piled in a certain order, words were spoken, and then the blood of two chickens and a goat were dripped onto this shrine while words were spoken, and everyone prayed. I was thanked, and ITT was relieved of the responsibility to take eternal care of this village.

The airlines serving Nigeria would all schedule a flight leaving Lagos on Friday evening as everyone would want to be back in Europe for the weekend. As a result, Friday nights were always busy. There would be crowds pushing and shoving in all areas. Especially bad was the security clearance leading into the boarding areas. This consisted of a plywood box with doors on both ends. You had to stand in line to enter this box, which could accommodate two people at one time in the box. On a Friday there would be 15 to 20 flights leaving between 10pm and midnight. Most were large planes, so there would be several thousand passengers passing through this two-man security box. It was time-consuming, so you needed to get to the airport early.

Driving to the airport was also a challenge. There was a single road leading to the airport and it would be congested with traffic. This was a two-lane road with people selling their goods from small stalls on the side of the road, and people coming and going to all of these stands. There were many intersections and no traffic lights, so drivers were forced to push their cars forward at every opportunity. This drive was more complicated during the rainy season as the market stalls, normally located along the flood-prone sides of the road, would be moved onto the road itself, leaving only one lane open to traffic. This made an already congested road even more difficult to navigate. It was 14 kilometers from our living quarters to the airport. If you had an evening flight you needed to leave early in the morning. It could take up to twelve hours to get to the airport.

Choosing which airline to use was up to each individual. Sabena only flew twice each week and was usually fully booked. Lufthansa and Swiss Air had flights that were good but not every day. My main choice was British Caledonia, which offered daily service. This gave me more flexibility as I could fly on any day. I got to know their staff in Nigeria, so they treated me as a VIP. They also had a Friday night flight which left three hours before the huge mob booked on the later flights. The flight time between Europe and Nigeria was only six hours, but the ITT headquarters people were allowed to use first class due to the huge problems with airports and overcrowded planes. A lot of people flying in economy class would be denied seats as someone would bribe the airline staff for a seat.

Delayed Flight

British Caledonia had a flight at to London at 9:00 pm on Friday. This was my choice as I could go through security before the huge crowd would arrive for the later flights. I joked with several of my colleagues as they were booked on other flights that left around midnight. I had a connecting flight Saturday morning to put me in Brussels early morning.

I arrived at the airport, checked in and was through security by 7 pm. There was a new airport building just completed so all of the chairs had been removed to the new airport. There was no place to sit, nothing to eat or drink, just a huge empty space. I didn't worry, as I would soon be in a first-class seat enjoying some refreshment and a nice meal. I sat on my suitcase and waited for my flight to be called. An announcement came that the BCAL Flight would be delayed. I continued to wait and then others for the later flights began to arrive. With all of these people now crowding into the airport, the temperature began to rise. The air conditioning was not working.

The later flights began to be called, and my flight was still delayed. I watched my colleagues board their planes and leave. Then an announcement was made that the scheduled BCAL flight was changed, and we would be flying to Accra instead of a direct flight to London. I later learned that the scheduled plane had broken its nose wheel when landing in Lagos and would have to be repaired. We flew to Accra, and everyone had to get off the plane. Now there was something available to purchase to drink, but you could only purchase things with the local money. I didn't have any, and there was no money exchange available. I found another person who was boarding in Accra that had local funds. He was kind enough to let me exchange some dollars with him so I could get something to drink. It was now early Saturday morning, and I was in Ghana.

We were scheduled to leave at 10 am Saturday morning, but then that flight was delayed. There was heavy fog in London, and we would have to wait for the fog to lift. I used the limited amount of local currency I had left to buy something to eat and waited. At about 2 pm, we were advised that the fog in London had lifted, and we would go. Happily, I settled into my first-class seat, and enjoyed some good wine and food. We would be in London about 9 pm and, with luck, I could catch a connecting flight to Brussels.

As we were approaching the UK, the pilot announced that the London weather forecast was for more fog. He said we would try to land, and we began to circle the airport. After some time, it was announced that we would be landing in Manchester.

After landing in Manchester, we were met by some buses. We were advised that we were all to be processed in London because of all of the checked luggage. The luggage was loaded onto trucks and off we went, convoy style, to the London airport. It was midnight when we arrived and cleared customs. The ticket counters were closed, and people were leaving the airport. Instead of sitting all night in the airport, I decided to take the underground into London and get a hotel room. To find a vacant room in London at 1 am was a challenge, but at 1:30 I was booked into the Cumberland Hotel. I left a wakeup call for 6 am and went to bed. When I woke up at six am, I immediately called Sabena and made a booking for a 10 am flight. This was now Sunday morning. The weather was clear.

I checked out of the hotel and went to the airport. When I arrived, I checked in for my flight, cleared security, and went to the boarding area. We boarded the plane, and I had a glass of orange juice. There we sat—and nothing happened. An announcement came from the pilot, stating that we were waiting for clearance as there was heavy fog in Brussels. There we sat. An hour later, we were told that we should leave the plane and go back to the boarding area. Everyone would be given a one pound note so they could buy something to eat or drink. I looked, but there were no phones available to call Brussels.

Around 3 pm, we were told that Brussels had cleared, and we should board the airplane. After a short delay we took off and were on our way to Brussels. We landed. I claimed my suitcase and looked for a payphone. I called our home in Waterloo, but there was no answer. I went outside the airport for a taxi, only to find a long line with major delays. I then took the train to Brussels Nord only to find another long line waiting for a taxi. So, I walked down to the Sheraton hotel, again tried to call Waterloo, and again there was no answer.

The doorman at the hotel was able to find me a taxi, so off I went, destination Waterloo. We were on the ring road when traffic suddenly came to a dead stop. There had been an accident in the tunnel ahead, and a car was on fire. There we sat for at least 45 minutes before the road was cleared and we could proceed. I now had an expensive taxi bill. Arriving at home, I paid for the cab, the house was dark, and it was now Sunday evening. I unlocked the door, went in, made myself a drink, and sat down. About 15 minutes later, the door opened, and in came the family. I said hello to be met with, "Where have you been enjoying yourself this weekend?" I responded that I had a flight delay which was met with some very unkind words. I didn't say anything further as I did not feel like arguing. The family went upstairs and turned on the TV and I made a second drink. I was in the doghouse the rest of the week.

The challenges continued in Nigeria. We were asked to place one of the containerized exchanges in Abonnema in Rivers State. I was told that there were problems and that the installers needed help with this exchange. I flew to Port Harcourt and prepared to visit the site. One of the engineers had a 20-year-old son visiting and he asked if he could go with me. I agreed and the next morning we went to the Port Harcourt docks. Abonnema was on an island so the only way to get there was by boat. There was a ferry which took three and a half hours, so I opted to go with a speed boat. There were many available, some good, some bad, and all with aggressive drivers. I entered into negotiations and watched who belonged to which boat. There was a good-looking boat, and when this driver approached me, I accepted his offer.

Abonnema

Upon arriving at Abonnema we were met by a large crowd of people. We were a novelty as this was a remote island, population 72,000, all crowded into one main town. We selected a young boy as a guide and went to the local telephone exchange. Here I found a single operator with plugs that she would put into slots to connect the telephones. Further research revealed that there were no roads other than a single narrow road on the island. There were two small taxis on this road, which was seven feet wide. Now I wanted to see where this container was to be placed. This was a long walk with a huge crowd following us. The young girls kept taunting the 20-year-old boy and pulled on his pants. They wanted him to show them how a white boy made love. He became very embarrassed and turned red. I was able to shoo them away and we arrived at the destination site.

There was a concrete pad which had been made and some switching boxes to be used when the container was installed. I said let's have lunch while I think about what could be done. We were told that there was a small hut where they sold drinks and food, so off we went. This turned out to be a small hut with a porch, and no air conditioning, so we sat on the porch. He said he could make us a sandwich. I asked if he had anything to drink and he offered beer. I ordered two beers, and they were served frozen solid! They were stored in his freezer! We waited for the beer to melt and ate our sandwiches. In the meantime, a local hunter walked by with a monkey hanging on a stick over his shoulder, dinner for his family.

I did find a solution for where to place this container. There was a construction company building a road on a nearby island that was using a barge to transport their equipment. I was able to strike a deal with them to allow us to drive our truck with loaded container onto their barge and transport it to Abonnema. We placed some logs on the riverbank by the school as the ground was very muddy and marshy and then took down the fence around the schoolyard to allow the truck to access this site. Success!

We had many indigenous contractors constructing the buildings for the local exchanges. These needed to be inspected before we could begin installation of the telephone equipment. A site in Northern Nigeria was ready for installation so it needed to be inspected. Another person from our Brussels office was in the country so we were asked to make the inspection. We flew to Kano which is in the North and checked into our hotel. The next morning, we left the hotel at 7 am for the airport. We had chartered a small plane from Aero Contractors to fly us to the small city of Katsina. We were told that Katsina has a small airport.

It was almost 11 when we arrived at Katsina and looked for the airport. We flew around several times and the pilot said, "that looks like a radio shack next to that grassy field." We made several passes over the field to be sure there were no hidden obstacles. We learned that no plane had landed in Katsina in the last three months. We buckled our seat belts tight, and the pilot landed on the grass, which turned out to be two feet tall. Bill and I walked over to the radio shack; there was an antenna on the roof. We found a Nigerian sound asleep next to a radio. We woke him and asked where we could find a taxi to go into town. Answer: walk three miles down what looked like a footpath to the main road.

We began walking through the grass and mud. We saw a shack with some horses grazing next to it. There was a man sitting there so we spoke to him. In the discussion I asked if we could use his horses to go into town. We agreed a price to rent the horses. There were bridles but no saddles, so off we went bareback on horses. Executives from a large corporation performing an inspection. Needless to say, we attracted a large crowd as we entered the city. We tied the horses at the exchange and began our inspection.

This was a cinderblock cement building. There were numerous problems. The upstairs floor was very weak and would actually move when you jumped. There was no way that this would ever support the weight of the equipment to be installed. The door to the generator room was too small to allow the planned generator to be installed. There was no proper drainage so the building would flood when there was heavy rain. There were other numerous problems, so we did not accept the buildings. A new building would have to be constructed. We asked where we could find something to eat and drink. Nothing was available that we could eat, and there was nothing to drink other than local water.

We mounted our horses and rode back to the airport. We paid the man for the horses, found the pilot, and started to fly back to Kano. It was late when we landed and returned exhausted to our hotel. The restaurant was closed so we went to the bar. We had not had breakfast as we left early, and there was nothing in Katsina. Maybe in the hotel bar? There was nothing available to eat. We asked for a beer, no beer as the delivery truck did not come in today. The whole town was dry. What about a soft drink? Same answer: no delivery truck. What do you have? Some fresh orange juice for $12 a glass! We each had four glasses; it had been a long hot dry day. The next day, our return flight to Lagos had a six-hour delay.

When we returned to Brussels and submitted our expense reports, both Bill and I placed "horse rental" on our expense reports. We had told everyone in our section about this experience, so it was well known what had happened. A week later our expense reports were returned with the comment that this was a business trip, so the horse rental was declined. We both wrote back with a long explanation about why we had rented horses instead of using a taxi. In Nigeria it was impossible to obtain a receipt from a taxi so if we had put "taxi" instead of "horse rental," it would have gone through without comment. There was a further exchange of information and finally it was approved. The amount was only $20. Everyone had a big laugh about this affair. Then, about a month later, this charge was again rejected, this time in the head office in New York. Again, an exchange of information, and New York still refused to honor the charge.

It was finally approved after Dan Weadock wrote a memo. I believe he enjoyed this episode even more than some others. We still laugh

Containerized exchange in transport

about this story when we are together.

It was important to be familiar with the European ports and trucking agencies that were being used for the Nigerian project. This required that I visit all of the companies involved in the project. In Italy there were three companies, CET in Milan that supplied generators, FACE in Battipaglia with various factories, and SIETTE in Florence, who were working on electrical transmission lines. I spent many days in Genoa, which was the main port for these companies. The generators being supplied by CET based in Milan were to be sent by air. One day, I planned to fly to Lagos aboard a DC 10 that had been scheduled from Martin Air to transport a load of generators to Lagos. The plane was configured for cargo and there were two pilots, a radio navigator, and a loadmaster aboard from Martin Air. My Italian logistics manager had all of the cargo loaded and we were ready to leave for Lagos. Going down the runway we were gathering speed, but the plane was not lifting until the very last moment when we barely cleared some buildings. In a later discussion, I learned that my Italian manager had falsified the weights and had overloaded the plane by 23 tons. It almost got us killed.

In Belgium we worked with BTM (Bell Telephone Manufacturing) which was the main supplier of the electromagnetic switches in the exchange buildings. They shipped via the port of Antwerp and also Rotterdam. They also produced the 39 containerized exchanges which were stored in Lagos for distribution. TEVES in Frankfurt, Germany supplied special equipment and SEL in Stuttgart supplied some exchange materials and switches.

The coaxial cable was supplied by STC in Cardiff, Wales. STC also had other locations in the UK which were involved. The other major supplier was CITESA in Madrid, Spain. This company had 28,000 employees. All of these system houses had shipping departments and my responsibility was to ensure that everything ran smoothly. When there was a problem, I was called to come and fix whatever was wrong. As you have read, there were many problems encountered with this project that required assistance. There was always a condition I had to remedy.

ITT also had companies working in other countries in West

Africa. I was asked for assistance in Ghana, Benin, the Ivory Coast, and Senegal. We were receiving materials from Senegal which needed to be shipped to Lagos. This would be shipped from Dakar to Lagos, however, there were problems with trucking in Senegal. I really got to see a lot of places in Africa where a tourist would never go. Many roads and infrastructure were very crude, and this required thinking out of the box to find solutions. There were many challenges to overcome and solve.

The Nigerian PTT (Post Telephone and telegraph) requested that we install strong security locks on the warehouses where their equipment was stored before installation. These warehouses had steel doors, and they now demanded that we put strong security locks on these doors. We bought some very heavy-duty locks in the UK and shipped them to Nigeria. They increased the security at the warehouses. However, losses were experienced. The walls of these warehouses were built with cinder blocks. These were not of good quality so when the thieves wanted to enter and steal, they simply broke through the wall and took what they wanted. The steel doors and the special locks were never touched.

Another challenge thrown onto my plate was when I was informed that one of the warehouses could not be entered as it was full of wasps. Upon investigation, we discovered three huge wasp nests in this warehouse. Using special clothing and a lot of smoke these nests were removed. This warehouse contained generators, all on pallets. These pallets were no longer usable as they were full of termites and would collapse when being moved. There was always something new in every day. A person would say today I will do these 10 things. At the end of the day, you might have done two or three, but you would manage to do five or six other tasks that you hadn't thought about but would take an opportunity to accomplish.

When trying to meet contractors and other individuals you had to drive to their office only to find that they were going to your office to meet you! There were no telephones to use, so you were forced to meet in offices. You would pass each other in traffic without knowing that the other party was driving to your office. For this reason, you had to be an opportunist, and do what you could when there was a chance.

Caribbean Cruise

In the fall of 1979, the ITT corporation chartered a boat to reward its valued employees for special efforts and achievements. In the AME division, I was selected to go on this all-expense paid cruise as a thank you for the service I had rendered in Nigeria. Rosa and I were flown from Brussels to London to join the European group flying from London to Miami, Florida. As I was in the headquarters of AME, we were given first class seats for this flight.

In Miami we were all taken to our cruise ship for a six-day cruise in the Caribbean. We had a first-class cabin on the ship and were treated to wonderful meals and all of the drinks we wanted. We sailed to various islands and spent one full day at sea. The final stop was in the Bahamas where we were taken to an island by special boats that met our ship. Here we were treated to a wonderful cook out on the beach and then viewed a presentation of native culture and dance. We enjoyed an afternoon on the beach, and, in the evening, we had a special dinner.

We sailed back to Miami and spent one night there before returning to Brussels via London. This was a very special treat, and we met a lot of the top executives from the ITT headquarters In New York. There was music, dancing, and various entertainments aboard the ship. This was a great honor and there were only three people selected from Brussels.

A special request was made to have me assist CITESA, our Spanish system house in Madrid. They had received a contract to place telephone exchanges in 12 cities in Iraq. They were having problems with the logistics involved and they asked for my expertise on this project. Sadam Hussien was the president in Iraq and I was not sure how my visit would be received. I went to the Iraq embassy in Brussels and applied for a visa, which was refused. I gave this information to CITESA and said I was sorry that I couldn't help them. They responded for me to send my passport to Madrid so they could get a visa for me.

The American Embassy in Brussels issued me a second passport, which I sent to Madrid. They took this to the Iraq Embassy in Madrid, which refused to give them a visa for me. A week later, I received a call from Madrid that they had been able to obtain a visa for me to visit Iraq. As the embassy had refused to issue a visa, the managing director of CITESA went to the palace and told King Juan Carlos about this problem. He was the one that had obtained the contract. I was told that the Palace had called the President of Iraq, Sadam Hussein, who then instructed his embassy in Madrid to issue a visa for me. WOW!

Iraq

Plans were made for me to fly to Madrid, meet the team going to Bagdad, and pick up my passport with my visa. I went to Brussels airport for my flight to Madrid to connect with the team in Madrid. Upon arriving at the airport to check in, I was told to go to the customer service counter. Here I was told that the flight was overbooked, and I would be flying on a later flight. This resulted in a very long conversation with me explaining why I had to be on this flight. The flight was boarding, and I was still arguing at the counter. Finally, they found a solution. There was a lady in first class who had a baby that could be carried on her lap, and I was given a seat assignment and a boarding pass.

I took my suitcase into the jetway way with me as the flight was being closed. I gave my suitcase to an agent who took it down the stairs to be loaded into the plane. I entered the plane, sat down, and was given a glass of champagne. Then the flight attendant said that the captain wanted to see my ticket. She returned and told me that I had to get off the plane, the captain would not take me. I tried to explain but there was nothing I could do so I had to leave the plane. I was not in a very good mood, and I had to go back to the customer service counter.

Now we had a new conversation. They already knew in detail about the problem, and they tried to be very accommodating.

They could book me on a flight to Frankfurt and Lufthansa had a direct flight from Frankfurt to Bagdad. I could meet my colleagues and they could give me my passport with the visa. I said no. What happens if I arrive in Bagdad without a visa and miss connecting with the Spanish team that I had yet to meet? Too high of a risk.

Finally, it was agreed that Sabena would bring my passport with visa from Madrid to Brussels and would return my suitcase which was in the plane flying to Madrid. I was then booked on a flight to Frankfurt with a connection to their Bagdad flight for the next day. I returned to the office and related the story so Madrid could be advised. That evening, I went home and packed another suitcase as a backup for the Iraq trip.

The next day, I arrived at the Brussels airport to find my passport with the Iraq visa waiting for me. But my suitcase had not been returned, so I checked my backup suitcase and flew to Frankfurt. I caught my connecting flight and flew to Bagdad. I received a lot of attention as an American arriving without diplomatic status. I was allowed to enter Iraq and was met by the ITT representative in Iraq, who was an Austrian national. He said only speak about personal and family things, which I did. We drove to his house and went out in his garden. There was a hose fastened to a tree which fed into a bucket. He turned this hose on and then standing close to this flowing water he explained that everything he did was monitored. They used directional microphones to pick up conversations and would place magnetic devices on his cars to hear conversations in the car.

I then checked into my Bagdad hotel and had the first meeting with my Spanish team. We had dinner and agreed to meet at 10 am the next morning. CITESA had also hired an in country Iraqi manager. There was no office at this point, so we met in the second-floor lobby area. We had to decide where our installers would reside, how the equipment would be shipped and stored, what medical facilities were available, what food would be available locally and what was the situation of the buildings at the various exchange sites. CITESA had a contract for 12 sites in Iraq, most in the south with three in the north. Our meeting began with the in-country Iraqi manager, the Spanish director for the project, and the chief installer.

We had been meeting for about two hours when two beautiful young Asian ladies came in and sat down at a table in the room. One Spanish installer immediately left our meeting and went to their table. He was back in a few minutes and said they were waiting for someone. An older Iraqi gentleman entered and joined the two ladies. They ordered champagne and snacks. Each time they were served, this gentleman would give a 30- or 40-dollar tip to the server. Then they entered the restaurant, and we could see a lot of attention being given to this party and a lot of tips being given to everyone. They finished lunch, left, giving huge tips to the staff, and entered the elevator. The doors closed. There was a lot of activity with the staff on the telephone and running down the stairs. Five minutes later, the gentleman and his two friends were back in the lobby. This man was well-educated, dignified, and had a lot of money—and yet this was not enough to "get lucky with the ladies." My Spanish employees had none of these resources, and even less opportunity to get a date. How would my Spanish installers cope with this situation? Another problem to be addressed.

We agreed to leave at 6 am the following morning to begin a visit to the various sites. Our Iraqi manager said we would have breakfast along the way. We drove south and reached the Hanging Gardens of Babylon. The manager opened the trunk of the car and we enjoyed a breakfast of bread, jam, honey, and a lot of tea. We were able to view this site, which also allowed us to see the stone upon which the code of Hammurabi is written. It was a very enjoyable meal and a unique way to visit a special place. We then proceeded to the various sites to decide how to manage the project. It might be of interest that we were always followed by at least one black car and sometimes two. We were observed at all times and had very little privacy. There were always directional microphones pointed at us.

We were having dinner at a very nice restaurant in Basrah when a huge rat ran over my foot. Iraq was full of rats. All of the hotels were infested with rats. Our hotel in Bagdad didn't have a problem as it was full of cats. They would be in the hallways, and you could see them in the air conditioning ducts and the kitchens.

I was able to visit seven of the twelve sites under the contract. We could not enter the port areas as they were very closely guarded and sealed. In Nigeria, we had to pack everything in huge boxes that couldn't be moved by a single person. In Iraq, I recommended using smaller boxes so the installers could carry them into the exchanges. Theft was not a problem; things were very secure and safe.

Returning to Madrid, I went to CITESA and gave them a report along with my recommendations for their project. This included recommendations on how to pack their equipment, where to store materials in Iraq, what transportation to use in the country, where to house their employees, certain foods that they should send to Iraqi to feed their employees, what medical facilities were available, and what vehicles they should purchase for the project. I also recommended that the young Spanish men should work 21 days nonstop in Iraq and then be given a week's leave back in Spain each month. This was accepted as everyone realized that this would solve any problems of young men misbehaving in a country where there were very tight restrictions on society.

There was a major change in ITT in Brussels. The Nigerian project was in the ITT AME (Africa Middle East) Division. The President of ITT Europe received a telephone call from the New York World Headquarters. He was told to have the head of ITT Security come to his office. This was done and there was a short conversation. You are no longer working for ITT, you have 20 minutes to remove your items from your office, Security will then escort you out of the building, we will be in touch, and the call ended. The next morning Dan Weadock was seated as the new president of ITT Europe. As a result, all of us in the ITT AME division moved into the ITT Europe tower and assumed additional responsibilities.

ITT Europe

I now had the oversight for logistics over the 167 system houses owned by ITT in Europe, in addition to overseeing the Nigerian project. The previous office of AME on Avenue Lloyd George was closed. I now had an office on the 19th floor in the ITT Tower. The 20th floor was reserved for the top senior executives of ITT. The 21st floor contained the office of the President and the Director of Human Relations. Additionally, there was a large conference room with a large oval desk which seated 21 people, backed by two rows of chairs for support personnel during official, top-level meetings. There were also some smaller conference rooms for side talks. There were two underground levels used for parking. The mail room was located on the upper level of the underground levels. There were elevators that went to the ground floor. Located here was an entry area with security guards. We all wore an identification badge to allow entry. The second floor contained the cafeteria and the medical unit. There were doctors and nurses in a medical unit and then from floor three and higher were offices.

ITT used a grading system for its employees. The lower floors would be for low-level employees, the higher floors were used for high-level employees. There was no floor 13. The floors from 18 down were managers and other employees. Floors 19, 20 and 21 all had locked restrooms. You had to have a special key to use these restrooms. There were two levels of parking at levels of minus two and three. We were all issued a special pass which would open the gates blocking access to these levels. There were elevators that exited on the ground floor where guards would check your identity passes. Everything was tightly controlled.

One of the perks I enjoyed working for the ITT corporation in Europe was that all employees received a Home Leave trip once a year. We would receive round trip tickets for ourselves and our immediate family to our home country. As we received four weeks of vacation under Belgian law, this meant that we could now take a four-week vacation to Wyoming each year.

One of my goals in life had always been to build a house

with my own hands! When I was growing up, my father had trained me in woodworking and doing repairs around the house. My grandfather Thomas and I had worked together in his workshop, restoring a roll top desk that we had in the family home on Pershing in Cheyenne. It was my mother's desk, and I was very proud of the part I had played in restoring it. I had spent many hours sanding the various parts and helping in their assembly. My father was very skilled in woodworking and made many closets, cabinets, and alterations to our Pershing home.

I would use this vacation time to build my dream home. In 1976, we were able to find a seven-acre parcel of land close to Woodslanding which we bought.

The first goal was to find water. We drilled a well and found water. In Denver I found a used 28-foot house trailer that we brought to Woodslanding so we could live on the property. I had power brought to the property, so we had electricity and water. For sewage we dug a big hole, and now we could live in our trailer. It was powered by a butane tank so we could cook.

The construction began by digging a hole for the foundation and basement of the new house. We hired a backhoe. I was able to borrow some forms and constructed a basement foundation and basement walls.

We also installed a septic tank complete with a leach field and built a floor over the basement. This we covered with tar paper, drained water from the trailer, and left to go back to Europe.

The next year, we found frozen, leaking water lines in our trailer, but the basement and floor of the house were all in good shape. Then we constructed the log walls, rafters, roof and shingles, doors, and windows, built shutters for the front doors, and went back to Europe. The following year, we again found frozen leaking pipes in the trailer which we repaired and then we began the interior work. We sold the trailer and moved into the basement. In this fashion, the house was constructed in stages and paid for as we progressed.

Dan Weadock was the AME Project Director before his promotion as the new President of ITT Europe. In AME, Graham Davies was the Director of Project Support Services, and he was promoted to be the new Project Director. Then Peter Sommer was moved to be the new Director of Project Support Services. I reported to Graham on European matters, and Peter for Africa. Peter reported to Graham, and Graham to Dan Weadock. This arrangement would cause some problems in the future.

To give an oversight of everything, I organized a physical distribution council for all of Europe. I visited all 17 countries in Europe where we had multiple system houses and organized a country council. Then each country would select one individual to represent their country when a meeting of the European Distribution council would meet, usually in Brussels. This way I had a direct line to all 167 system houses in Europe and was able to be aware of developments. If there was a smaller problem, I would receive a report from the country manager. When a program was required to be installed in all system houses, I could do this via my European Council. It was easier to meet with 17 individuals rather than take 167 separate visits. When a major problem was encountered, then I would take action where required.

As an example, we had a serious problem in Sweden, as warehousing costs were huge. I spent some time in Sweden, visiting all of the sites handling our materials. As a result, I closed 14 of the sites where goods were being handled and stored and everything now moved through the five remaining sites. Material handling costs were reduced by 46 percent. We had improved efficiency with fewer locations and less staff.

Another example was a company in the Netherlands producing light fixtures. I discovered that they were making 520 articles in their catalogs. They had three large warehouses containing their products. I reviewed production and sales reports for each item. This had to be done using printouts from their records and was a long, tedious procedure. I found the problem was that as it took them a long time to retool their manufacturing equipment, they would make a large amount of each item. Some were sold, but most were in storage, which was costing them money. My solution: the 520 items were reduced to only 103 items, the others were cancelled, and the remaining items in storage were sold at a reduced price or scrapped. Two of the three warehouses were closed. The company began making a profit.

I continued my responsibilities for the Nigerian project. Additionally, I visited the ITT offices in Ghana and the Ivory Coast. Based on the logistics for Nigeria, I also made visits to Senegal, Gambia, Togo, and Benin. At one point, we had a major problem in storing equipment in the northern city of Kano, which required several visits to solve. I continued to visit the various site around Nigeria in all parts of the country. There were problems encountered all over the country and we had 316 sites where we were installing equipment.

As previously stated, we were given first class air travel when visiting Nigeria. On one occasion I had to visit Hamburg prior to flying to Lagos. In the first-class section from Brussels to Hamburg there was only one additional passenger. When landing, we stood up to get our luggage and I saw his coat. Being polite, I retrieved his coat and handed it to him. He said thank you and I asked him where he was from. He said Nigeria. I responded, "My friend, how can I help you? I have had many great experiences in your country." He was pleased and we talked. He was booked into a first-class hotel. I said, "I go right by there, why don't we share a cab?" to which he agreed. He then asked how much money he needed to exchange, and we discussed what he wanted to do in Hamburg. We then drove into the city and stopped at his hotel. I went in with him to be sure he was taken care of, and then he asked to meet the next day. I said I would pass by when I finished my appointments.

The next day I arrived at his hotel about 4 pm and he was there. He wanted to have a drink, so we went to a famous bar on the Alster. He ordered a whiskey which surprised me, as normally Muslims don't drink alcohol. Then he said he wanted to visit the Reeperbahn but was afraid as he was black and didn't speak German. We spent an interesting evening together, and I took him back to his hotel. He said thank you and said that I should contact him when I came back to Nigeria. I took his card and returned to my hotel. His card read "Honorable Alhadji Kaltungo, Speaker of the House of Representatives, Nigerian Federal Government." I had no idea who he was.

After that when I would visit Nigeria, I would visit him. He lived in the 1000 Estates which housed all of the government employees, including the President. I was the only white person I know of to be allowed entry into this heavily guarded seat of government. We became good friends and spent many evenings watching movies, having drinks and conversations. I met many important people when visiting Alhadji. He always reserved the seat to his right for me. This was the seat reserved for important visitors. One evening, the door flew open and in came a team of high-level military leaders all in uniform. They informed Alhadji that there was a breach on the border with the Cameroons and six Nigerian soldiers had been killed.

There was a heated discussion, Nigerians are like Italians and get fired up when speaking. I sat there quietly and listened to all of the Generals and politicians discuss what action to take. Should they bomb the Cameroons? Should they invade with their troops? Everyone was very excited and believed action should be taken. After a 30-to-40-minute discussion on the subject, Alhadji turned to me and said, "What do you think we should do?" WOW. What should I say? I asked, "Were your troops killed on our side of the border? Were there alcohol, drugs, or women involved? Who fired the first shot?" They all looked at each other, no one had answers, so a decision was reached that they would ask for more information and meet again tomorrow. Everyone left. Alhadji and I had a drink, and I went home.

Another interesting tidbit involving Alhadji: it so happened that we were both booked on the same flight from Lagos to Frankfurt one day. Alhadji said he would pick me up and we could go to the airport together. I said thank you, and the next morning I was outside my apartment waiting for Alhadji. Chief Abiola, the ITT executive who had obtained all of the contracts, happened to come by our complex. He asked me where I was going, and I said to the airport. I told him that I had a Nigerian friend who was picking me up. The Chief was horrified and said, "I cannot allow you to be taken by a Nigerian, my driver will take you to the airport." Around the corner came a jeep with a mounted machine gun, followed by a staff car, and then a larger limousine followed by more military vehicles. The convoy stopped, a Nigerian second lieutenant emerged, came over and picked up my bag and I said goodbye to Chief Abiola. I was treated to first class treatment at the government lounge at the Lagos airport.

On my very next trip to Nigeria, I was summoned to the Chief's office and was asked to explain why I was speaking to government officials as he was the one with the contacts. I gave him an explanation and we went quietly back to work. Chief Abiola and I had a tighter relationship after this incident. I continued to spend time with Alhadji Kaltungo on all of my visits. He was a good friend, and we enjoyed each other's company. He was from Bauchi state.

East/South Africa

ITT had factories in Zambia, Zimbabwe, and South Africa. They used the name Supersonic and manufactured radios, televisions, and some other appliances. Graham came to me and said he wanted me to visit these factories. I agreed, went to our travel bureau, and decided to take Rosa with me as she had never been to Africa. She was surprised but agreed to go. Tickets were issued and we both got visas in our passports. Two days before our scheduled trip Peter Sommer came to my office and informed me to cancel my trip as he was going to make the trip. I was not happy and received a bad reception at home.

I was never told in detail about what transpired in Zambia, Zimbabwe, and South Africa, but Peter Sommer did not make any more trips and I was again asked to visit the factories. My first trip was to Livingston, Zambia where I was able to solve some problems they were experiencing. This location was close to Victoria Falls where my hotel was located. Over the years I was able to view the falls in the dry season and also the rainy season where a trillion gallons a second would cascade over the falls. There is a single bridge from Zambia to Zimbabwe which I crossed on several occasions.

On the highway in Zambia. 4wd is required!

The factory in Zimbabwe is located in Bulawayo. The operation was smooth running with a few minor things that were easily corrected. In addition to working with the factory, I was invited for dinner at an executive's private residence. We had a cocktail and then he came into the room with a baseball bat in hand and asked if I would help him. I agreed, we went into the living room, and he said "stand to the side and pull the food cart away from the wall quickly; I did as he requested, and this revealed a large cobra. He swung the bat and killed the cobra! I asked if this was a common occurrence. He said, "No, that this was only the second one they had seen in the four years they had been living in this house."

I continued on to South Africa and first visited the headquarters in Johannesburg. Supersonic has a factory in the north and seven locations around the country. When I visited the factory, I found it located next to a factory which processed all of the ivory collected legally from Kruger National Park, the national game preserve. I was introduced to the manager of that factory and was able to legally purchase a carved ivory elephant which was an unusual piece, and also a tusk which was engraved using a dentist drill. We had dinner in a game lodge which was being renovated. There were many heads of various animals which I could have bought cheaply, but I had no way to transport them. The factory visit went well. I was able to give them some advice for logistics and also production which they thanked me for and put into their system.

The next step was to visit all of the other locations to assess what was being done at each one. Other than Johannesburg, the factory in the north, the only other location that was worthwhile was in Durban, where their materials were being received. Here we were able to establish a free trade zone, which saved a lot of

There were no bridges--river crossings were by ferry

money for the company. As a result of my visit, four locations were closed.

I saw a lot of changes in South Africa as apartheid was slowly coming to an end. One evening I was sitting in a local bar when a man came in with his driver, who was black. I could see that this driver was very uncomfortable being in the bar, so I asked the man if I could use his car and driver to run an errand. He agreed and the driver and I left together. I got in and the driver asked, "Where to sir?" I replied, "Drive around the corner and find a good place to park. I saw how uncomfortable you were in that bar." He thanked me, and I sat in the backseat and enjoyed a beer that the driver went and got for me. We had a nice chat. Thirty minutes later we returned, and the driver said he would wait in the car for his master.

ITT received a new contract to install telephone exchanges in seven locations in Zambia. I was asked to go to Zambia and set up arrangements for this project. I was met by two American installers and one Norwegian installer who would be working on the project. First, we had to visit the sites to see what problems they would present.

We hired a game guide and his assistant to take us to the sites. We had a 4-wheel-drive Land Cruiser pickup and another Land Cruiser SUV for transportation. There was a large box with a huge chunk of ice where we placed some food and beer to keep everything cool and fresh. The guide, his wife, and I rode in the pickup. His assistant rode in the bed of the pickup. The three installers and a driver rode in the SUV.

The first day we drove nine hours, were stuck in mud often, and had to pull each other out several times while traveling. We only passed two buses and one truck during this journey. We stopped for the night, drove into the bush, and set up camp. The assistants climbed a tree and attached an antenna so the guide could contact Lusaka and let them know our location.

There was a lot of friction between South Africa and the neighboring countries, and there were convoys of armed soldiers patrolling who would shoot a white man on sight. That is why we hid in the bush. In the morning, the Norwegian installer crawled out of his pup tent wearing silk pajamas, slippers on his feet, holding a toothbrush, and asked, "Where can I brush my teeth?" It was hard to keep from laughing as we had all slept in our clothes.

Suddenly, we were surrounded by soldiers holding their weapons on us. We were taken to the police headquarters and kept in cells while they checked to see who we were. We all had been issued an identification card by the PTT headquarters in Lusaka. It took several hours before everything was confirmed, and we were released in the town of Munilunga. This area is located in the northwest corner of Zambia next to Angola and Zaire. It is a nine-hour drive and only has bad roads, many impassible in the rainy season. This site presented problems.

We continued to the next site, Mongu, on the opposite side of the Zambezi River. To get there we had to cross the Barotse Floodplain. In the dry season, the road would descend 12 feet and then you would drive kilometers until you reached the Zambezi River, where there was a ferryboat that would take you across the river. Another two-to-three-hour drive would bring you to the opposite side where you would again climb up 12 feet and enter Mongu. This site did present some challenges as during the rainy season the flood plains would fill up and there was no way to cross from one side to the other. We had to schedule delivery of materials and make special arrangements for the installers who would be developing this site.

The visit to the final sites took us across the southern part of Zambia. It was interesting to travel with this group and observe all of the different lifestyles and problem solving. Both the guide's wife and the assistant would prepare meals and each night we would drive into the bush and contact Lusaka using the short-wave radio. We slept in tents and every evening there would be a bonfire used for cooking and afterwards to enjoy a cold beer and interesting conversation. After visiting these sites, we were happy to return to Lusaka and to have a shower and once again eat food from a normal table.

I was scheduled to return to Brussels on a British Caledonian flight the next day. I had planned to spend a few hours in the morning in the office and then go to the airport. That night I had a problem in my hotel room as the a/c would run hot and cold. I did not sleep well and the next morning I did not feel good. I cancelled my office visit and was later informed that my return flight had been cancelled as the BCAL flight had broken its nose wheel on landing and would have to be repaired. I was able to rebook on Alitalia via Frankfurt. I was in first class, but only drank a glass of orange juice during the flight from Lusaka to Frankfurt. I transferred and upon arrival in Brussels struggled to leave the airport. I arrived at the ITT building and collapsed in the lobby. The guards took me to our clinic who then sent me to the hospital.

I was placed in the emergency room, and they sent my blood sample to Antwerp. The results came back. I had a serious case of cerebral malaria. I was placed into intensive care. Fluids poured out, I was sweating, they changed my pajamas five or six times, until finally I calmed down. I was kept in intensive care for several days and later was released with the orders to stay home and rest. I had no strength and was unable to work for six months. Then I went back on a part-time basis. It took a full year for me to recover from this sickness.

Mozambique

On one of my trips to South Africa I was asked to visit Mozambique to check the ports and transportation possibilities. There were two ports, Maputo, and Beira, which was midway up the country. To enter Mozambique, you needed a visa. The only way to get a visa was to have someone in the country sponsor you. ITT had an office in Maputo, and they notified me that they had been able to get a visa for me which would be waiting for me upon arrival. Upon arriving at the Maputo airport, I discovered that there were three plywood cubicles, all having a long line, waiting to be processed. Which cubicle would have my visa? I chose the middle one and joined the line. I waited a good 45 minutes in line and then it was my turn. You enter this cubicle and sit on a small bench facing a window covered by a drape. A hand comes out and a voice says give me your passport. Luckily,

I made the right choice because this agent had my visa. The visa was entered in my passport, and I exited to go through security. They were not gentle, and this was a bad experience, as they went through everything I had with me.

Some other travelers informed me that there were no taxis because of a fuel shortage. I was stranded until a kind gentleman offered to take me into town in his car. There were five of us in his car and, as I did not have a hotel reservation, they offered to take me to my hotel. It was late in the evening, but I did manage to get a room. There was nothing to eat or drink so I went upstairs and went to bed. The next morning, I came down for breakfast to find the only thing available was a piece of bread and some hot water. I found an empty chair and sat down. I saw that the people would get a cup of hot water and would then make a cup of tea or coffee. They all had tea bags or a jar of instant coffee for this use. Most people also had a jar of jam for their bread. I was thankful that a kind gentlemen offered me some coffee and jam.

The ITT manager picked me up after breakfast and we went to the ITT office. It was on the 17th floor and the elevator wasn't working as there was no power in the building. The elevator shaft was in the middle and the stairs were around it. There was no light, so we ascended the 17 flights in the dark. The office was dusty and hot. The only window in the room was broken so there was a small breeze. I was told that they couldn't replace the windowpane as there was no glass in Mozambique.

We had some discussions about our activities. ITT was installing some signal lights on the railroads in the country. I gathered some information and then we went down for lunch. After lunch, I told them that I was meeting some freight forwarders and that we could meet the next morning at my hotel as I would be flying to Beira.

That afternoon I met the freight forwarder, and we had some positive discussions. I also learned that we would be on the same plane to Beira the next day. We agreed that we could sit together and have some further discussions. He was flying to Haare, Zimbabwe via Beira. This didn't happen as he checked in as an international passenger and I was an in-country passenger. The international passengers entered through the front door of the plane, and we entered using the rear door. There was a rope across the aisle that no one was allowed to pass. I saw my colleague and he saw me, but we were not allowed to sit together.

I went to my appointment which was with the Mozambique port authorities. They gave me a nice welcome and I felt at ease with them. I received a lot of information and learned a lot about the local circumstances. At one point there was a lot of noise coming from the street. We saw a pickup truck loaded with fresh fish surrounded by guards and followed by a huge crowd of people. They all wanted to buy some fish. The truck went next door, and the guards began unloading the fish while the crowd formed a line. I asked my companions if they wanted to get in line. They laughed and said, "We get ours via the back door."

They invited me for dinner and said that there was only one restaurant where we could get some food. Remember these are government officials so they had special privileges. There was no menu, tablecloth, or dishes on the old tables. The only food available was chicken. We each had a helping of chicken and my hosts had brought some beer with them. We were the only ones in this restaurant to have something to drink. We ate with our fingers from paper plates. There was a crowd of people standing in the street watching the restaurant. There was a dirt floor and no ventilation, it was open air. When a piece of chicken was finished and pushed aside, someone would run in from the street, grab the plates, and run back into the street. People, including children, would sit on the ground and eat the bones. These people were starving.

My hosts offered to drive me to the airport in the morning. I had a flight to Malawi scheduled for 1 pm. They picked me up at my hotel and we managed to have breakfast served in a government compound. Then, they insisted that they would give me a tour of Beira. I said that I wanted to go to the airport early. They kept delaying as they said there was more to see. We drove by the airport, the plane I had flown on from Maputo was sitting on the tarmac getting ready to take off. I asked them to stop but they said there is plenty of time and that there was something else they wanted to show me. So, an hour later, they finally drove me to the airport and dropped me. I entered and saw that my scheduled flight was ready to start boarding. I rushed to the counter and said that I was on the flight. The clerk replied, sorry, the flight is closed. I could see the plane and insisted that I be allowed to board. The clerk said that I couldn't as the customs officials had left for lunch! I watched three passengers board the plane, the door closed, and the plane left. I was not happy.

I asked to see the manager and was shown to an office. This was the airport manager and he apologized and said that they would book me on the next flight. I asked when that would be, and he said next week. It is a weekly flight. He went on to explain that they would find a hotel accommodation for me. Remember this is all being conducted in Portuguese. Needless to say, this was unacceptable, and I wanted to be booked back to Maputo. I knew that there were daily flights back to Johannesburg. He said that was not possible, so I just sat there and said that was the only acceptable solution. He again said that he could not authorize that, and I should leave and go to a hotel. I refused and sat in his office like a stone. He continually tried to get me out of his office, but I refused and sat there. He became angry and threatened me, I paid no mind and continued to sit in his office. This continued for several hours. I wouldn't budge.

Finally, he said that he would get me a return ticket to Maputo. I said when I have a booked ticket in my hand, I would leave his office and go to the airplane. There was an incoming flight, and he left his office to manage the flight. Passengers arrived and there were passengers who were waiting to board. He came to his office, handed me a ticket, and led me to the boarding gate. The flight was called, and I boarded. The flight was overbooked so the manager came on asking people to give up their seats. He looked at me and I glared at him. I stayed on the flight while others had to leave. Then we took off, not to Maputo but to Quelimane, which was further north and away from Maputo. We flew for more than an hour and landed. Then I discovered that this plane would fly on to Maputo. I remained onboard and all passengers left with a few exceptions. Then new passengers came aboard. The aircraft seated 220 passengers; we took off with less than 20 passengers. It was a four-and-a-half-hour flight, and we landed shortly before midnight. The Italian Ambassador was on board, and he offered to drive me into the city.

I learned that gasoline was rationed. A single car was allowed eight liters per month. No wonder there was little traffic. I went back to the hotel I had stayed in before to find there were no rooms available. I knocked on the door where the gentleman who gave me coffee was staying. He allowed me in, and I was able to sleep in a chair in his room. The next morning, he again treated me to coffee and jam for my bread. I managed to find a ride to the airport and was able to take a flight back to Johannesburg. I was back in civilization and enjoyed a wonderful dinner and a good night's rest.

Nigeria experienced a lot of corruption. The Naira was a blocked currency and was tightly controlled by the Central Bank of Nigeria. You were not allowed to take more than ten Naira out of the country. To do business overseas all Nigerian business deals would go through the Central Bank for foreign currency allocations. There were clever ways to get around this blockage.

An automobile dealer in Nigeria would apply for foreign currency to purchase some auto parts overseas. His relative in the UK would furnish paperwork that would show a sale of $10,000 in auto parts. The bank would approve the sale and send the $10,000 to the UK. The relative would get a container, go to the junkyard, and load the container with junk. Then, the relative could go to his bank in the UK and get the $10,000, showing that the materials had been shipped. The container would arrive in Lagos, and no one would claim it. Now the Nigerian auto dealer could travel to the UK and have money waiting for him. The ports in Nigeria were full of unclaimed shipments.

The government took action. A deadline was set on claiming cargo sitting in the Nigerian ports. When the deadline passed, the government would bulldoze all of the unclaimed cargo into the sea or pits that were dug for this purpose. Then they negotiated a contract with a Swiss company called SGS. The system was to control three things in a shipment: price, quality, and quantity. They developed a form M that would have to be filled out for each shipment coming to Nigeria and the form M was part of the required documentation to allow the shipment to enter

Nigeria. All shipments were then subjected to inspection to see if the price was correct, to see if the quality of the items being shipped was up to standard, and to see if the quantity of the materials being shipped was correct. A form M would then be filled out and would accompany the shipping documents to allow entry into Nigeria.

I became aware of this development and wrote several messages to headquarters and the system houses of this new procedure. There were a lot of discussions and a lot of meetings concerning this form M. It was decided by the ITT lawyers that this did not apply to our shipments as we were shipping government cargo. I disagreed but company policy followed the advice of the attorneys. Life went on until suddenly the installers in Nigeria couldn't do any further installations because they didn't have parts and materials. These were all being held in the Nigerian ports waiting for clearance which required a form M. My phone rang and I was directed to solve this problem.

Form M

I flew to Nigeria, and spoke with many people: both ITT employees, as well as government officials. The lawyers were still holding firm saying that we were not required to use the form M. Then I flew back to Europe and visited the system houses that were involved in this problem. This took a three-week period to visit everyone, to obtain information, and to develop a plan for the project to move forward. I returned to Brussels and spent the next two days compiling everything, and writing a report to prove to the attorneys that we did have to comply. This was a three-page report with 12 pages of attachments. My secretary was typing this for me. It was lunchtime so I asked her if was done. She said that she needed another 45 minutes to finish so I said I will go to the cafeteria, have a quick lunch, and sign it when I come back.

I returned from lunch and said I'm ready to do a final read through and send the report. She responded, "the report has already been sent." WHAT! I'm sorry, Peter Sommer took your name off the report, and he signed it and had it sent out. Needless to say, I was not a happy camper. My efforts were now known as the Sommer report as it was being read at high levels. My relationship with Peter Sommer was not a good one. Later, I was asked to attend some high-level meetings as Mr. Sommer could not answer some of the questions being asked. I no longer had to report to him, and I now reported directly to Graham Davies.

I was visiting Zambia on an extended tour when our local manager, Tony Johnson, invited me to go fishing with him on the weekend. He said he had a new boat and wanted to try it out. We would go and fish on the Kafue River. Fantastic! He was to pick me up at my hotel at 6 am on Saturday. I was waiting and waiting, and finally he arrived at 8 am. He said that there had been some complications but that we were all set. He was driving a pickup which I shared with his wife and baby in the front and a helper riding in the back.

When one enters the Kafue National Park there is a wide cleared area to keep the tsetse fly from spreading. Every vehicle entering or leaving the park is inspected and sprayed.

Visitors to the park are required to register and stay in one of the lodges. Tony was an honorary Game Ranger so he could go where he wanted. We drove about 45 minutes along the highway when he turned onto a path going into the jungle. We drove another 20 minutes and arrived on the bank of the Kafue River. We selected a camp site and began unloading the pickup. Tony and the crew set up the camp and my job was to pump up the rubber dingy which was the new boat. When the dingy was inflated we took it to the bank and placed it in the water. We had to wade to the boat with the motor and then attach it. Barefooted, Tony and I got into the dingy, started the motor and off we went. We cruised down the river and caught a few catfish. It was very enjoyable. Along the way there were herds of hippopotamuses in the water. These we avoided and would go to the other side of the river to pass them.

The hippopotamus has killed more people in Africa than any other animal. They are very territorial and protective of their territory. They are not meat eaters; they forage on grass, but they have extremely large mouths. They will not attack, but if you invade their territory they will come after you. They simply crush a person and then leave them to rot or be eaten by the other animals in the park. The park had lions, tigers, large snakes, crocodiles, and other meat-eating animals which were living in the wild. A person had to be cautious at all times. Most animals will avoid human contact unless they are threatened or hungry.

We continued downstream and I was enjoying this close up view of nature as we motored along. Then we decided to go back to camp as it was getting late in the day. When we turned around, we discovered that our speed was dramatically reduced as we were going against the current. Slowly we motored along when suddenly the motor quit! Luckily, we were close to the bank, so I was able to grab a tree branch while Tony worked to restart the motor. He got it started and we continued upstream. Then a mother hippo with her baby surfaced about 30 feet behind our dingy. Then she disappeared and was under water. They run on the riverbed and come up for air. She appeared again, about the same distance and again went down. This went on for about six to eight minutes until finally she was gone.

It was beginning to get dark, so we were anxious to get back to camp. Then the motor quit again. This time we were in mid-stream, so we were carried by the current. Tony kept trying to get the motor started by pulling on the cord, it was not starting, he pulled harder—and fell over the side of the boat into the river. There was an oar which I was able to grab and extend to Tony. He grabbed this and I pulled him back into the dingy. Using the dingy seat and the oar we paddled back to shore. Luckily, we did not run into a herd of hippopotamuses as we came to the riverbank. We moored the dingy. Tony said he had a friend who had a boat, and they could get it on the next trip. Now we had to walk. Whoops, we had left our shoes and socks back at camp. We had a canvas mail bag we had been using for the fish. This we cut into four pieces, tied onto our feet, and off we went.

The hippopotamuses come ashore at night to forage and eat. We had to be careful not to walk into them. As we progressed it was getting dark. There were also some estuaries feeding into the river. Some of these were small but others required wading through them Here you had to be careful of alligators. It was now dark and hard to see. Tony kept calling but received no answer. We continued walking for another 30 minutes when suddenly Tony's wife answered his call. He said turn on the truck lights and we made a beeline for them. We arrived on the other side of a huge estuary while Lorna was looking on the riverbank for us. I said I don't care what is in that estuary I'm going to camp. We waded through a 3-foot deep, 15-foot-wide body of water and arrived at camp, with very sore feet. My feet hurt for the next 3 weeks. Tony had a bottle of Scotch which helped to calm down.

The next day we headed back to Lusaka and did find two tsetse flies in the pickup which the park rangers killed. Along the highway we saw a Land Rover with an empty boat trailer parked. On Monday, when I arrived in the office Tony said, "do you remember that empty boat trailer we saw on the way home?" I said yes and he continued "that belongs to my friend. He was attacked by a hippopotamus who took a big bite out of his boat. He was able to get to shore safely, but his boat is a total loss." My response was, please don't take me on any further walking tours of your national parks. We all laughed. We were happy to be safe.

In the USA a company had been formed to handle all of the logistics expenses in the USA. It was based in Florida where all invoices concerning freight movements were centralized and paid. ITT had been able to negotiate contracts with the major trucking companies and related services. All of the ITT US companies were directed to have all invoices for shipments paid by this company in Florida. In the US there are rules and tariffs established for what can be charged by freight companies.

ITT-TDS

A system for handling and paying freight and related invoices was developed in the United States. All invoices would be handled by a company in Florida, ITT-TDS (Transportation Distribution Services)

This company would receive all invoices for ITT-owned US companies, check them against existing rates and tariffs, approve them, and then pay from Florida. They would also negotiate rates with US carriers for international shipments. Most invoices could be checked against published rates and tariffs that were controlled by the government for trucking and related services.

A decision was made to implement this system in Europe. I formed a new company which would be located in the Netherlands. The new corporation, ITT-TDS (Transportation Distribution Services) was incorporated in Den Hague. I rented an apartment in Scheveningen and hired an assistant. The family remained in Waterloo, so I was asked to drive back and forth each weekend. As the company was new it required some long hours, but I did my best to comply. This was extremely complicated as there were no set tariffs for many shipments, everything was based on negotiations, each company had their own negotiated rates, and there were different countries and currencies involved.

During this period, I had to work long hours to build this new company. The traffic on the Dutch highways was heavy, especially on Fridays when everyone was going home from work. It could take as long as two hours to drive from Den Haag to Rotterdam, which could be done in 15 minutes when traffic was normal. Working late in my office and then facing a three-to-seven-hour drive to Waterloo was demanding. If I had dinner before I left to avoid the heavy traffic, my arrival in Waterloo would be late. This was always a dilemma, especially as I would be tired from working long hours. There were always things to be done at home and then I had to be back in my office at 7 am on Monday.

I had a lot of pressure from all sides on how to spend my time. The director of the TDS facility in the USA could not understand why I couldn't get all of the European companies to join the program as he had in the United States. Simple, the US had a system of tariffs and rates for the whole country. I had to deal with many countries, each with their own systems, plus we were dealing with various currencies. In the USA it was all in dollars. The European logistic managers in each company were not in agreement, they all had their own deals with shipping companies and were resisting central control. ITT Europe was pushing for this new company to be profitable; headquarters in New York was monitoring things closely, and I was getting a lot of family pressure. There were a lot of balls to juggle, but I kept going.

In 1986 a new company was formed, Alcatel. ITT joined with the Compagnie de General in France. ITT was the minority, so the top executives were French. A decision was made to only have French leadership, so all Americans working in Europe were given termination notices. When I received my termination notice I went home to tell Rosa. I was met with the comment, "Well, Thomas, how are you going to support me?" Only parts of ITT were to be sold. My company was listed on the "to be sold list" as it was decided that we were part of the telecommunications division. ITT retained their other companies, such as insurance, manufacturing, automobile parts, etc.

I was the only American based in the Netherlands and was able to negotiate an agreement to stay as an employee until the end of 1988. This allowed me to qualify for a pension and for Alex to finish her education in Brussels. I would remain on the Alcatel payroll, but I would not have employment duties. This meant looking for a new job. I decided to return to the US for a job search. ITT would give support to the fired European employees. I would receive assistance from a company in Denver, the closest office to Wyoming.

Woodslanding

Returning to the USA on a permanent basis required a lot of adjusting. I had been living in Europe for the last 23 years where there were different rules and laws that Europeans had to live with. There were some differences in culture and requirements of daily life. The family remained in Belgium. I prepared a resume and made weekly trips from Woodslanding to Denver where I received support in my job search. I sent out a lot of applications but did not have any success. I filed for divorce and tried to reach an agreement with Rosa. She came to Wyoming and hired an attorney which forced me to do the same. I made my last trip to Belgium the end of 1987, leaving December 31st so I could have a fresh start in the USA on January 1, 1988. I agreed to return to Belgium in March 1988 so we could sort out our personal belongings.

Then in February of 1988, I received a phone call from Cowboy Moving and Storage who said that they had a container for me. A 20-foot container was delivered which had been packed in Belgium. I had not authorized any shipment, and this was a complete surprise. When I opened it, I found personal belongings from our house in Waterloo. The items were placed in my garage, and I signed a delivery receipt. I began to open some boxes and when I saw the contents, I became very sad and depressed.

I was alone when I began living full time in Woodslanding. At the time I moved in, the house had been developed to the point where there was a basement, a first floor and a garage which could be entered with an outside door. I soon discovered that there were major problems in the winter using this garage. The front of the garage would have a snow drift from 3 to 6 feet in depth. To get to the garage one had to shovel a path from the basement door to the garage door and then shovel a path for the vehicles to exit the garage. This was a lot of shoveling so I decided to construct a new garage which could be entered without going outside. I created a sunroom which was connected to both the old garage and the new garage. The new garage was at a higher level and faced east. There was no drift that formed in front of this garage, and I could use the vehicles without having to shovel. I also could access both garages via the sunroom. I was able to acquire an additional plot of land, so I had a total of 17.6 acres.

My job search continued so I made many trips to Denver. I met a young lady in Laramie who was having some problems. She had two daughters, aged 13 and 14, who were both in Denver in a hospital. They were both pregnant and expecting to give birth. She heard that I was driving back and forth to Denver and asked if she could have a ride. I agreed, I would pick her up and drop her at the Denver hospital so she could be with her daughters. On one trip we returned to Laramie and her house was found with water inside. There was a litter of eight puppies standing on a small, raised area with the mother dog out searching for food. She asked me to take the dogs to the kennel as she could not care for them. I agreed and took the mother and eight puppies to the Laramie city dog shelter. The puppies were cute, so I kept one. I named him Spotty.

During this period, I was able to spend time with my mother and sister in Cheyenne which was rewarding. Then I lost my mother in February 1989. In her will my mother left some money for me and my sister and the family home at 109 West Pershing. Using some of this money I made a $30,000 down payment on a fourplex in Laramie. This meant I became a landlord. This investment proved to be a good one and I used the rental income to pay the mortgage. I hired an individual to manage the property and collect the rent each month and this was an additional income to other earnings. I took a ten-year mortgage on this property and the rental on the four units paid the mortgage. These were all three-bedroom apartments; three of the units included a garage. There was a shortage of three-bedroom apartments in Laramie, so I had very few vacancies.

The divorce proceedings with Rosa became very messy and I was severely depressed. I had requests coming for support money during this process. As long as I was still receiving a paycheck from ITT, I would send $3,000 a month to Rosa. When the paycheck from ITT stopped, things became very nasty. I held my new puppy and cried a lot; it was an earth-shattering experience. In the end, this divorce was finalized in April 1989 with my life savings being lost. I was forced to use the rest of the inheritance money I had received when my mother died in February 1989 to pay the personal debt created by the divorce decree. Now I was penniless with no employment. I had my dog Spotty to keep me company. My sister and I became very close, and our sibling relationship became very strong. For the first time in my life, I finally had a woman who truly cared for and supported me. I was blessed to have this experience. I miss her.

Growing up in Cheyenne I had a fox terrier Sparky who was my companion. He and I were always together. As a paperboy delivering newspapers Sparky was always with me. He was hit by a car when I was in high school. When I was married to Carmen we had a beagle dog, Mike. In Brussels the only pet we had was Fido who was given to Rosa by her sister Karola. When I was traveling in Africa Rosa returned him to Germany where he was killed when a horse kicked him. Rosa did not like dogs. Then, in Woodslanding I was lonely, so I adopted Spotty. His mother was a combination Germen Shepherd and Doberman mix, and his father was an Akita. I felt he needed a companion, so Rusty joined us. He was a full-blooded German shepherd. These two dogs bonded and were allowed to run free on my property. I placed Spotty in a police dog training school for 2 weeks and he was well trained and very protective. Later they were joined by Yogi, a Basenji who was Tonia's dog in California. She was moving to New York and Yogi would be temporarily with us in Wyoming. He stayed!

When Yogi first arrived, he had to adjust. Living in California and New York he was used to being on a leash. When he would break free Tonia used to chase him. The first day we opened the door, and he took off like a shot, then stopped and looked back, like well aren't you going to chase me? To him it was a game. He soon learned from the other dogs how to act; however, he chased some antelope which is a no-no. This caused him to go to jail for a day (locked in the garage), which he didn't like. He was convinced that he was the Alpha dog and continually tried to show Spotty that he was in charge. I came home one day to find Yogi covered with bite marks, he then allowed Spotty to be the Alpha dog. They evidently had a discussion about who was the alpha dog. There was never any question in the future.

Mayme Lestum, the owner of the Woodslanding resort, died and our neighbor Lorraine Wicklund was named as the executor of her estate. I was a pallbearer for Mayme Lestum at her funeral and the resort was put up for sale. Lorraine asked me if I would help her maintain the property and I agreed. The dance hall and restaurant were closed, and we kept a small fire burning in the wood stove to keep the building from freezing. Then the property was sold, and the new owners said they would open a gambling casino. I told them that Wyoming would not allow this, but I was told, "I have a friend who says that there will be new legislation soon that will allow this."

The people that had bought the Woodslanding resort defaulted and so control went back to Lorraine Wicklund. They had moved the bar into the restaurant dance hall building and there was a small store, post office and gas station in the original building. Lorraine asked me to run the resort for her and I agreed. We closed the dance hall and concentrated on the store and cabins. I was able to enlarge the groceries and items being sold in the store and rented some of the cabins. The people who had purchased the resort had operated the store on a minimal basis. It was closed a lot and people had to get someone from the restaurant to open it when they wanted to buy something or to get gas. I opened the store seven days a week. I kept a fire burning in the large building so it wouldn't freeze.

Again, I stocked the store and was able to keep it open seven days a week from 7 am to 7 pm. The locals gave me good business, and all was going well, except I was working 84 hours a week. When a local wanted something, I would tell them that I would carry that item in the future. I went to Laramie every two or three days so I could have fresh dairy items including milk. I made weekly trips to Sam's club in Cheyenne to buy canned goods and other items for sale. I used my purchase price plus one-third, which made the price competitive to Laramie stores. I bought cigarettes, candy, and other related items at a wholesale dealer in Laramie. There was a bakery truck which passed on a daily basis, and I always had fresh bread. I priced the gasoline 12 cents above the prices in Laramie, this was for the tourists. I sold gasoline to the locals for the same price as was paid in Laramie. I had a great business and was doing well. Then the resort was sold a second time, and I was unemployed again. I did have my apartment house in Laramie producing some money (there was a mortgage to pay) and now I received a pension check for $670 from my employment with ITT.

I found a job selling cancer insurance in the rural communities in Wyoming. I had to drive to various locations for 8 am

Monday morning meetings, usually in a restaurant, and then spend the day calling on farmers and ranchers. We were required to be in the field Monday through Thursday and would have to turn in the day's results in the evenings. This required driving from Laramie to Sheridan for the first area, and later driving to Riverton for the next area. We would meet at 8 am to plan the day's activities, then we would each work a certain area. We sold two types of policies, a monthly and a yearly, depending on how the payments were to be made by the customer. We were paid a commission on the policies we sold.

Most salesmen would only sell one or two policies a week, as it was a difficult sell. I was able to do better. One day we were visited by the regional supervisor, and he would motivate the salesman. He rode with me, and I was able to sell $3,000 of insurance in one day. He was impressed. He said he would give a prize to anyone selling three or more policies the next day. In the evening, he asked for results, I said that I had sold two monthlies AND 2 annuals. He was shocked and I won the prize, a collection of motivational lectures by Zig Zigler on how to sell.

The company held a convention in Puerto Rico which Bob Bumford and I attended. This was all smoke and mirrors and I felt it was not serious, only a lot of dog-and-pony shows. So, I left and went to Saint Martin, where I enjoyed nice beaches and good food. When In Puerto Rico I had been charged $10 for a hamburger which was a patty between two buns. Ketchup, mustard, and onions were available in small packets on the counter. I flew back to Wyoming and didn't sell any more cancer insurance. Bob and I discussed the situation and decided that was nothing but a fraud and a scam. Along with two other men who also had been selling insurance we hired an attorney and sued the company. Bob Bumford was the lead person in the filed complaint, so we worked together. We had two attorneys, one in Cheyenne the other in Riverton.

While the lawsuit was being processed Bob and I formed a private detective agency in Cheyenne and did investigative work privately and for several Cheyenne attorneys. We rented an office and registered with the Cheyenne Police Department. We carried formal identification and had official badges to carry. We were able to obtain some cases. The office paid for itself but was not rewarding to any great degree. We did have employees and compiled some valuable information which was used by law enforcement and attorneys. Then another opportunity was found in the insurance business.

The four of us involved in the lawsuit decided to sell life insurance in Cheyenne. Bob had found a life insurance company based in Utah that we could represent. We rented an office in Cheyenne and went to work. We found that selling these policies did not do well and was not successful. The other three individuals were using credit cards for funding this office which they maxed out. I refused to put funds into this enterprise, so I walked away. Shortly thereafter the office was closed and two of the participants left Cheyenne. I returned to building my house in Woodslanding.

Professor 1992-2012

University of Northern Colorado

One day I saw an ad in a northern Colorado newspaper advertising for a professor to teach at the University of Northern Colorado. They wanted someone who had worked in the real world to teach a TQM class. I applied and was invited to Greeley for an interview. I was hired on a one-year contract as a Monfort Executive Professor for the 1992/1993 school year.

The Monfort company owned meat processing and packing plants. They funded a special program to help students in the real world. They hired three professors, one in Marketing, one in Finance, and I was hired to teach in Management. All of these hires had real life working experience. The Department of Management wanted to introduce a new course in TQM (total quality management) which dealt with manufacturing and engineering. My background in logistics is what helped me to be hired. I could have an apartment on campus, but dogs were not allowed. I found a small house in Ault where I could keep my dogs.

I was given an office and asked to prepare a syllabus for my classes. My first class on Monday, Wednesday, and Friday was at 9 am, the next one at 11 am. These were both classes in management.

On Tuesday and Thursday, I developed a TQM class. The management classes were large, 80 students in one, and 75 in the other. My TQM class had 35 students. I commuted back and forth to Woodslanding. It was a two-and-a-half-hour trip each way. I would leave after my last class on Friday and return for my first class on Mondays. This allowed me to be in Woodslanding Friday afternoon until late on Sunday. The dogs traveled with me. I built a fenced-in yard in Ault where they could stay when I was teaching.

I enjoyed teaching and working with these young students.

I told them that classes didn't have to be boring, we could have fun and learn at the same time. I would give them reading assignments from the textbook and then we would discuss how these principles would be applied in the real world. I was able to develop a strong rapport with my students and many would come visit me in my office. Sometimes there would be a line waiting. Some of the other professors got annoyed with this as no students would visit their offices. I wondered why this was happening when my daughter, Alexandra, gave me the answer.

She said, "Dad, when a student has a problem, they seek advice. They ask their fellow students for advice but find they don't have answers, they can ask their parents but maybe it is something that they don't want their parents to know about or there is a bad relationship, or they can ask a caring professor for advice, and that is you." That made sense as many of the other professors were demanding and not caring. I taught at UNC (University of Northern Colorado) for the 1991/1992 school year. I was very popular, and the students wanted my contract to be renewed. The professors were unhappy because they didn't have popularity, so they blocked my contract from being renewed. I was named the best professor by the students at the end of the year. This also was not appreciated by many faculty members.

After my contract ended, I was asked to conduct some courses as part of a federal program that was monitored by UNC. I agreed and taught classes in Helena, Montana and Pierre, South Dakota. Later, in Laramie, I met Jerry Haenish who had a contract for teaching state programs in management. I spoke with him and was assigned to teach classes in Rock Springs and Casper. These were only one week in length.

Preston University

I returned to Woodslanding and continued working on my house when a wanted ad appeared in the Cheyenne newspaper. In 1994, a new school was planning to open in Cheyenne and was looking to hire teachers. I drove to Cheyenne and met with Dr. Basit, who was the owner of Preston University. He explained that Preston had campuses around the world and was planning to establish its US campus in Wyoming. I liked the international aspect of this school. I was hired to teach management but also to be the Administrative Director for this school. WOW. The first office was in a real estate office run by Roger Greenlee. He was appointed to be the Director of Finance. Two other men were hired, one as the Dean and the other to be the Registrar. After a short time, Roger Greenlee wanted to control everything. It became clear that he had no idea about higher education and was making bad choices. Dr. Basit then signed a lease for a building by the airport that had offices and classrooms. Roger tried to be the boss here but was quickly removed from the school.

We tried to build a student body but were unable to attract many students. We hired some others to handle paperwork and soon had many foreign students who were studying at the various foreign campuses. As I had an extensive international background I was asked to visit the foreign campuses.

Dr Basit was from Pakistan and had several thousand students and a large faculty there. I traveled to Pakistan, met with the professors, and visited campuses in Islamabad, Rawalpindi, Peshawar, Karachi, and Lahore.

The concept was to build an educational system where students could take classes in different countries on Preston campuses. We hired staff and began processing the paperwork for students worldwide. I was selected to visit various campuses around the world to develop this program. In Germany I was able to contact Dr. Friedrich Frei who was selected to head up our German programs. We selected three professors to be our deans and eventually had a faculty of 30 professors. In Spain, France, Georgia, the Canary Islands, and Morocco we worked with the ESM (European School of Management) which had campuses in these countries. I arranged a meeting in my cousin's beer garden for professors from various locations.

I made trips to and lectured in Tbilisi, Georgia, Casablanca, Morocco, Tenerife, Canary Islands, and several cities in

Germany. In The Netherlands we had classes located at the Amsterdam Airport.

At one point we rented the Hohenzollern castle and had a formal graduation ceremony with caps and gowns. Everyone had to take off their shoes and wear special slippers to protect the floors. There was a dining room in the castle where we had a gala dinner. There was a band hired and I surprised everyone by sitting in and playing the string bass.

Dr. Basit arranged to have a booth at the International Educational Fair which was held each year in Dubai. He and I would man this booth and meet with potential students. This also gave us the opportunity to make contacts with schools from different countries. From Dubai we would fly to Karachi, Pakistan. I remember that I had been given a special bottle of vodka by some Russian professors. Entering into Pakistan, your luggage is run through a scanner. Dr Basit and I were together as our luggage was scanned. The guards went into high alert when they saw the vodka, and everything went quiet. I picked up my luggage which contained the vodka, and everything was back to normal. It is an offense for any Pakistani to have alcohol in their possession, however as a foreigner I was OK.

I made several trips to Pakistan and visited Preston campuses in Islamabad, Rawalpindi, Lahore, Karachi, and Peshawar. There were students at all of these locations. There was an orientation for potential new students held in the Marriott Hotel in Islamabad. I was on the stage along with other professors. At one point I had to give a speech, which I did in English which was then translated into Urdu, the local language. There were more than 600 people in the audience. In Pakistan the only place allowed to serve alcohol was in the international hotels. Pakistanis were not allowed to be served but foreigners were served. I enjoyed the visits I made to Pakistan,

While working at Preston I was still living in Woodslanding, so I commuted every day. It was a one-and-a-half-hour drive when the weather was good but take longer in the winter. One day I arrived in Laramie to find the road to Cheyenne was closed. Highway 287 was open, so I drove to Tie Sidings. There was a gravel road that went up to the Ames monument and then connected to Interstate 80. The snow was deep, and we were experiencing a blizzard. I put my Jeep in 4WD and started up the road. It was difficult driving. When I reached the high point I saw a big drift ahead, I put the Jeep in low gear and floor boarded it. The drift was four feet deep. I busted through and then churned my way to a spot where the wind had cleared the road. I was lucky to have gotten through this drift. When I reached the Interstate, I proceeded towards Cheyenne. There was a highway patrol car parked at Buford.

When I reached Cheyenne and contacted my sister she asked, "how did you get here?" I explained my trip and she responded that there were several cars stuck on that gravel road and that emergency crews had to be sent out to rescue the drivers. The road was officially closed, and everyone was being given a ticket and fined. Evidentially some drivers had attempted to follow my tracks but didn't make it through that big drift. I was happy to be in Cheyenne and stayed overnight with my sister so the road would be cleared, and I could go home.

Another time I was in Cheyenne when a bad storm hit, and they closed the road to Laramie. I needed to go home so I drove north on Interstate 25 and took the exit that connected with the highway to Horse Creek. The road as far as Horse Creek was passable with no problems. However, at Horse Creek the gravel road connecting to Laramie presented some problems. I had a sleeping bag, water, and some food I bought before leaving Cheyenne in case I got stranded. I climbed the hill heading towards Laramie and encountered deep blowing snow. Using 4WD I proceeded and was doing ok. Then there is a big saddle on the road that I knew was going to be a problem as it would fill with snow. I left the road and drove through sage brush on the side of the road. Suddenly I saw a man ahead waving me down. He had stayed on the road and his pickup was buried deep in the snow. You could see the cab, but the hood and bed of the truck were covered with snow. He wanted me to pull him out, I said no that is impossible. I gave him a ride into Laramie, and he was very thankful. I called my sister to let her know I was safe at home.

This also gave me the opportunity to spend time with my

sister who lived close to the Preston building. I feel blessed to have had this opportunity as we became very close. I learned that Regis University in Denver was offering classes at the LCCC (Laramie County Community Center) so I put in an application and I was hired to teach some management classes. These were evening classes so sometimes I would stay over, sleeping at my sister's house.

I traveled to Preston campuses worldwide. I also visited the ESM campuses that were offering the Preston programs. The head of the ESM network lived in Seville, Spain to I visited there many times. There was a local campus there and then we would go to the campus in Tenerife in the Canary Islands. I made two trips to Tbilisi. Georgia and lectured there. It was interesting as this had been part of the Soviet Union. The city streets did not have showroom windows as we have in the west; you had to get close and peer through a small space to see what was inside. One store sold broches made from the tusks of a Wooly Mammoth. Different atmosphere than that of western cities.

We were contacted by a school in northern Sumatra in Indonesia. I flew to Medan and upon arrival at the airport I found students and faculty waiting for me with a big welcoming sign. They were anxious to show off their school. I was treated to a tour of the school and a nice dinner. Then I was informed that there was an orientation planned for the next day for some 500 potential students, I was to be the guest speaker. The next day I was seated on the stage with a big flower on my chest along with five faculty members. The day began at 8 am and I spoke about 9 am for 20 minutes. Then all of the faculty began speaking, all in Bahasa, the local language of which I understood nothing. I had to sit there, smile and look interested.

We broke for lunch and then resumed in the afternoon. Finally, at about 4 pm the session ended, and they set up tables to sign up students. I said I was going to take a break and left the meeting.

I went to the hotel bar and ordered a drink. There were two men at a nearby table and I could sense a heavy accent which sounded like German. I finished my drink, and as I was leaving, I asked if there was someone from Europe. The one gentleman was a German and they invited me to sit down. There was a German, and the other was from Malaysia. I told them I was here from a university to set up a new school. They looked at each other and said they were looking for a way to be able to have their employees earn a college diploma. They invited me to visit their oil palm plantation located in Padang, Indonesia. I told them I had other commitments planned but they insisted. They said they would pay all expenses. Arrangements were made for me to modify my itinerary and to visit the plantation.

When I arrived in Padang, I was met by Mr. Goh Ing Sing who was the director of the plantation. We drove to the plantation which I learned was only one of many located in Indonesia. Their problem was that they had Malaysian managers at each of the plantations and the Indonesian government had passed a new law that required all foreigners to have a university degree to work in Indonesia. I received a red-carpet treatment. The plantation facilities were first class with a private bedroom, well-furnished living area and servants serving meals and serving guests. Each plantation had living quarters for the managers and housing complexes for the workers. Each plantation was like a small town surrounded by fences and protected by guards. There were guard posts at the entry roads.

There were processing plants that transformed the fruit of the trees into palm oil and other products. The waste of the processing was used as fuel, so each plantation was self-sufficient. There were more than 40 plantations with 50,000 employees total in Indonesia. They also had plantations in other countries. We had discussions and I agreed to send professors to the main plantation to teach classes there. I would be one of those professors and I taught two classes there. The program was a success, and we were able to award diplomas to the managers of the plantations.

Back in Wyoming I developed a program entitled "English in the Rockies" for students from other countries to develop their English skills. The students would attend classes in Cheyenne and then would be given a tour of Wyoming including various sites and Yellowstone Park. Goh in Sing and his wife took part in this program. We also had graduation ceremonies in

Cheyenne for graduating students. They had to pay their own expenses, so we had limited attendance. Goh Ing Sing wanted to earn a master's degree, so I personally enrolled him as a distance learning student and taught all of his required classes. He was a good student and received his master's degree in management.

A decision was made to have a board of directors for the University. We held a meeting in Germany and elected the managers from Germany, The Netherlands, and South Africa as the new board. Then Dr. Basit hired Jerry Haenish to be full time as a vice president. Things went downhill. Barry Bota from South Africa was selected as President, and we moved forward. There was a lot of friction, and tempers flew back and forth. Things changed with Barry Bota as president. We settled into the new routine. Then one morning Barry did not appear in the office. Thinking that he might be sick we checked his motel to find that he had checked out and left. The company car was there but he was gone. We then learned that he had gone back to South Africa.

Discussions were held. I was given the title of President, and we moved forward. About two weeks later Dr. Basit flew in from Pakistan. Everyone assembled for a meeting. This got nasty, Gary Lane attacked me and made some accusations about what had happened with Barry Bota leaving and the way I conducted myself as president. Then Jerry Haenisch supported his accusations. I defended myself but was not happy with some actions taking place at the University. I learned that Diplomas were being awarded without any classes being taken. Individuals in South Korea paid money for their PhD diplomas. The original concept I had admired was no longer there. So, I resigned and went back to Woodslanding.

Goh Ing Sing contacted me and asked if I would come to Indonesia and hold some seminars to help his managers and staff. We discussed this possibility and decided that I would develop some seminars to focus on team building and management. I developed some lecture notes and put together some team exercises that could be used for the students to solve some problems as a team. I notified Goh that I had everything prepared and he should set the schedule. These were to be two-to-three-day seminars at various locations. I would stay on the plantations and Ku Su Bing would travel with me as an interpreter as some students only spoke Bahasa, a language used in both Indonesia and Malaysia.

In February 2001 I traveled to Indonesia and our first seminar at the AMP (American Malaysian Plantation). There were 40 students in this seminar, and all went well. I lectured in English and both Ku Su Bing and Goh Ing Sing would translate into Bahasa. I would speak about management and how it should be used in their industry. We would use some actual issues related to the plantations and how they could be handled and solved. A lot of problems that were being experienced were presented and discussed. It was amazing to hear what some of these managers had to cope with at the various locations. The second day we would discuss team building and then divide the students into groups and give them problems to solve.

The next seminar was held at the GMP Plantation (German Malaysian Plantation). This plantation had been founded and organized by Dr. Helmut von Uexküll who was from Germany. Again, there was a class of 40 students, and we followed the same format as in the first seminar. We soon discovered that these managers were encountering some of the same problems as our first seminar but also brought to light some additional problems they had to solve. This was beginning to be a learning experience for the senior executive as well as the local managers. Everyone agreed that it had been a good idea to have these seminars. Goh Ing Sing was very pleased as this had been his creation.

We next moved to Palembang where the seminar was held in a local theater that also served drinks and food. This plantation was in the southern part of Sumatra and the local people were from different tribes than the ones on the previous plantations. Goh Ing Sing was not present for this seminar, so everything was handled by Ku Su Bing and me. We used the same format with Ku doing all of the required translations.

This seminar went extremely well and at the end, we had a gala dinner with a lot of drinks. Then everyone was asked to sing as they had a karaoke session. It was a wonderful experience.

The final seminar was held at the Burnai Timur Estate plantation. We followed the same format and this time some new problems were discussed. Each of the plantations was like a town and had its own housing, medical facilities, grocery store, gas station, schools, and water and gas supplies. All of them were protected by fences and guards. There were gates at the entrances with guards checking everyone in and out. This final seminar went well and then they wanted everyone to pose for a group picture. There was a stone camel in front of the building, and I was asked to sit on this camel. To put it mildly, it hurt to sit on the camel without any way to adjust your private parts. I was happy when that photo session ended.

I returned to Wyoming and began working on building my house, mowing my acreage, and feeding my dogs. Was also able to earn some extra money with my tractor mowing the grass at a Cold Storage facility. A month later I received a phone call from Dr. Ted Dalton, the owner of Newport International University. He asked me if I would be able to help him obtain a license from the Board of Education. He was going to close his operations in South Dakota and move the school to Wyoming. His main campus was in Newport Beach, California with US students. He wanted to have his international students separated in a Wyoming-based university. I agreed and in 2002 I completed the paperwork to obtain a license. The license was issued, and we made plans for the new University office to be based in Wyoming.

Newport International University

The president of the California Newport University, Dr. Clive Grafton, came to Wyoming and we looked for and rented an office in Laramie, Wyoming. I hired one girl to work in the office. We opened the door and began operations. Dr. Grafton controlled the finances in California, and we reported to him. We had a lot of students as Newport University had overseas campuses in Europe, Asia, South America, and Africa. Dr. Dalton and I flew to Europe and held a meeting in Budapest. Hungary with the directors of the European campuses. Newport had campuses in Hungary. Turkey, Latvia, the UK, Spain, The Netherlands, and Italy. I told everyone that I would visit their campuses.

I was able to establish good relations with the directors and we were off to a good start. The campus in Budapest was in Pest. The city is made up of two separate cities, Buda on the left bank and Pest on the right bank of the Danube River. The owner of our campus was crippled as he had polio as a child. He walked with two supports which he called poles, and his car was fitted with hand controls when he drove. He had a swimming pool in his house where he exercised and built muscle strength in his arms. He always had help with him when traveling. There were seven bridges in Budapest, I set a goal to walk over all seven. I accomplished walking over five. Still two to go.

Back in Laramie I began processing students' records and issuing diplomas which I signed as Chancelor. My first hire was excellent, and the office got off to a good start. Then she moved and I had to find a replacement. The next girl did an adequate job but I became suspicious with how the funds were being handled. I went to the bank and discovered that she had written some checks forging my signature. I went to the police department and was told that I would have to contact the District Attorney. I was told that I should immediately fire her and that his office would issue an arrest warrant. This I did, and a warrant was issued. She went into hiding and the police were unable to arrest her. Three weeks later they arrested her and she appeared before a judge and was released on bond. Eventually, she was tried and released on probation.

Regis University

I was working on my house and was kept occupied with my other activities. Then I received a phone call from Regis University in Denver, asking if I would teach some classes on their campus in Denver. These would be adult classes for MBA students and would be a four-hour class once a week in the evenings. This worked out fine as I would leave Woodslanding at 2 in the afternoon arriving on campus around 5 pm. I would have one-hour office time for any students that wanted to see me. We would then have class from 6 pm to 10 pm. After class, I would drive back to Woodslanding arriving home before 1 am

This meant an 11-hour day once a week. Sometimes I would have two classes on consecutive days, in which case I would stay overnight in Denver. Regis would pay for my mileage and motel room. In total, I would teach over one thousand students on the Denver campus. The students would read the textbook and in class we would discuss how what they read would be used in the real world. Most of my classes would be international subjects and many of my students were already dealing in international business in their jobs.

At NIU, the next person I hired was originally from the Philippines and she turned out to be a real gem. She would be permanent. The volume grew so I hired a second person to handle the financial records. We were obligated to follow guidelines from Dr. Grafton in California concerning the transfer of funds. I was not allowed to visit campuses in Asia as Dr. Grafton would visit them. I did visit the campuses in London. Riga. Amsterdam, Budapest, and Istanbul.

Then there was a big change in the Department of Education in Cheyenne. A new Superintendent of Education Jim McBride was appointed. He vowed to rid Wyoming of illegal degree mills. He and his finance director began looking at the operations of those schools with licenses issued by the state of Wyoming.

The state of Wyoming passed new legislation in 2006 concerning the licensing of higher education in the state of Wyoming. This new law required all schools be accredited or in the process of securing accreditation. The new State Superintendent of Education decided that all institutes of higher education were diploma mills, so he began a campaign to force all of them to close and leave Wyoming. Dr Dalton was of the opinion that this was not correct. He hired an attorney and filed a lawsuit contesting this law. He came to Wyoming and there was a trial. Dr.

Dalton lost and the law remained in effect.

They would make accusations against the schools which then had to be defended before the Wyoming Board of Education. I successfully defended Newport at a Board meeting in Casper and again in Saratoga. One day I received a phone call from Phil Kautz who worked in the department of Education in Cheyenne. He told me that a gentleman had traveled all the way from Malaysia to apply for a license to open a school in Wyoming. Phil told me that this man had been rudely handled and told to get lost by Fred Hansen. He was going back to Malaysia and felt he had made a wasted trip. Would I be able to help him? He had a flight booked from Cheyenne to Denver. I spoke to the man and agreed that I would drive him to Denver, and we could discuss the situation.

EC Council University

I drove to Cheyenne and met Mr. Sanjay Bavisi at the Cheyenne airport. We discussed what had happened and I agreed to help him. He was the President of the EC Council which specialized in the security of international internet operations around the world. He wanted to establish a school to educate students about his programs. The EC Council was composed of security experts from different countries. His programs were being used in many countries and many governments.

He flew back to Malaysia, and I prepared the paperwork to apply for a license. Jim McBride refused to accept the application, so we had to hire an attorney. The application was accepted but we were told that no license would be issued. Our attorney then contacted the Board of Education. It was agreed that the Board would hold a special meeting to hear the case. Sanjay flew back from Malaysia and the meeting was held in Cheyenne. It was a nasty event with Sanjay presenting his reasons for opening a school and outlining his intentions. Jim McBride and Fred Hansen were both there and very negative in their presentations. The meeting took a break and when we returned, the Board instructed the Department of Education to issue a license.

We then proceeded to rent an office. We rented space on the fourth floor of the First National Bank building, and we bought some furniture. The Department of Education had a Laramie office located on the fifth floor, so we were able to establish a good working relationship. We visited each other and everything was positive. I was able to handle many things in my Newport office but spent some time in the EC Council University office each day. My days were full, and I worked long hours. The dogs were happy to see me when I came home at night.

Dr. Dalton returned to California and then I was informed that there had been some problems and Ted had fired Clive Grafton. Sanjay Bavisi was uneasy about the EC Council University, so he asked me to look for another location. I contacted many states and found some interest in New Mexico. I drove to Sante Fe and met with the Secretary of Education's office. I found a warm reception and people willing to work with us. I took the necessary paperwork to apply for a license and drove back to Laramie. I told Sanjay that I had found a solution and he said he would come over when we submitted our license application in New Mexico.

There had been a problem brewing in Nairobi, Kenya for some time. I had told Clive Grafton that I should go there, but he said no, that I should not go. Now, since Grafton was out of the picture, I decided that this was necessary as we had a lot of students there. We had been receiving complaints from many students. In 2005 I flew to Nairobi and met with the Director of the school who reassured me that everything was fine. I then met with the students who gave me a different story. The problem was with the Department of Education, which was going to declare that the school was being closed and their diplomas would be useless. I tried to contact the Department of Education to be told that this decision was being made by the Secretary of Education who was unavailable.

I knew that Goh Ing Sing had a plantation in Kenya, and I had met the owner so I called him and asked if he could do anything to help. He said that he knew the Secretary of Education and he would contact him for me. A short time later I received a message that the Secretary of Education would come to my hotel and meet me. We met, and he was a very nice intelligent individual and we had a good discussion. He informed me that the decision would stand but he would help the students. The problem was that the Director of the school was married to his right-hand lady, and he had been caught cheating on her. She was on the warpath and was determined to destroy him and his school. He could do nothing to stop her.

I flew back to Wyoming. I honestly believe that if I had gone there earlier that we could have solved the problem. We waited too long. Kenya canceled all of the NIU degrees in that country.

Sanjay arrived from Malaysia, and we drove to New Mexico and submitted our application for a license to open the school. We looked for and found a large building which we rented. It had offices and classrooms, so it was perfect. Sanjay asked me to move to Albuquerque, but I said no because I had my house in Wyoming. I agreed to make visits to Albuquerque as often as possible. I was now the Chancelor of this University.

In Laramie I had Candice doing the student records with another girl as her assistant and Trisch handing the financial records. I came to the office one Saturday and found mail waiting to be opened. There was a letter from a credit card company. I had authorized a credit card to be used when I was traveling. I opened the envelope to see it was the monthly bill to be paid. Included on this bill were charges for perfume, women's clothing, medicine, and other personal items. Trisch handled all the finances, so I called her and asked her to come to the office. I confronted her with what I had found, she confessed, cried, and said that she would pay it all back. I asked how and found out that she was receiving money from another source. I told her if she made good for the items, she had purchased that I would allow her to keep working and not press charges. She agreed and took the credit card, destroyed it and canceled the account. She did pay everything back as she had promised.

I had to cancel the lease Sanjay had signed for in Laramie and move the EC Council University to Albuquerque. All of the student files, paperwork and some office furniture were loaded into my Dodge Ram pickup, and Candice and I drove to

Albuquerque, Candice was going to organize the new office and I was going to interview some people that had applied for employment. I would conduct the interviews in the Hilton Hotel as our campus was in the process of being organized, buying new furniture and desks.

One of the ladies scheduled for an interview called and said that she couldn't make the interview as she had a problem with a dog and needed to put the dog to sleep. I asked what kind of dog and she said that it was a Basenji, I told her that I would come to her house. Yogi, Tonia's dog, was a Basenji so I was hooked. Turns out that she had two dogs, and they didn't get along. Then the Basenji had tried to bite her husband when he was holding their newborn baby. She was probably jealous and wanted attention. She was planning to take the Basenji to the pound. I told her I would adopt the dog. We had an interview (we didn't hire her), I loaded the dog and her lease and the dog mattress and went back to finish setting up the EC Council University building.

Driving back to Wyoming the Basenji dog was in the camper in the bed of the pickup. We had been driving for a long period, so we stopped at a rest stop on Interstate 25. I told Candice that the dog probably needed to relieve herself. I sat down and Candice said she would take the dog for a walk. Next thing I knew Candice was running and pulling the dog behind her. The dog made a sudden stop, and her collar came off. Here we were at the side of the Interstate with cars going by at 75 mph chasing a dog who was scared to death as she was being chased by a bunch of strangers. It took almost 15 minutes before we caught her, everyone stopped at the rest stop helped so we were able to corner her.

I now had an office in Albuquerque and Laramie. I would go back and forth between these two schools and would be in charge of both offices. New people were hired in Albuquerque, and we opened the office. We had a receptionist, a secretary, and an accountant in the beginning. This number would grow as time passed. We had adjunct faculty and then we hired some local faculty and began giving classes. I was able to supervise both offices as there were competent people at both locations.

Then Dr. Dalton called and said that he had sold Newport and that the new owners would be visiting me. The new owner, Hooi Yeap, lived in Hayward, California and had several nursing schools that she owned and operated. She was planning to offer a University Education and to include nursing programs. She was married to a Chinese national who had contacts with high level educational authorities in China. We had long discussions as plans were made for the future. We looked for and found a building for sale which she purchased. This building on Sheridan occupied 25 percent of the block and had offices, classrooms, a kitchen, and a conference room. We moved our furniture and records from our current location and began planning for the future. She wanted to start the accreditation process and asked to look for help in this endeavor.

Candice and her assistant were assigned a large office for their record keeping. Trish moved into the office next to mine which was the corner office. There was a large reception area when one entered where we set up a reception desk. There were other offices in this portion of the building. The other side was a split level with the kitchen, laboratory, and classrooms on the upper level and classrooms and the conference room on the lower level. There were bathrooms in all areas. The building had been used as a medical building previously. We ordered furniture for the classrooms as well as some additional office furniture. I was able to hire the Director of Personnel who had recently retired from the University of Wyoming to be our Director of Personnel. I was able to find a gentleman who knew accreditation procedures and arranged to meet him in Denver. I interviewed him and thought he was a possibility.

Hooi made another visit to Wyoming, and it was arranged to have Dr. David Oxenhandler come to meet her. They had a private meeting and Hooi announced that she had hired him to handle the accreditation procedure. I was not involved in their discussions and didn't know any details under which he had been hired. We gave him an office and he began to assemble all of the information that he would need for the accreditation application. Wyoming was assigned to the North Central Accreditation Council located in Chicago. We had discussions and I said that it would be a good idea if we made a visit to the overseas locations so everyone would know what was planned for the future. This would also allow everyone to meet Hooi. Arrangements were made for Hooi and her husband, David, and me to visit our campuses in London UK, Budapest Hungary, Istanbul Turkey, Riga. Latvia, and Chisinau, Moldova in Europe. We would then travel to China where Hooi's husband made arrangements for us to have a campus there, visit several locations in China, then on to Tokyo, Japan Kula Lumpur, and Malaysia.

I was the President of Newport International University, but all the accreditation work was done by David and Hooi—I only saw what they had produced to present to North Central in Chicago. As we could show that we were in the process of accreditation, Dr. McBride and Fred Hansen didn't bother us, In the meantime I also visited the Wyoming Nursing Board which was separate from the Wyoming Board of Education and also had a licensing procedure. Hooi had found a nursing professor in Denver who would move to Wyoming and buy a ranch near Laramie. Hooi also applied for a license for her nursing programs. Things were coming together, and the future looked bright. The accreditation package was completed and Hooi and David flew to Chicago to present their application. I stayed behind in Wyoming.

The planned trip went well. Hooi met the directors and visited their campuses. London was well established and had a big sign promoting Newport on their building. Beautiful classrooms, a large library, and a large computer lab. Amsterdam had two small classrooms and an office. Budapest had excellent classrooms, a good computer lab, and a nice library. Turkey had two locations, one on the Asian side and the other on the European side of the Bosphorus. The schools had nice classrooms and good computer labs. The classroom in Chisinau, Moldova turned out to be a room in a local hotel. They did have computers, but the classes were small, not too many students. Riga had a local lady who was well connected and wealthy. She was aspiring to be the Educational Director for Latvia. She had classrooms and computers.

When we arrived in China, William, Hooi's husband, had us booked into a local hotel in Beijing. It was not very nice, so

David and I went to a Marriott and booked rooms on our own. We were then scheduled to fly to Xian as we were to have our programs given on their campus. In Xian we received a warm welcome and had meetings with the President of the Xian University and individuals of the Chinese Bureau of Education. Xian University had a student body of 250,000 students. William had arranged for Newport classes to be held on campus and there was a sign on one building that gave the location of the Newport International University. It looked like we would have a campus in China endorsed by the government.

The next day we had a free day to explore the city and surrounding area. The highlight of this day was a visit to the tomb of the emperor Shihuangdi, which contained the famous terracotta soldiers. There are 8,000 soldiers in this exhibition, which is inside a huge building protected from the weather. For a person from Wyoming to be able to view these soldiers was amazing. It was a breath-taking experience. We then flew back to Beijing to catch our next flight to Shenyang. Unfortunately, there were problems with our bookings, so we had a long layover at Beijing airport. We spent the night sleeping on benches at the Burger King. The next morning, we were able to take a flight to Shenyang. We were met on arrival by a group that was going to show us properties that could be used as a campus. There were professors from local schools as well as real estate agents. It looked like Hooi and William had big plans for China. We were treated to a wonderful lunch and viewed several properties. All of them would require major renovations to become useable. Much of the discussions were in Chinese, so David and I were not always aware of what was being discussed. That evening, we flew back to Beijing. David and I went back to the Marriott.

We then flew to Kuala Lumpur, Malaysia and visited the Newport campus there. We spent the night in Kuala Lumpur and then flew to Georgetown in Northern Malaysia. Hooi had arranged for a directors' meeting to be held there. It was anticipated that the directors from Asian campuses would come to this meeting. The director from Hungary and the director from Japan were the only ones who came to this meeting. I did, however, meet a lot of Hooi's relatives as this was the area where she was born and grew up. We spent several days enjoying this part of Malaysia and then we all flew back to the United States.

Things settled down in our new building. I made visits to the Presidents of both LCCC and the University of Wyoming. Both were very positive and said they would be happy to have us, as that would give students some additional educational opportunities. A second European directors meeting was planned, this time to be held in Turkey. In Turkey we received a warm welcome from our local school and had a productive meeting. We were on our way to achieving a global education for our students.

I then planned to have a grand opening of our campus in Laramie. Invitations were sent to all of our directors, and I arranged to have coverage by the Cheyenne television station channel 5 as well as the local newspaper. The Directors began arriving and everyone was in a positive mood. Life was great!

Then we received a letter from North Central concerning our accreditation application. This was two days before our planned grand opening. There were seven areas in the application, we had failed four of them, and changes would be required before we could resubmit. This was followed by a certified letter from the Department of Education saying that our license would be canceled as we were no longer considered to be in the accreditation process.

Directors from Turkey. Moldova, the Netherlands, Latvia. Hungary, Colombia, Japan, and Ecuador had all arrived in Laramie for our Grand Opening. I called the TV station in Cheyenne. I called the President of LCCC who had planned to come and other local officials who were planning to be there for our Grand Opening. We had our directors' meeting as scheduled, David Oxenhandler, our accreditation expert, and Hooi were both present. I informed everyone what had happened, and we made plans for the future. We had discussed the situation with our attorney, and we planned to use Hooi's school in Hayward as the address for Newport International University and to have an administration office in Laramie. Now I had to find a new location and sell the building Hooi had purchased.

The directors were all going to Denver the next day, but a huge snowstorm arrived and the shuttle service was canceled.

David and I offered to drive them to Denver. He had a 4wd Yukon and I had a 4wd Dodge Ram. We loaded 8 directors in the Yukon, 2 directors and all the luggage in the Ram, and left for Denver. The highway was under a no necessary travel alert and there were very few cars on the road. There were times when we had to use 4wd and it was a difficult trip. We arrived safely at Denver airport, said goodbye to the directors, and I left for my return trip to Woodslanding. The conditions had gotten worse, and it was difficult driving. Colorado had plowed the roads up to the four corners but there were drifts even in the cleared sections. From the four corners on, there had been no plowing, and I was in 4wd all the time. When I reached Laramie, I found all the roads were closed. The highway to Woodslanding is the only road that doesn't have a closing gate, so, using 4wd, I was able to reach my house. The dogs were happy to see me. The roads were all closed for two days.

I found a three-room office for Newport on North 3rd Street, so we moved the student files, some office furniture, and closed the building on Sheridan. I was lucky. Working with a real estate agent I knew, we were able to sell the building. Newport International University was now located in California, with only an administrative office in Laramie. Now I had an office in Laramie and also in Albuquerque. I would spend time in both offices and life continued forward. For the EC Council University, we hired three more people and engaged an accountant to handle the financial records.

I was keeping busy with two Universities to watch over and teaching an occasional class at Regis. Then, EC Council scheduled a conference to be held in Miami. This was a four-day conference, so I flew to Miami.

There were a host of events and workshops to introduce attendees to the EC Council programs. The one that was most popular was the CEH (Certified Ethical Hacker) which taught the good guys how to hack computers so they could catch the bad guys. There were textbooks published by EC Council used around the world. It would become a requirement for US military and officials to earn their CEH license when they were in the intelligence branches of the United States. The conference ended with a gala dinner. Sanjay presented some awards, and then I flew back to Wyoming via Albuquerque.

Everything was going well in both Laramie and Albuquerque, and I was able to teach more classes for Regis on their Denver campus. I was enjoying life in Woodslanding, working on my house and spending time with my dogs. Candice was extremely busy in our Laramie office, so we decided to hire an additional employee to help her. We advertised in the local newspaper and received several resumes. As this individual was going to report to Candice, she was corresponding with the candidates. I was unaware of this, but she used the title of Registrar of the University. It turned out that one applicant was actually working in the Wyoming Department of Education and reported this title usage to Jim McBride. We then received an official letter to cease operations, or we would be fined and possibly be imprisoned. I contacted our attorney and advised Hooi of what had happened. Our attorney said we could probably win if this went to a trial. Hooi had had enough. She said to close the Wyoming office and move everything to California.

Then Sanjay called me and said that the EC Council University had been asked to make a presentation in Monterrey, Merico. He asked me if I could go to Mexico and handle this request. I agreed and flew to Monterrey. I was met at the airport and given a tour of the University. We had lunch and a free afternoon. Over lunch, they were proud to tell me that they were opening a new program to be taught in English. It would be for a Bachelors and MBA program.

The next morning, I made the presentation and answered questions about international business and the programs we offered at the EC Council University. I was awarded a thank you letter, and a trophy issued by the school. At our departing lunch I was asked if I would like to come back and teach in their new English-speaking school. They would offer me a permanent position and pay my moving expenses. I said that I would think it over. I later learned that was the University where Debbie had studied and earned her MBA degree. Strange how things develop—I was back in the area where I had found Carmen.

Back in Laramie preparations were made to move Newport

University to California. I rented a large truck and loaded all the furniture, student files, records, and computers. printers, plus other misc. items. The next morning, I left for California. I was alone in the truck and so I would stop along the way for food, gas, and toilet breaks. I drove straight through with an occasional break on the side of the road to take a cat nap in the truck. Interstate 80 was an easy drive through Wyoming, Utah, and Nevada but the Donner Pass in California was a different story. There was a lot of construction with narrow lanes. There were only inches separating vehicles, especially when there were trucks in the opposing lanes as there were many two-lane stretches in the construction zones.

I arrived safely after a 28-hour drive, and we unloaded the rental truck which I returned to the Hayward office of the rental company. Hooi loaned me a car to drive, and I went to a motel and went to bed. It had been a long time without a bed to sleep in. The next day I went to Hooi's Nursing school, and I helped her move furniture and unload boxes. We called Candice and told her to come to California to organize the office and to acquaint everyone on the Newport filing system, student records, etc. I was given an office with title of President on the door. Candice agreed to stay for 10 days to train everyone on procedures used by Newport International University.

Candice was able to train the Nursing school staff on the Newport procedures. Then Hooi hosted a dinner at an excellent Chinese restaurant which the staff attended, along with Candice and I, as well as a professor from Stanford University who was to be a dean of the business school for Newport. Plans were made for the future operation of Newport, and everything was now in place, so we were officially removed from Wyoming.

Now I had an office in Hayward, California and in Albuquerque, New Mexico. Additionally, I continued to teach classes at Regis University in Denver. Depending on circumstances and where there were issues to be handled. I would allocate my time between Hayward and Albuquerque around my classes at Regis and continue building on to my Woodslanding house in what little spare time I had. I also handled requests for working with my tractor: mowing grass in the summer and snow removal in the winter. There were a lot of balls to juggle during this period of my life.

After I moved Newport International to California; I spent more time in Albuquerque. Some additional faculty were hired in New Mexico, and some new administrators were hired when I was in California. Then there was a power play by some new hires. To keep the peace and to allow Sanjay to have a smooth-running operation, I decided that I had helped him enough, that he now had his license, and he could build his school. I resigned and turned the control over to his new staff.

Today, the EC Council University is still located in Albuquerque and is now accredited. Wyoming lost a gold mine with the actions of Jim McBride and Fred Hansen. The EC Council degrees are now a requirement for the US Military who protect the security of the United States. I am proud to have been a part of this! EC Council University has achieved accreditation in the United States.

To have Newport be legal in California we had to apply for a license to operate a university in that state. During this process it became apparent that there were some areas that needed to be corrected. A major issue was accreditation by a federal agency. I worked on this and was fortunate to be able to have one of the officials from the agency agree to come to Hayward and help us in what needed to be done. We spent two full days working with this gentleman. He worked out a procedure with certain goals that had be met in a certain time frame schedule. This was going to be a difficult task, but we began to do what was needed. It soon became clear that Hooi was not up to allocating money and didn't want to do some of what needed to be done. I struggled with this and then Hooi announced that she wanted to sell Newport. A buyer was found who would move Newport International University to Los Angeles. My time with Newport ended and I went back to Wyoming.

Tim's Award Trip

When my mother graduated from High School, her father, my grandfather, took her on a trip to Europe as a graduation reward. I thought that this would be a great thing to do for my grandchildren. The first one to graduate was Tim, Tonia's son. He finished high school in 2009, and we discussed where he would like to go. He had taken a summer job, so we agreed to make the trip when he had his holiday break from his university. Tim and I spoke, and we agreed on the dates. I made the bookings, and we would start in Singapore. The next day I received a very angry call from my daughter who said she was planning to see her son during this break. I said I was sorry, but the airplane tickets had already been purchased. She was not happy. The next day she called and said that she would meet us in Singapore and go on the trip with us.

Tim and I met, and we flew to Singapore. The next day Tonia and Chris arrived. We spent the night in Singapore and the next day took a bus to Johor Bahru, Malaysia. At the border you have your passport checked to enter Malaysia. Goh Ing Sing met

Standing on the equator in Sumatra, from left: Christopher Carson, Tonia Ries, Timothy Carson, and Tom Ries

us in Johor Bahru, and we drove to his home in Malacca. We had a wonderful visit seeing many sights in Malacca. There was a large sailing ship to visit and a lift that went up in the air and revolved so you could see the city from on high. We spent two days in Malacca and then flew to Padang, Indonesia, where Goh managed some oil palm plantations. One highlight here is a look-out high up in a tree overlooking the acres of palm trees that have been planted.

Next, we flew to Sandakan on the island of Borneo. Goh was dealing on another oil palm plantation to be added to his company. He has a plantation there where we stayed and enjoyed great hospitality with food and drinks. We visited the prospective new plantation and then drove to Sapi, the hometown of Goh's wife Flora. Here we were treated to ride in boats as roads were limited. Goh knew a restaurant that served fresh fish directly from the fisherman's boats. You could choose what you wanted, and it would be prepared for you. This was a very primitive area, accessible only by water. We had a delicious dinner and then spent another night in Sapi before returning to Goh's plantation.

It was an exciting trip enjoyed by everyone and made possible by Goh Ing Sing. We returned to Singapore, and everyone caught their flight back to the USA: Tim to his university in Texas, Tonia to New York, and I flew to Wyoming via San Francisco and Denver. I believe that everyone was happy that we made this trip. It was also wonderful that Tonia was able to come and join us.

Woodslanding Construction

Now it was time to get serious about finishing my house that I had planned. I had found the property and designed the house using a notebook and ruler. I was happy that I had insisted on having a basement although there had been some resistance. It was nice to have your own creation.

There were still ceilings that needed to be installed, garages that needed to be finished, meadows to be mowed, and many other projects that I had been putting on hold.

There were projects that needed to be done. I wanted to have a barn that could be used for livestock and storage of my tractor and other equipment and materials. I designed a structure to be 100' long, 60' wide, and for one portion to be 80' wide. This portion was intended to enclose a guest cottage. I hired a friend that I knew, Bob Honekan, and it was decided to build a pole barn. This required leveling a space to accommodate the barn. To do that, we had to level the south end and then bring in dirt to build up the north end. Dirt had to be found, so we began digging a hole close to the barn.

Then I got the idea that this hole could be made into a swimming pool in the future. As the guest cottage would require water and sewage, we dug trenches and installed copper pipes for water and plastic PVC for sewage. These we extended beyond the barn's exterior and we capped them to be used at a later time. The next procedure was to drill holes for the poles to be erected. I ordered trusses which were to be delivered. Then the holes w ere drilled, and the poles were inserted and leveled. The poles were held in place by some 2x16 planks at the top to support the trusses, and then a series of 2x4s down to the bottom of each pole to be used to attach the siding. The trusses arrived and were put in place and held together with 2x4s to be used to attach the roof. We used metal sheets for both the roof and the sides, with clear plastic sheets to be placed on the roof for light. The metal sheets

The house Tom built in Woodslanding, Wyoming. From top: back of the house; Tom's Bar

were 4x8. I would stand them on end, push them up to Bob, who would pull them up using a pair of vice grips.

Another project I was thinking about was to build a small cottage by the irrigation ditch which could be a playhouse and sleepover house for my grandchildren. This was put on the back burner and never came to pass. However, it remained in my head and was always a dream. Additionally, I was able to purchase some additional land, so I now owned a total of 17.6 acres of property.

There were still projects that needed to be completed inside the house. The basement was not finished—there was no ceiling, and it needed to be divided into separate rooms. I made my plans and divided the basement into two bedrooms, a laundry room, a bathroom, and a bar room. Additionally, I replaced the stairs and made two separate storage areas. There were closets in both bedrooms. The ceilings in the bar area were covered with beer coasters, which I had collected on my travels. Both bedrooms and the bathroom had knotty pine ceilings installed, and there were 4x8 tile sheets used to finish the walls and ceiling in the laundry room.

Both garages were unfinished, so I used 4x8 sheets of birch plywood for the walls and ceilings in both garages. I also installed electric heaters in both garages for heat. The lower garage served as my workshop. These projects all took time, and the house was completely finished by the end of 2014.

1976 to 2014 meant that I spent more than 35 years building this house, but I accomplished my wish of building my own house. It was a lot of work, but I also learned a lot in the process. I also was able to fulfill another wish of mine, to live in the country. I had lived in cities for all my life. Now I had a family home to pass on to my children!

In addition to spending time in Woodslanding, I was able to visit my daughters and spend time with my grandchildren. I also made trips to Asia to see my good friend Goh Ing Sing, and to Europe to see relatives in Germany and my good friend Acki Schultze. I was able to add several more countries to my list of where I had been. When I would visit Germany, I booked side trips to various locations. One time I booked a side trip to South

Tom's house in front of Sheep Mountain

Africa to retain my 1K status with United Airlines. I also used this opportunity to visit Central and South America. Using miles, I flew to Argentina and Uruguay in business class. I also visited Costa Rica and Peru. So, I had a wonderful time living in the country but still being able to travel and see friends and relatives.

United Airlines had a program for frequent flyers based on miles flown each year. 25,000 = silver status, 50,000 = gold status, 75,000 = platinum status, 100,000 = 1K. I ha d been 1K for several years because of the traveling I did each year. Now I became a million miler as I had flown a million miles on United. As a benefit, I could name another person on my account who would then automatically have the status I had. They had to live at the same address. I had been using Kym's address for my United account, so I named Kym. She was awarded 1K status and could enjoy the benefits.

Nina's Award Trip

In 2012 Nina, Graces's daughter, graduated from high

school. Time for another graduation trip from grandpa. Discussions were held, and it was decided that we would go to Asia. I spoke with Goh, and he said to include Malaysia and Indonesia on our itinerary. We met Goh and were treated to a wonderful reception in Malaysia. We went to Jonker Walk, which was an area in Malacca that I had never seen. There were numerous restaurants and booths selling a large assortment of items. There were also stages where artists were performing. A memorable walk and evening.

The next day, we went to Indonesia and visited a plantation. Grace was not on this trip as she was on duty at the Mayo Clinic, however Jorge, Nina's father, was with us. We were taken into a factory where they processed the fruit of the oil palm trees. First, we viewed the harvesting of the fruit from the trees. Next, we saw how the fruit would be transported to the processing plant. The fruit would be placed in small special railway cars which were then drawn into a large oven where they would be cooked for 24 hours. Then, one by one, these rail cars would be lifted with a huge crane that would turn them upside down and dump the cooked fruit into a large press. This would then extract

Nina in Sumatra

the oil, which would run into large vats. The leftover residue would be carried away on a belt to be used for fuel to run the plant. A self-operating, stand-alone facility.

They had a barbeque with all kinds of food being prepared. They used coconut shells as fuel instead of charcoal. There was music, so people were dancing and having a real banquet and party. Everyone was invited to sing karaoke music and a good time was had by all. The next day Nina, Jorge, and I went to Singapore. In one of the big shopping malls there was an indoor skating rink. Nina was a good ice skater due to her ice hockey experience. She rented some skates, went on the ice, and fell down. The skates she had been given were dull. Armed with good skates she went back on the ice, and everyone was amazed and were watching this girl whiz around with no problem. She was the star of the show.

Andy's Award Trip

Andy, Debbie's son, graduated high school in 2013, so it was his turn to have an overseas trip courtesy of grandpa. We had some discussions and he said he would like to visit Europe, including France, Germany, The Netherlands, and Italy. Based on the time allowed, I said we couldn't do all of those countries, so we agreed on an itinerary to include Germany, the Netherlands, Belgium, and France.

We flew into Frankfurt. Acki met us at the airport, and we drove to Marburg to stay at the Fasanerie, a hotel owned and operated by Acki and his family. We received a warm welcome with a nice lunch and then took a nap. That evening we enjoyed a great dinner in their restaurant. The next day was for sightseeing. Marburg has a castle which we visited, and there were other visits to various sights. We went to another hotel owned by a friend of Acki, and Andy drank his very first beer! He loved it and was happy to be able to legally drink.

We spent one more day in Marburg and then took a train to Frankfurt and caught the bullet train to Amsterdam. The TGV train was a positive experience for both Andy and Debbie. Traveling over 100 mph, enjoying a snack while watching the scenery go by was something new for them. We arrived in Amsterdam and walked from the train station to the hotel where we had rooms reserved. Upon arrival we were told that the hotel was full, but we had rooms in their annex which was across the street on the corner. This was a four-story building with a single room on the 2nd floor which I took, one on the 3rd floor, which was allocated to Debbie, and one on the 4th floor for Andy. There was no elevator, and the stairs were narrow with turns. It was quite difficult to go up and down.

We left our luggage and began to explore Amsterdam. We were close to the canals and narrow pedestrian streets. We found a restaurant that served good food and Andy was able to sample Dutch beer. He said he preferred the German beer. He wanted to do some more exploring so I told them, go explore and I will sit at a table outside of a local pub. They explored and I relaxed. We spent two days in Amsterdam and then took a train to Brussels, Belgium. They were having a flower festival, and the Grand Place was covered with flowers. We visited the Mannequin Pis, and Debbie rubbed the swan which brings good luck. That

Debbie Ost, Acki Schultze, Andy Ost in Marburg, Germany

evening we had a delicious dinner on the famous Rue de Bou-chée. They were happy that we stopped in Belgium.

We went to the Gare Midi and took another bullet train to Paris. Upon arriving at the Gard de Nord, we walked to our hotel which I had prebooked. We visited Notre Dame and the Louvre. We took a sightseeing bus and toured Paris. We also went to the Sacre Coeur cathedral, and visited the artists community in Montmartre which was close by. Then we descended using the funicular which took us to the Pigalle neighborhood. We were then able to walk back to our hotel. The next day we took a train to Frankfurt and caught our return flight to the USA.

Ackitoberfest

Working with Ed Lewis, we put together a library of Ger-man songs for a German brass band. The scores were written for two trumpets, a French Horn, a trombone and a tuba. We played a few concerts in Laramie, and I decided to host a typical Ger-man Octoberfest. Each year I would buy real German Bratwurst and Weisswurst from a German butcher in Wisconsin. We would stock a large supply of beer, and order special beer mugs for the event. I would invite locals and friends and relatives from around the world. Tom's Bar would be the location. This event grew to an attendance of 100 to 150 people. Music was provided by our German band.

This became popular, and Acki would come from Germany. Then Hans Ullrich started to attend also from Germany. Goh Ing Sing would come from Asia along with his sons. One year, Mark Schneider from North Dakota renamed our annual Octoberfest celebration to "Ackitoberfest," in honor of our friend Acki Schultze. The name stuck, and every year I would host an Ackitoberfest with beer, bratwurst, and music.

I had card tables, folding chairs, umbrellas, and a large grill for preparing the food. I would have porta-toilets delivered and set up the furniture for everyone to enjoy the events. I would make arrangements for people to stay overnight, and some would come with campers and tents. I also made friends with the owners of a German restaurant in Denver and was able to obtain kegs of real Octoberfest beer shipped from Germany.

As a special gift, Goh Ing Sing had special handmade shirts made for relatives and close friends and brought those with him from Malaysia. I would run Tom's Bar and Acki and Hans would prepare the Bratwurst and Weisswurst to be served. Acki would tap the kegs and serve the beer in mugs that I had made for the occasion. We would start at noon, and it would be midnight or later when it would end.

In 2014 I was honored and pleased to have all of my daughters and their families attend the Ackitoberfest. I divided my garage into sections and made separate bedrooms to accommodate everyone. This was a large event also attended by Mr. Goh Ing

Tom's family at Ackitoberfest in Woodslanding, Wyoming, 2014. All four daughters and six of seven grandchildren attended, along with extended family members. From left: cousin Brandon Holcombe (with unknown guest); granddaughter-in-law Soledad Villar and grandson Tim Carson; cousins Kasey Ries, Brian Holcombe, and Eric Ries; daughter Tonia Ries; cousin David Ries; grandsons Jack (front) and Sam Leach, daughter Alexandra Leach; Tom; granddaughter Katherine Leach, son-in-law Mark Leach; niece Kym and nephew David Zwonitzer; granddaughter Nina Arteaga, son-in-law Jorge Arteaga, and daughter Grace Arteaga; grandson Dante Ost, daughter Debbie Ost and her husband, Ben Ost.

Sing who came all the way from Malaysia, Acki Schultze and Hans Ullrich from Germany, David Ries from Idaho, and Mark Schneider from North Dakota. We had a keg of real German beer from Germany via a friend in Colorado and Bratwurst from Wisconsin. Our German band played German music. I believe it was after 3am before the last beer was served. It was a wonderful event.

This was the last Ackitoberfest we held. It was a wonderful experience to have them all visit at the same time. My daughters had grown up in two different households. They were not aware that they had additional sisters as they grew up. It was a wonderful, emotional experience for me to see them all together for the first time.

It was my fault they had not met before, and I'm the only person responsible for that. I continually beat myself up for this failure, but nothing can replace this as I was avoiding responsibility. I was weak where I should have been strong and, as a result, my children suffered. When I began living alone in Woodslanding, I realized that I had let my children down, and I vowed to be a better father moving forward.

Many of my grandchildren also attended. David Ries, son of Carl Ries and his wife came from Idaho, Dan and Kym

Ackitoberfest 2014 with my four daughters: Alexandra Leach, Tonia Ries, Tom Ries, Grace Arteaga, and Debbie Ost

Zwonitzer came for Cheyenne, plus many neighbors from Woodslanding and Laramie were in attendance. It was a successful Ackitoberfest, and everyone enjoyed themselves.

Planning for Retirement

After everyone left, I sat with my dogs and contemplated the future. I was struggling with my COPD and realized that I might be better off living at a lower altitude. Through conversations I had with my daughters, it became clear that none of them had any interest in the Woodslanding house.

I was proud of this house as I had built it with my own two hands. It was supposed to become a family home, but I realized that was not going to become reality. So, after much consideration, I decided it might be best to sell this property. If I were to die, then my daughters would have a problem selling this property long distance, and if it were sold then it would be easy to divide the funds. OK, now to make plans.

The first question was: where would I want to live? A US state or a foreign country? I thought about moving to a Spanish-speaking country to learn more Spanish. How about Europe, or Asia? I began to make a list of possibilities. Mexico, Costa Rica, Malaysia, Germany, St. Maarten, California, Florida, the Gulf Coast. By process of elimination, I narrowed the choices down and decided it was best to stay in the USA.

Now, what about the sale of the house? It was full, as were the two garages and the barn. Oh my, what should I do with all this stuff? This was 2015.

I began by walking through each room and selecting things I would give to my daughters. I would move these items into the garage where I designated an area for each daughter. I tried to find things that would have meaning for each daughter plus any special significance for each of them. These piles grew until I thought that that was the best I could do. This area was then closed off, so it was secure.

Then, I prepared everything that could be sold. I set up tables and exhibits in the upper garage and advertised a garage sale. I also placed a separate ad for furniture items such as bedroom furniture, cabinets, chairs, etc. I had some success in selling furniture and a few items from the garage sale.

My friend Acki came over from Germany to help me. I rented a truck and we loaded everything I had for my daughter Debbie, who lived in Lakewood, Washington. This load included some table saws, tool chests, and many tools. I knew that Debbie's husband Ben would put these to good use. The first day, we drove as far as Boise, Idaho where we spent the night with my cousin David Ries.

The second day, we drove to Washington via Oregon. The eastern part of Oregon was a boring drive with not much scenery to speak of. We arrived in Lakewood and unloaded the rental truck, which we then returned to the U-Haul office. We spent two nights in Lakewood and then went to Seattle airport. Acki flew back to Germany, and I flew to Wyoming.

Then I rented a bigger truck and loaded it with everything I wanted to give to my other three daughters. I drove this truck from Laramie to Rochester, Minnesota, where my daughter Grace was living. Jorge helped me unload things for Grace, and I rested. I had driven nonstop and was tired. The next day Mark (Alex's husband) arrived so we could drive together from Minnesota to New York, where my other daughters lived. We planned to drive straight through, taking turns driving the truck. The trip went smoothly and Mark drove when we entered New York City. He knew the routes, and we arrived safely at Alex's house in Larchmont. New York. We were tired so we went to bed.

The next day, we unloaded everything for Alex, and I took off for Tonia's house in Montauk, New York, the very end of Long Island. I was able to make this drive on my own as I had been to Tonia's house before. We unloaded the truck and Tonia followed me to drop off the rental truck. In addition to the items I was giving Tonia, I had also brought my own belongings as it was planned that I would come and live in Montauk until I found my new home. I then flew back to Wyoming.

My real estate agent had been able to find a buyer for the

Woodslanding house, so it needed to be emptied. I had one final garage sale and sold what I could. Then I ordered a 20-foot trash container to be delivered to my property. I had Cowboy Moving and Storage pick up some items—a couch, chairs, bed, TV, and desk, that I was placing in storage until I had a new home. My niece and nephew came over from Cheyenne and offered to help me clear the house. I said, "everything I want is out," take whatever you want and throw everything else away. I am going to sit outside, drink a beer and ignore what is happening. I knew there were things that meant something to me but would be junk for other people. And I sat quietly while my life's material things were thrown into the trash container.

My nephew had an auction house in Cheyenne, so he took some items that he would sell at auction. My collections of 28 lighted beer signs and other signs went to Cheyenne. The people buying the property didn't want some items. I had a collection of barnwood stored in my barn for future construction projects which they didn't want, plus other items. Everything went into the 20-foot trash container until it was filled. So, I had this container picked up and another one put in place. The second one also got filled. The people buying the property bought my John Deere tractor and my Jeep Cherokee. I sold my Dodge pickup to a construction company in Laramie.

The house was empty, the new owners walked through, and everything was to be finalized the next morning in Laramie. We met, the paperwork was signed, and I received a check. We said goodbye and I went to the bank to deposit the check. I ran into a problem at the bank I had been using. They wanted to put a hold on the funds and would only release the full check after a 10-day period. I said no as I was leaving town and wanted access to my funds. I then went to another bank which was more accommodating and proper arrangements were made.

Retirement

Montauk

I flew to New York and settled down in Montauk to let the dust settle. Tonia let me move into Tim's room, so I placed my clothes in his closet and put my computer on the desk. Life in Montauk was very pleasant and relaxing. I could enjoy sitting on her back deck and garden during the day, and then enjoy the specular sunsets from her front porch in the evenings. It was always entertaining to see everyone trying to find a place on the beach to watch the sunset. We had a prime reserved seat. Another benefit was that I was able to enjoy some delicious home cooked meals made by Tonia. There were also visits to local restaurants, The Dock being among the favorites, as well as enjoying music in some local places. Tonia had a friend, Sarah Conway, who was a gifted singer and who would give shows.

However, the question remained: where should I live in the future? I decided to travel and explore options. I flew to Germany and stayed in both Gamburg where I had relatives, and Marburg with my good friend Acki. I thought about both of these locations, but decided these were not really what I wanted for the future. My good friend Dr. Friedrich Frei had a house in southern Germany that no one was using. He offered to give me this house, but it was in an area that did not appeal to me. I went to northern Germany but again, did not feel any connection. Using Germany as a base, I made side trips to other European countries looking for possibilities. Portugal was interesting, as was Italy, but both required a new language and different lifestyle. I crossed Europe off my list.

I flew to New Orleans, spent a few nights there, and then rented a car and drove the Gulf Coast thinking this could offer some possibilities. I drove through Mississippi, Alabama, and Florida. I did not find anything that looked promising. My mother had purchased a plot of land in Cape Coral which I had inherited after my mother's death. I visited this and did not like the area. I sold this. Driving back to New Orleans, I came to the conclusion that there was nothing here that appealed to me. I considered New Mexico, Arizona, and southern California. Again, I had no desire.

What about South America? I had heard that Uruguay was the Switzerland of South America. United Air Lines offered a special deal for a business class trip to Argentina. I was able to add Montevideo to this trip while I was still living in Woodslanding. I had a desire to learn more Spanish, so I flew to Costa Rica and enjoyed that country. I wanted to see more, so I booked a flight to Lima, Peru, and made arrangements to also visit Machu Picchu. I enjoyed Lima, had some good food and exciting experiences. I took a sightseeing bus and was able to see the parks, beaches, and other sights of this city.

The visit to Machu Picchu was an experience to remember. First you fly from Lima to Cusco. This city is at a high elevation, and the hotels all have oxygen tanks in the lobbies for the guests to use. I was able to visit what is classified as the highest Irish pub in the world. It is at over 11,000-foot elevation. I had a nice hotel room and enjoyed exploring the city. The next day, I took the train which goes along the river to Agua Calientes, which is below Machu Picchu. There are no cars in this city, and the train is the only connection to the rest of the country. There are no roads connecting this city to the rest of Peru. To reach Machu Picchu, there are some Mercedes Benz buses. These were brought in by train. There is one road that goes up the mountain to Machu Picchu that has a large number of switch backs. It is a 30-minute commute. Or you can hike up the mountain which takes over 3 hours.

When you reach Agua Calientes, the train station is like a marketplace. You have to walk through various stands selling fruits, vegetables, meats, clothing, and souvenirs. There are no taxis, so you walk to your hotel. Everything is within walking distance. There is a stream running through the town, and the bus stop to Machu Picchu is on the other side from where the hotels are located. There is also a hot spring you can visit. I was able to find a decent restaurant and had a satisfying dinner.

The next day I had a ticket to visit Machu Picchu, which you have to buy in advance. There is a long line to board the limited buses that go up the mountain. Off we went, only to stop about halfway up the mountain. There had been a landslide, and the road was blocked. We left the bus and climbed up a path that went past the blockage. There we entered another bus that took us to the entrance of Machu Picchu. There are no toilet facilities inside the park, so use the restroom before you enter. You present your ticket and are allowed into the park. It was an interesting day. On the return train ride to Cusco, a meal was served, and they had entertainment.

I liked Lima, so I decided that Peru was a possibility for retirement. There was a lot to do, good medical facilities were available, and I liked the food and atmosphere. I had previously been to Costa Rica, so I booked a trip there. I rented a car and drove along the coast. There were a lot of Americans living in Costa Rica. The prices for housing were low and there were good medical facilities with several good hospitals. I enjoyed my visit and met some nice people. I was able to visit a nature park which contained a lot of wildlife. The country had good housing, good food and friendly people. I put Peru and Costa Rica as possibilities.

Another location I was considering was the island of St. Maarten. This is the only place in the world where France and the Netherlands share a common border. I was introduced to this island when ITT had a conference there which I attended. There was a direct flight from New York, so I booked a flight and made a hotel reservation at a beach resort. My flight was late arriving. I rented a car and drove to the resort where I had my booking. When I arrived, everything was closed and there was a gate with a guard so you couldn't enter. I explained to the guard, told him I had a booking and he said I would have to wait till morning when they opened, and I could check in. I said no problem I will sleep in my rental car here in the parking lot. I went to sleep in my rental car.

About 2 am there was a banging on my car. There was a change of guard and this new guard said that I couldn't sleep there and would have to move. He was very insistent, so I left, starting onto the highway, and driving on a dark road. There were very few cars on the road. Suddenly, a car moving very fast with bright lights came up to me. It slowed down when it was alongside, and two men with umbrellas began hitting my car. I made a quick stop and the other car stopped ahead of me. I put my car in reverse. Two men jumped out of the stopped car, which was 100 feet ahead of me, and started running towards me. I waited until they almost reached me, then I floored my car in reverse, took off down the road, was able to change the direction I was heading, and with a high rate of speed headed down the road. They turned around and chased me. I could see no one to ask for help, so I headed into the next town. They were gaining on me when I came to a narrow section of road where there was almost one-way traffic. There was a car coming the other way, so I drove into this narrow spot, so we had to stop. There were two French policemen in that car. I told them what was happening, and the car that had been chasing me took off in another direction. A short distance down the road was a night club that was open. I stopped there and spent the rest of the night in the nightclub where I was safe. The next morning, I went back to the resort and checked into my reserved room.

I enjoyed Saint Maarten. There were beautiful beaches and some nightlife. There were nice restaurants, and it was easy to drive around. Warm water and plenty of sunshine. A paradise. I thought this is great—but what if I wanted a change of scenery? You can only drink so many pina coladas, and then what is there to do? Lay on the beach all day? What if you felt like going for a drive someplace? You were stuck on this island and were limited to what it had to offer. As nice and appealing as all of this was, I felt that I would need to have better access to the rest of the world. I scratched Saint Maarten off my list and flew back to New York.

I was still undecided as to where I wanted to retire, I had considered Europe, South America, Australia, and North America. I had seen a lot of Africa and had no desire to live there so off I went to explore Asia. Singapore was attractive but very expensive. I met my good friend Goh Ing Sing, and we looked at possibilities. Indonesia was cheap but there were political issues.

Thailand was considered, but the language would be a major hurtle and there were political issues and medical conditions. We looked at Malaysia, and there was a possibility. Goh was considering buying a new property in Kota Kinabalu on the northern coast of the island of Borneo. There was a villa on the property plus some outbuildings. Nice property but was in a remote area. Not a good location.

I spend some more time with Goh visiting his oil palm plantations in Malaysia and Indonesia. We spent time at his home in Malacca and his apartment in Kuala Lumpur, the capital of Malaysia. There were many individuals I knew on the various plantations from the training seminars as well as previous visits. I also had the opportunity to visit the headquarters of the EC Council and renew relationships. It was amazing to see how many friends I had in this part of the world. All in all, a wonderful experience. I was happy to have made this trip.

I returned to Montauk and enjoyed the good food, home cooking, and all of the entertainment that was available—especially the evenings, watching the beautiful sunsets. I no longer had to sleep alone as Milo, Tonia's dog, would be on my bed every night. He was a welcome guest. In the mornings I would sit in the kitchen. I would have a shot of tequila and Milo would enjoy a treat. This became a morning ritual for both of us. I realized that it was time to make a decision. I had looked at and researched many locations, now I had to decide. I told Tonia that I was going to retire to New Orleans.

I arrived in New Orleans, took a room in a hotel in the French Quarter, and began searching for a place to live. I made one side trip to Ocean Springs, Mississippi as I heard some good stories about living there. I looked at three places there but decided that New Orleans was where I would be the most content. A lot of live music, excellent food, many different cultures, many things to do, no snow to shovel, and a low altitude. I wanted to be close to the action, Bourbon Street, and the French Quarter. Possibilities were limited in this area. I visited and looked at apartments in the downtown area. They were all expensive, and there was little opportunity to be outside. I found nothing that appealed to me. On my last day I found an ad about

Bienville Basin, so I decided to try it there.

Bienville Basin Development was previously called the Iberville projects. It was an area known for criminal activity, drug use, prostitution, and vice. There were gangsters living here who would go in the French Quarter, rob people and then run back to the projects. This was a dangerous area and even the police were reluctant to go there. Hurricane Katrina had devastated this area, and it was badly destroyed. To recover, the Iberville Projects were taken over by private companies, and everyone had to leave. The buildings were gutted and then renovated into nice apartments.

I was received in the property management office and told them that I was interested in a two-bedroom apartment. Nothing was ready to be rented, but one had just become vacant. They hesitated but then agreed to let me look at it. It needed to be repainted, cleaned and made ready for the next tenant. We returned to the rental office, and I was left sitting while they handled other people. When everyone was taken care of, they then asked me what I thought. I said, 'I will take it," which surprised everyone. I explained that I did not have an immediate need and that they would have time to get it ready before I moved. In August 2016, I completed the paperwork, paid a deposit, and, at age 84, had a new home.

Upon returning to New York, I told Tonia that I would be officially moving to New Orleans. I had been living in Montauk, so I had my personal belongings and clothing there. I thought about a rental truck but then realized that there was not enough to justify that. What about a rental car? That was a possibility, but then I decided that I would need a car in New Orleans, so I decided to buy a used car. The search was on, and we found a 2008 Honda Accord with low mileage at a decent price. Temporary licenses plates were placed on this car, and it came to me in Montauk.

New Orleans

When I received notification that my new apartment was ready, we loaded everything, including my string bass, into the Honda and I left for New Orleans. This was a two-day drive, so I stopped for one night in Tennessee. The next day I arrived in New Orleans and took possession of my new apartment. There was no furniture, but I had an air mattress I could blow up, and pillows and a blanket. When I went to blow up the mattress, I found a huge hole and it would not hold air. So I spent my first night sleeping on the floor.

The next day, I flew to Cheyenne and spent the night at Kym's house. Then I rented a truck and drove to Cowboy Moving and Storage in Laramie to pick up the things I had in storage there. I left, driving the truck on my own. I drove straight through, stopping to catch some sleep in the truck when I got tired. I had made arrangements with some movers to help me unload the truck in New Orleans. Both my bed and my desk had to be taken up three flights of stairs and then the couches and TV had to be taken up two flights with twists and turns. It was a difficult move, but everything was in place, and I would be able to sleep in my own bed.

I bought a kit to make a nice cabinet upon which I could place the TV. This had a lot of pieces and took two days to assemble. I bought a table and four chairs as well as a chest of drawers for my clothes. I was kept busy assembling all of these items. I had a 40-foot-long balcony off the living room, so I ordered wrought iron furniture: three tables and 12 chairs. I needed pots, pans, dishes and silverware, so I was kept busy settling into my new home. This apartment had a lot of stairs which I wanted as they would be good exercise. The new balcony furniture arrived, and it took more than a full day to unwrap the chairs and assemble the tables. I had also ordered three umbrellas, so now I had to order three bases to put them in. The results were worth the effort.

Now to get acquainted with my new home. I started by visiting Bourbon Street which was a 10-minute walk from my apartment. There I found live music, bars, and restaurants. I found the Upper Quarter, a bar used by locals, and there I met people working in the area. I learned where to go and where not to go. I found that when you became a local, you would be treated specially instead of the tourist routine. The Upper Quarter bar was about halfway on my way to Bourbon Street, so I became a local.

There were a lot of bars featuring live music, however much of it was simply guitars with amplifiers turned to high volumes, not what I was seeking. I found some traditional live music in four clubs. Those I would visit, and I met and became acquainted with the musicians. I began to make friends in the music business and was able to sit in and play with several different bands. I began to feel at home and think that I had made the right decision about where to retire. Another wonderful feature of this city was the variety and quality of the food being offered. You soon learned which were the good restaurants and which were tourist traps. I love sea food and found some great restaurants.

Then I began driving around to learn the streets and byways. As in any city there are the main routes followed by everyone and then there are the side streets you can use to get around the traffic jams. New Orleans offered a special challenge as there are many twists and turns to many of the streets and avenues. The Interstates running through the city have some special intersections that need to be learned. It helps to know which lane to be in when approaching these connections. New Orleans is a unique city and has a lot to offer. The more I saw the better I felt about moving there.

Sam's Award Trip

Alex's oldest son graduated from high school in 2018, so he was to be awarded his trip. He wanted to visit Greece, so I asked around for information. I finally decided on Athens, then the islands of Santorini and Mykonos. This itinerary was accepted so I began making arrangements. I was able to get some good seats on United from Newark to Athens. In Athens I found a central hotel that we could easily reach by using the rail network from the airport to the city. I booked three nights; we could rest the first day and then have two days to explore Athens. Then a boat to Santorini, another to Mykonos, and then a return boat to Athens for our return flight home.

I made bookings for hotels in both Santorini and Mykonos. Alex then texted back that she had found a different hotel in Santorini, so I cancelled the booking I had made and put the one Alex had found on our itinerary. The trip was planned, and the dates were set. I had confirmations for the hotels, seats and flights reserved and the boat tickets all bought and paid for. We would leave on a Friday and arrive in Athens on Saturday morning. Then I planned our itinerary from Larchmont to the Newark airport. Everything confirmed: we were on our way.

Friday morning, we were scheduled to take an 11 am train into the city, connect with the Newark Express bus, and arrive in Newark in plenty of time to clear security and catch our flight to Athens. Arriving at the Larchmont train station, we found that there was a delay on the trains. I was a little concerned, but both Alex and Sam did not seem to be concerned. The train was delayed 45 minutes, but I didn't worry as we could still catch a Newark Express bus to the airport. When we were on the train and on our way, Alex informed me that we were going to meet Mark at the Grand Central Train Station for lunch. We arrived and found our way to the food court at Grand Central Station where we met Mark.

It was a long lunch, and I was really getting concerned, but I told myself; hey, it is their trip so why should I worry. When we finally finished lunch, I said we needed to rush to the bus stop. The goodbyes took some time and we finally got to the bus stop. There was one person at the bus stop, and he said the buses were not running on schedule. The last one had left five minutes ago so we would have to wait for the next one. We had a 5:30 flight to catch. It was now after 2 pm. Alex suggested we take a taxi, but I said we should wait for the bus. We waited for the next bus which finally arrived around 3 pm. We boarded the bus, finally we were on our way. When the bus turned onto 42nd Street, there was a huge traffic jam with traffic just inching along. We got to 7th Avenue where the bus turns down to 41st Street to pick up passengers at the Port Authority Terminal. Total blockage. It took almost an hour to transit that one block. We stopped at Port Authority, the bus filled, and people were left standing.

We left and went to the tunnel under the river to New Jersey. There we found the interstate backed up with slow moving traffic. The bus driver did his best, even going through a parking lot on the side of the road to get ahead of a lot of traffic. It was after 5 pm when we finally reached Newark Airport for our 5:45 flight, which left from Terminal C. The bus stopped first at Terminal A, and then at Terminal B. We reached terminal C about 5:20 for our 5:45 pm flight. Our bags were in the luggage compartment of the bus. I said "give me your passports and I will check us in." I ran into the terminal and, ignoring everyone, I went to the front of the line and told the attendant of the problem; I asked her to call the gate. Her supervisor came over and I had to explain everything again. There was a long delay before they agreed to call the gate at which time they said the flight is closed.

Sam and Alex arrived with the luggage, and I started asking about the next flight. They only had one flight a day to Athens, and Saturday was booked solid. After a lot of back and forth they found three seats on the Sunday flight. No longer business class, but I was able to book us in three different parts of economy class. While this was going on I didn't see my suitcase to discover that Alex had grabbed to wrong suitcase. There was a luggage tag on the case with a phone number. Sam called to discover that the gentleman had gone through security and had left my suitcase with security, Sam left and went to retrieve my suitcase.

We finalized everything for our Sunday flight when Sam called and said that they wouldn't let him have my suitcase and I would have to come to security and prove my identity before they would release my suitcase. I said OK and to give me directions. He said, hold on, I spoke to security and was told to stay where I was and wait. Ten minutes later here came Sam with a TSA official and my suitcase and I was able to retrieve it. By this time, I had enough and said let's go sit down, have something to drink, and decide what to do next. There was nothing to drink in Terminal C, and we were directed to Terminal B, where we found an Italian restaurant that served food and drink. I had a glass of wine. We had dinner, and then took an Uber back to Larchmont.

We spent Saturday in Larchmont instead of sightseeing in Athens. Sunday, we took an Uber to the airport and checked in for our flight to Athens. Upon arrival, we cleared customs and went to the baggage area. I had Sam and Alex wait for the bags, and I went to change money. There was only one place and there was a long line. They arrived with the bags, I changed money, and we caught the train into the city. It was a short walk from the train to our hotel. We checked in and made plans. Our boat left the next morning, and it was already Monday afternoon. The Acropolis was within walking distance of our hotel. I said that they should go, and I would wait for them in the hotel. I rested and when they returned, we had dinner in a nice restaurant on the top floor of the hotel.

Tuesday morning the hotel ordered a taxi to take us to the ferry to Santorini. The driver knew the city and was able to get us to the ferry ahead of some huge traffic jams. We boarded and found seats at the front of the boat where we could view the scenery. Some people from Asia set up a cooking stove and cooked their meal next to us. We were able to purchase good food and snacks. Upon arriving in Santorini, we took a taxi to the hotel Alex had been able to find. Then, Alex revealed that she had been here before. She and Mark had spent their honeymoon on this island! The hotel was excellent and served good food.

On Wednesday we took a bus into the city center and caught a connecting bus to Oia, where there were shops, restaurants, and a beach. To get to the beach there was a very long set of stairs going down the hillside. I found a restaurant that had a courtyard and was due to open soon, so I told them to do their thing and I would meet them in the restaurant. There were narrow streets and a lot of people. The restaurant opened and I was one of the first to enter. This was a family restaurant; they spoke English and we became friends. I enjoyed some wine and snacks while waiting. Had some nice conversations and felt very comfortable.

Sam and Alex were exhausted when they arrived, so we began with some drinks. When we ordered we were treated like family. The food was delicious, and after eating the Greek family came over and sat at our table. It was like being at home. We all had a good time and a very relaxed evening. Oia is famous for its sunsets, and we enjoyed that. We found a taxi to take us back to our hotel. We could sit outside at our hotel, so it was a wonderful day.

The next day we visited the city of Akrotiri which had been excavated and was now housed in a large structure as a museum. You could see the old buildings, how they were constructed, and how people would have lived in those ancient times. This was a large exhibit and required a lot of walking combined with some up and down pathways. I looked at the section that was easily accessible, and let Sam and Alex explore the rest. Alex came back, and Sam covered the whole exhibit. It was hot and exhausting, so we decided to take a local boat to the beaches of Akrotiri. There were many beaches. At one of these, Alex and I watched Sam make a long swim to an underground cave, which he enjoyed. We made another side trip to Delos, another ancient city that had been uncovered. There was a lot of history in this area.

The ferry from Santorini to Mykonos was very different than the one we had been on before. You enter on the lower deck, which had racks for storing luggage. You were not allowed to take your suitcases to the passenger deck. You were told to remember where your suitcase was stored to be able to retrieve it when you disembarked in Mykonos. You climbed a staircase to the passenger deck, and no one was allowed access to the luggage deck once the door to the passenger deck was closed. We did not have a window seat on this ferry. Upon arriving in Mykonos, we retrieved our luggage and joined a line to take a taxi. We finally got a taxi and were driven to our hotel which was on a high point and overlooked the city. The hotel had a swimming pool which we enjoyed.

After checking in, Sam and Alex wanted to explore the city. This required going down some stairs and going down a sloped area. I told them to go ahead, and I would wait in the hotel. I spent the afternoon at the swimming pool. That evening we had a nice dinner in the hotel, saw a beautiful sunset and sat outside by the swimming pool. Very pleasant and relaxing. Then I discovered that my reserve money I had in my suitcase was missing. Probably taken by the crew on the ferry boat where we had to leave our luggage. Nothing I could do; the money was gone. Luckly, I had enough in my wallet to cover our cash needs. Slept well in a comfortable bed and woke up to a nice breakfast in the hotel.

There were sights to see, the windmills on Mykonos were famous, and were a tourist attraction. We took a taxi down to the town center which was full of shops selling a lot of tourist items. I found a nice restaurant where I could sit outside. Sam and Alex went shopping and Sam gave me a T shirt that said, "Save Water, Drink Wine!" I loved it! They went off to see the windmills, and I relaxed with a glass of wine. We had a nice dinner and then took a taxi back to the hotel to enjoy the sunset.

There was an airport on Mykonos which had a flight to

Alexandra Leach and Sam Leach in Mykonos

Athens where we could connect for our flight home. We had booked seats for our flight but had some discussions with the airlines before we were able to get our boarding passes. This was a popular flight, and some people would pay extra to get a seat. We took off and headed to Athens. We arrived safely and checked in with United for our flight back to New York. We were met at Newark by Mark, who then drove us to Larchmont. A happy evening with a lot of stories brought this Greek adventure to a close.

Musician Again

Back in New Orleans, I continued to explore music venues and restaurants. I was concentrating on the Franch Quarter as that was withing walking distance. I got acquainted with the bars that featured live music and was amazed at the large variety of musicians playing. One of the first bands I got well acquainted with was the Loose Change Jazz band which played at the Maison Bourbon Jazz club. This group was led by Phil Campo, who played trumpet. We spoke about some of the musicians we had both known in the 1950s. The piano player, David Hull, and I became good friends, and we would go eat together. He lived on a small boat in the harbor. The trombone player, Dave Ruffner, and I would cross paths many times in the future. I sat in and played with this band many times.

Another club which was nearby was Fritzel's European Jazz club. They featured great musicians with standard Dixieland and traditional jazz music. This club would get very crowded and would have a crowd that appreciated what was offered. The other clubs on Bourbon featured guitars and large amps. Many people liked these clubs, but I found them to be loud, noisy and not always with people I cared to be around.

As I had the money, I received for my Woodslanding property, I decided to invest in some real estate in New Orleans. I began looking online and contacted a couple of real estate agents. I looked at fourplexes as a possibility. Then a seven plex was offered and I considered that as a possibility. It was a tight squeeze, but I managed, so I bought a seven-plex at 2110 Bienville. Six two-bedroom apartments and a one-bedroom apartment, plus a washroom with two washers and two dryers and a storage room. I hired a property management company to manage this property. Now I was a landlord in both Laramie and New Orleans.

I continued to travel, with trips to see Goh in Asia and Acki and family in Germany. I would add side trips to explore countries I could add to my list. When I would visit Germany, I would make side trips to Bulgaria, Estonia, Lithuania, etc., so I could add to my list of countries. I wanted to travel enough to keep my 1K status with United Airlines. And I enjoy experiencing different cultures, foods, and ways of life. I would look for opportunities to visit new places. One time, on a trip to Asia I saw a promotion to visit New Zealand. Air Asia was offering special fares from Kuala Lumpur to Auckland, Australia. I booked a flight in their first-class section. The lady sitting next to me was from Auckland and we became friends. She owned a business offering perfumes and oils made from plants that were native to New Zealand. When we arrived, she drove me to my hotel, and we agreed to meet for dinner.

She picked me up, gave me a tour of the seafront area of Auckland, and treated me to a wonderful dinner at a very nice restaurant. The next day I booked a city tour on a sightseeing bus with stops where you could get on and off. I stopped at the wildlife sanctuary. I saw live penguins, local wildlife, and sea life. I was also able to visit a museum, and experience local cultures and native people, My daughter. Alex had been to New Zealand and had told me how beautiful it was. She was right! I loved my experience there. The sights, the food, and, above all, the very friendly people.

My life continued in New Orleans. I had been told that Frenchman Street was where good music could be experienced. Correct, I found a lot of live good music there and no guitars. Here was the music I had heard on my first visit to New Orleans in 1957. No booming amplifiers and loud noise. Here were musicians who loved their instruments and who were putting their hearts and souls into their music. What a wonderful experience! Then I heard about Buffa's Jazz Brunch so off I went. Another great surprise, and they were playing the music I had grown up with that I loved. This became my favorite club.

I was contacted about my fourplex in Laramie. There was an interested buyer who had just purchased the one next door and was interested in mine. They made a good offer, which I accepted, and I was no longer a property owner in Wyoming. I looked around New Orleans and found a five-plex on South Galvez, a four-plex with a one-bedroom cottage in the back, I bought this, so now I had 12 apartments in New Orleans. I used the same property management company, so they collected the rent and took care of renting any units that became vacant. My main concern was maintenance.

I had hired one of the maintenance workers from Bienville Basin apartments complex where I was living, but he was not reliable. A problem arose with a clogged sewer line on my Bienville apartments, I contacted the maintenance people at the Bienville Basin complex and was introduced to Richie Williams, who was in charge of this crew. He came to my rescue and was able to solve the problem quickly and efficiently, I developed a good relationship with Richie, and we became good friends. I used him for all of my maintenance needs on my properties.

I started going to Buffa's on a regular basis, and I would sit in and play every Sunday. One day I came in and they said that their bass player was sick and would I play the gig. Luckily, I had my tuba in my car, so I said yes and played all day. It felt good to once again earn money as a musician! I also met a musician who sat in, and we talked. He was also a member of a Legion band and said they needed a tuba player. I joined the American Legion Band, Post 350, and began playing concerts around New Orleans. We played in the City Park, several retirement homes, and in Gretna City celebrations. They rehearsed every Monday night in Metairie from 7:30 to 9:30. There were 30 band members.

A new French Horn player joined the band, and she said she also played with the New Orleans Volunteer Orchestra, and they didn't have a tuba player. They rehearsed on Tuesday evening, so I joined as their only tuba player. This was an 80-piece orchestra made up of mainly string instruments. A true symphony orchestra. The first concert I played with them included Dvorak's Symphony No. 9, "The New World Symphony." Later concerts included 1812 Overture by Tchaikovsky, Beethoven Piano Concerto #1, The Blue Danube by Johann Strauss, and many other choices from the classical music library. I was now able to play music. Sundays, sit-in at Buffa's. Mondays, the American Legion Band. And on Tuesdays, the New Orleans Volunteer Orchestra.

The Saenger Theater in New Orleans is where all of the major plays and visiting groups are presented. It is the leading stage in New Orleans. My apartment was a five-minute walk, and I did not have a parking problem. There was always a large crowd at the events and parking was limited. I enjoyed this theater and was able to see Mamma Mia, The Lion King, An Evening with Cirque Dreams Holiday, The US Marine Band, The Wizard of Oz, Cinderella, An American in Paris. Great Russian Ballet's the Nutcracker, Les Misérables, The Book of Mormon, Aladdin, the Phantom of the Opera, and Hamilton. This was wonderful to be able to enjoy all these plays and wonderful music. I could book my tickets online and have an easy stroll back and forth while others had to battle parking and traffic.

Another great benefit was the number of visitors I received. To visit Woodslanding was a large undertaking as it required some planning. They would have to fly into Denver and then drive a car. It was time-consuming, and sometimes included flight delays, traffic, etc. New Orleans was easy to get to and had a lot of attractions. I had visitors from New Zealand, Germany, France, the Netherlands, the UK, and many US states. Three of my four daughters came and spent time with me as did my niece, Kym Zwonitzer, from Wyoming. Everyone would visit the French Quarter, listen to live music, and visit the Café de Monde to have a famous New Orleans beignet.

One attraction that everyone liked was a Mississippi River cruise on a paddle steamboat, The Natchez. We would board and go to the upper deck for the upriver portion of the cruise. We would see various sites on the west bank and enjoy a drink while enjoying the breeze. Some would go to the rear of the boat to watch the paddles push us up the river, others would visit the engine room. The boat would continue, and we would go down one deck where lunch was served. There would be live music while one enjoyed a delicious meal. As we returned to New Orleans one could have excellent views of the New Orleans skyline and the Cresent River bridge, which connects the east and west banks of the city. Then a causal stroll through the Franch Quarter to my apartment.

Another favorite of many was the Swamp Tour. This required a one-hour drive south from New Orleans to the town of Lafitte. There, a company operates a fleet of air boats for the tours. Leaving the dock area, they go slowly as they are noisy, and the town has complained. Once they are away from the town, they increase their speed and cross a large lake that can be choppy when the wind is blowing. You then enter a series of canals going through the swamps. Alligators are attracted with marshmallows; you also see birds and a lot of cypress trees. On my first visit I was with Acki. In addition to the normal sights, we saw a raccoon stealing marshmallows from an alligator. The

Buffa's Jazz Brunch

alligator was on land, and our boat captain would throw marshmallows at him, and the racoon would dart in and steal the marshmallow. It was an exciting show, as the alligator would love to eat the racoon for dinner. These were both wild animals.

I went on many swamp tours with family members and friends. On one tour, I was with a colleague from my days working with ITT in Belgium. Graham Davies and I had been through a lot together in Europe and Africa. We were on a two-hour tour when we were hit with a monsoon-type rainstorm. There was no shelter on the swamp boat, so we headed back to the boat dock at a high rate of speed. It was a terrible 25-minute ride that I will never forget. The rain would hit your face so hard each drop felt like a rock. By the time we got back to the docks I was drenched. Even the dollar bills in my pocket were soaked. From the boat we ran through the rain into their office. We were given paper towels to dry off. When we got back to New Orleans both Graham and I had to put our shoes into the clothes dryer. I have never been so wet. Every piece of my clothing was soaked with rain.

I joined the Deutsches Haus, which was located on Moss Street, across from the New Orleans City Park. They had purchased a property which was previously used by the National Guard. It was a large property, and they constructed a new building, As I enjoyed German events, it felt like being in Germany. Every year they would host an Octoberfest. In 2018, as a volunteer, I was assigned to the entrance gate, and would assist in allowing guests into the grounds. The following year, I worked at the parking entrance, and would collect entrance funds for parking.

In 2020, using the music I had from my German band in Wyoming, I offered to organize a German brass band to play at the Deutsches Haus. There was a German who played trumpet, the president of the Deutsches Haus also played the trumpet, so

New Orleans Volunteer Orchestra

that was the beginning. We found a trombone player and used a saxophone to play the French horn part. I played the tuba, so now we had a house band for the Deutsches Haus.

From its founding in 2020, the band has developed into a well-respected band which has been named the Deutsches Haus Musikanten. This band now has 14 members, has played for many events at the Deutsche Haus, and has been invited to play in other locations. I am proud of this band and am happy to have founded this wonderful group of musicians.

My five plex on Galvez experienced flooding. It was about five inches deep in the two lower apartments. We had to cut and replace the bottom 18 inches of the wallboard. I had insurance, so the damage was covered. In one upstairs apartment, we had to replace some of the floors which had termite damage. I replaced the stove in one apartment, and we had to run a new sewer line to the free-standing unit in the back. One new tenant was having a lot of visitors, and neighbors were being bothered by all the strange people. I did some checking and discovered that he was using the unit as a short-term rental for visitors. I was able evict him and rent it to a normal couple.

In 2019, LSU Medical purchased three buildings on Galvez Street, adjacent to my building, tore them down, and made a huge parking lot. They approached me and offered to buy mine for an appraised amount. I refused, and life went on as usual. Then in 2020, the restaurant building on the opposite side of mine was sold. First to a person who planned to open a Chinese restaurant, but shortly thereafter to the LSU Foundation. Later I was contacted and asked if I would sell my property. I met them on numerous occasions, and they kept increasing their offer. I finally agreed and this property was sold on November 11, 2020, at a price I found acceptable.

Life in New Orleans changed when the coronavirus arrived. All the bars and restaurants were closed. Bourbon Street became deserted, with all the venues boarded up with either plywood or shutters. The city shut down, and people were advised to stay home and to shelter in place. Grocery stores and gas stations were allowed to stay open; hotels, barber shops, salon, etc. were all ordered closed. A big change was that I had been playing with the American Legion concert band and with the New Orleans Volunteer Orchestra. I had rehearsals on Monday and Tuesday evenings, and we would play concerts in the City of New Orleans. On Sundays I would go to Buffa's Jazz Brunch and play with the band there. All of this stopped when everything was closed because of the virus. Both the American Legion band and the New Orleans Volunteer Orchestra could not rehearse as there were too many people in one room.

I used the money from the sale of the Galvez Street property and purchased a fourplex in eastern New Orleans. This property had been gutted and required a lot of work before it could have renters. This became a problem as it required many permits. I was able to get a permit to connect the electricity and we did this by using an outdoor pole. I purchased wallboard to finish the walls which we loaded inside the building. We installed safety bars on the doors and windows for security. We hired an electrician to do the electrical work, which needed to be inspected before we could install the wallboard. We also had a lot of plumbing work done to be ready for the inspector to turn on the water.

We continued to do what we could to make progress. I bought bathtubs for all the units and installed plumbing pipes

The Bier Musikanten. Tom is 3rd from left. Photo by Katherine Leach.

and drains. Again, we waited for an inspector to approve what we had done, but to no avail. I had invested a lot in materials and manpower and still, we had to wait for an inspector to issue a certificate. I spent a lot on electrical wiring and purchased new meter boxes for the apartments.

Still, we were waiting for inspectors to approve certificates. At this point, I said enough is enough and decided to put the building up for sale.

At the same time, insurance rates and property taxes had huge increases. Then the cost of building materials and replacement items had a huge increase for my Bienville property, so I decided to sell everything. I was able to obtain a price to cover the expense I had in the Eastern New Orleans property and a favorable price for my Bienville property, so in 2022 I sold both properties. Life was good!

I received a big surprise in October 2022 when my daughters announced that they were coming to New Orleans to celebrate my 90th birthday. They rented a property that would sleep 22 people. The Stierle family came from Germany, Kym and Dave came from Cheyenne, and my daughters and their family came from New York. The property had a courtyard, so the first evening as everyone was arriving, we prepared food on the property. The next day, people went sightseeing, and there was a lot of coming and going. Then in the evening, we enjoyed a catered dinner with a beautiful birthday cake. It was a wonderful evening with friends and family.

On Sunday, we all went to Buffa's Jazz Brunch for breakfast and New Orleans music. I sat in with the band and everyone took pictures. In the afternoon we went to the Deutsches Haus, where we were all seated together in the main banquet room. We enjoyed catered food and then a very special birthday cake decorated with a string bass and tuba. Suddenly, in marched a typical New Orleans Street band arranged by Richie which gave us a New Orleans style concert and sang happy birthday to me. He grew up with these musicians. We returned to our courtyard and spent the rest of the evening enjoying drinks and each other's company.

Life continued on, but I was beginning to have more

Tom's 90th birthday cakes

problems with breathing and other issues. My daughters became concerned as I was living alone with no one to help me if I had an emergency. Tonia came from New York, and we looked at options. We visited many retirement communities and were not impressed with what we found. Then we looked at Woldenberg Village, which we both liked. It has no stairs, is all on one level and has 24-hour assistance for residents. I have a two-bedroom apartment, each bedroom with its own bathroom, a dining room, a living room, a kitchen and a beautiful outdoor patio. There is quality landscaping, well maintained, and very secure. I am happy living here and am enjoying my final years.

In closing, I want to say that I have been blessed with four wonderful daughters and seven fantastic grandchildren. I have had the opportunity to see the world and to enjoy life's pleasures. All my daughters are doing well, and I hope and pray that all of my grandchildren will have a good life.

Appendix A: Ries Family

Grace Ries Visits Europe in 1956

In 1956, Tom's parents, Anthony and Grace Ries, traveled to Europe to visit Tom, who was stationed in Wiesbaden, Germany. They left New York on August 30 and returned November 18th of that year. This is her account of the journey and her impressions of the many places they visited. It has been transcribed from the original typed document, preserving the original spelling and grammar.

♦ ♦ ♦

Our Second Honeymoon August 30, 1956

The Stogsdill family picked us up and took us to the station on Thursday August 30th, 1956. We boarded the Pacific Challenger at 6.20 pm and started for our European trip. We had breakfast on the diner. Arrived in Chicago at 11 am Friday morning.

Having 7 hours to spend in Chicago, a sightseeing trip was in order, so we got to see a bit of Chicago. Lunch and dinner in Chicago, boarding the train (New York Central) that evening at 6pm.

Arrived in Rom, New York at 7:40 Saturday morning were Ethel and Spencer Snyder met us, taking us to their home for breakfast. Spent the day visiting, in afternoon visiting Sadie Spriggs at her cabin on Delta Lake. She took covers from her beautiful antique furniture that we might see it. She had sent one of her tables to Mamie at the White House as furniture came from the Doud family. Ethel had prepared a grand dinner, we spend the evening with Snyders.

Up fairly early Sunday am and Spence drove us to Cato NY to see Burton Gallants and Cousin Jennie. Ester and Helen were away visiting her parents. Kenneth and Nellie Gallant came in for a while.

Ethel Snyder had prepared a picnic basket (fried chicken, etc.) which we enjoyed in a pleasant spot on the edge of Delta Lake. Monday morning we got an early start for the Vosburgh cabin at Caroga Lake. Ethel and Spence drove us in their car. Travelled on the Throughway. Llora had a chicken dinner prepared which we all enjoyed and the Snyder's then left for home. George, Jr took us around both lakes to see the lights, going thru the narrow, shallow channel by help of a flashlight. Had breakfast on the screened terrace Tuesday morning; had another motor boat ride on the lake (in my housecoat and waded in the lake at the end of trip). Llora put down the top of the convertible red car and we rode thru all the neighboring towns, stopped to see Sarah Darrow in Sprakers; visited the Farmer's museum in Cooperstown (the home of baseball), then to Balatine Bridge and thru the Vosburgh home and gardens. Picked up George Vosburgh at his office and took us to dinner at "Nick Stoner's Lodge". We had cocktails in the lounge first. Another night in the Vosburgh cabin in our cozy room overlooking the lake.

With our bags all packed and breakfast over, we bid good bye to the Camp on Caroga Lake and headed for Fort Plain and the lift on the Barge Canal, where we watched several boats pass thru the lift. We again visited Llora's home which is located between the main highway, the Thruway, barge canal, Mohawk River and railway. Visited Mac Winne and went thru her home, saw all her lovely antiques, her poodle "Beau" and she joined us on the ride to Albany. Getting a late start, Llora had to drive like mad to make the train and we barely got on it and hurriedly said goodbye to Llora and Mac. Then what a hunt we had for seats, couldn't even sit together.

Another hassle to get a taxi once we arrived in New York City. (Remember the man that tried to keep us from taking our cab and how the driver put our bags in for us?). A telegram was awaiting us at the Roger Smith Hotel, telling us of Lew and Nina's wedding the day after we left home.) We visited Rockefeller Center, saw the Rockettes at Radio City Music Hall, combined with the movie "High Society" with Bing Crosby, Grace

Kelly and Frank Sinatra.

On Thursday we took a sightseeing trip thru Manhattan and along the shore line drive, visiting piers and fishmarkets; thru the Bowery where we saw drunks sleeping in doorways, others fighting in the streets; some carrying their clothes over their arms on the way to pawn shops; along Fifth avenue, thru the Wall Street canyons.

We secured tickets for the "Big Payoff" where Tony was selected as a contestant and we got front seats so we could see the workings of a television program; had close up on Beth Myserson, the former Miss America. It was raining when we came out so we slowly worked our way to 42nd St. and a movie where we saw "Moby Dick" with Gregory Peck. After getting our raincoats from the hotel we retraced our steps to see Cinerama "Seven Wonders of the World".

Friday morning we took the bus to the Empire State Building and viewed New York City from the top, could see our ship, the "Ryndam" laying at anchor. We then strolled down Fifth Avenue, window shopping. Then to Roxie's Theatre to see "Bus Stop" with Marilyn Monroe, plus a beautiful skating pageant. We had dinner at the hotel and then walked down to the Post office and other places of interest.

Saturday, Sept 8th we took a taxi to the "Port of Authority" bus terminal, boarded another bus for the Holland-American Pier at Hoboken NJ which brough us to the "Ryndam", we identified our luggage and went on board. Luncheon was served at 2pm, dinner at 7"30 pm. There were 10 persons at our table, we were the only two that could not speak Dutch. Our table steward, Klaus, suggested that all speak English so we were included in conversations. We met Jack Van Hoff (a table mate) and his friend, Peter Flooy who became card partners for the trip. Dancing that evening.

Sunday, all church services in Dutch. Smooth seas, low swell. Life boat drill. Picture show "The Mountain" with Spencer Tracy. Played cards and attended horse racing.

Monday, rough seas, low swell, cold and damp.

Tuesday, have passed Cape Race and swinging north to avoid a hurricane; rough seas, high swells. I missed breakfast this morning but attended "Bridge Tournament" that afternoon; Tony won high prize. Picture show that night "The Naked Hills". Picked up 1 ½ hours by changing time.

Wednesday, sea very rough, many persons seasick. Paper bags hung in many places; ropes stretched to help in walking. Canasta tournament that afternoon. Picture show in evening "The Unguarded Moment" starring Ester Williams. Watched the Northern Lights from the upper deck.

Thursday, sun shining and the sea is smooth. Sat in deck chairs all morning. Played cards after lunch and watched the children's party. Picked up 1 ½ hours by changing time.

Friday, foggy, cold and damp. Played cards. Gala Night, all in full dress. Two bottles of wine at our table and everyone having a great deal of fun. Afterwards, talent show and dancing. Splendid talent, many students on way to Europe for study. Tony presented prize for bridge. 1 hour time change.

Saturday, again foggy; 1 hour time change. Movie in afternoon, "The Ship that Died of Shame", depressing for a foggy day at sea. Horse racing and Bingo in evening; sighted lights of other ships.

Sunday, foggy but smooth sea. Arrived Southhampton at 6pm, viewed landing from recreation deck, Dancing in Palm Court, tasted Dutch cognac, danced with the Dutch people.

Monday, arose early to see landing at Le Havre, France at 6:30. Played bridge with Mrs. Murrel and Mr Synrdrak. Again saw two Dutch women in their native costume with huge lace caps trimmed with gold. (Jack Van Hoff says these caps cost about $100 because of the gold clasps). We watched lights on the Hook of Holland and Rotterdam. I went to bed as I had a bad cold but Tony watched the landing at 12 midnight. At 2am we received a letter from Charlene.

Tuesday, (Sept 18). Jack called us at 5:45, went on deck to see if Tom was there. Breakfast at 6:45 then returned to deck and saw Tom standing on pier, waiting for us. We are a day late in landing because of rough weather. Passed through Customs and with tom about 8am. He surprised us with a Buick (we had expected to see a Volkswagon). We met Jack's father-in-law and brother-in-law, started for Wiesbaden, thru Breda, Tilburg,

Hertchbogeng, Nymen, Kleve, where we stopped for coffee, Krefeld, stopped at Dusseldorf for lunch, then went on Autobahn to Wiessbaden, arriving at 5pm. (Enroute we stopped at Siebenbierge Resthaug for fruitcake and coffee on the outside terrace) Registered at the Goldenses Rosse Bed (bath) House. Elevator has two open sides) Bed has elevated head, small feather quilts. After dinner, to the Chianti Keller where we had a bottle of champagne to celebrate meeting Tom, Char's letter, and Tony's birthday. Went to the Air Force Band quarters to see where Tom lives; then to Eagles Club for hamburger and soup; played Bingo and Tom bought us each a carnation.

Wednesday morning I took a hot mineral bath and gargled with the mineral water. My cold is so bad that I can hardly whisper. We had breakfast served in our room (rolls, coffee and marmalade.) We had our money changed and we had to wait for our International plate, so we went to the Air Base, walked thru PX and had lunch there. Down town again, walked down the Wilhermstrasse, priced ostrich purses, Having gotten International plate, we started for Reichelsheim in the Oldenwald forest. Beautiful country, small farms, many different kinds of trees, cobblestone roads. We parked on sidewalk in narrow street in front of Lissel's home. (She is wife of man played in band with Tom. Lives with her mother (Tom's girlfriend, age about 80 and looks like Mother Ries; and her brother Rudy.) The mother prepared coffee and kucken for us and the we walked up hill to view the little village. When we returned the mother had dinner ready for us, then Rudy and Lissel went with us to a tap room where we had wine and listened to music. Lissel's uncle came in and visited with us. He is 63 years old and seemed much older, has a heart condition and is unable to work. Told us he had been in a concentration camp in France. There were 2000 imprisoned and after the first 4 days, there were only 50 of them left.

Thursday, September 20 and Tony's Birthday. When we say down for breakfast, his plate was covered; when the mother removed the cloth, his plate was encircled with flowers and gifts of candy were on the plate, then we joined in singing "Happy Birthday", We bade farewell and started for Switzerland, driving through beautiful country along the edge of the Black Forest. We saw scores of women working in the files, along with their children; lots of horses and oxen; also cows drawing carts with produce and hay; everyone seems to be working and every inch of land under cultivation. We had lunch at Buhl Baden. When we arrived at the Swiss border there was some question over the extra gas cans that Tom could put that amount into his tank and had to be shown. We also had to purchase extra insurance since we failed to obtain the green card when we purchased the international plate. We arrived at Zurich about 5pm amidst heavy city traffic. Tom handles his car expertly and is a very careful driver. We secured rooms at Hotel Canova, opposite the Zurichsee. We had coffee and sandwiches at a sidewalk table and walked over the bridge, saw the swans on the water. Attended a European picture show (with English subtitles) Again strolled around Zurich to see lights, etc.

Friday, had breakfast in the Hotel dining room. It is very old and elaborate, carved mantel and posts, antique glassware, old paintings etc. Rolls and coffee with milk, for breakfast. Left for Como. Switzerland is a beautiful country, very steep, winding roads over the Alps; mountains on all sides and constant switchbacks. We had lunch on the summit and went shopping. Car is acting up and keeps stopping. Finally reached Como, after passing Italian border. Tom found rooms for us in a Pesione, very nice but different; hard beds and a long, hard pillow. There is running cold water in the room but no towels or soap. (We were given small bars of soap as we crossed the border and now we know why. There is a crucifix hanging over the bed; a beautiful glass door opens on a balcony overlooking the narrow, main street below and facing a beautiful old Church and Square. Had an Italian dinner of pizza.

Saturday, the Italian senora served breakfast in our room; coffee with milk (Tony said the cups looked dirty because there was such a small amount of coffee in bottom of cup), cookies (looked like Lorna Doone cookies) and chocolate bars (like Hershey bars). We took an excursion boat ride on Lake Como, landing at Bellagio where we had lunch and walked thru the open markets or shops. (Raviola and red wine for Lunch.)

That evening we went to a cinerama of "Tosca" with Italian

performers, which was held in their elaborate Opera House. We had last row seats in the Gallery (Tony couldn't figure why we were climbing so many winding stairs) but the Opera House had 6 balconies. As we left we stopped up to look at the beautiful lobby and the doorman switched on the chandeliers for us; they are only used for Operas and are kept covered with cheesecloth to protect them from dust; they are huge, containing hundreds of prisms and cost thousands of dollars. There was a band concert in the church square which we enjoyed after leaving the show. Then we had lemonade at a table on the promenade.

Sunday morning, Tom decided to try to start the car as the garages would not be open here when it worked, we started for Verona where there is an American garage. The car kept acting up so when we arrived at Bereschia, we drove into an "Esso" gas station and garage and the motor gave a final gasp and died. There was a beautiful girl in the restaurant, a daughter of the owner, who spoke some English and explained to the mechanics what Tom thought was wrong. The mechanics worked on the car for 4 hours Meantime, the girl took Tom to their home for lunch, served by maids on beautiful linens and crystal, with delicious food. Tony and I explored the city, saw beautiful parks, narrow streets and tall houses.

At the end of 4 hours, the mechanics decided they were unable to fix the car. (This labor cost $1.60) and insisted that we would have to get assistance from Verona, hiring a car to get the job done. Tom and his father decided to attempt driving our own car as long as they could get it started. What a trip, holding our breath not knowing when we would have to stop, what damage we were doing to the car and also joining in 2 different bicycle races enroute. How people do drive, as fast as they can make their cars go, no speed limits, hundreds of bicycles and motor scooters, plus huge trucks with two and three trailers narrow roads and hilly country.

As we crossed the bridge at Pescherio, the car completely quit for us. During a brief lull and with the help of some passing men, Tom and his father pushed the car into a driveway in front of an Italian Military Building. Tom put on his coveralls, took off the carburetor and did everything he thought possible with no success. It looked completely hopeless when up whizzed a little Italian Fiat and out climbed an Italian Colonel. In talking to Tom it was found they could both speak German and they became friends. He whistled at some passing soldiers and they pushed the car thru a narrow opening into his courtyard. The car grazed both sides but finally went in. He introduced us to his wife and daughter and we were invited to have coffee. (Tiny little cups with coffee as strong as lye) Also glasses of grapes prepared in wine, which we ate with our fingers, afterwards drinking the wine. He then took Tom across the bridge to a brand new hotel where we got lovely rooms ($3 for all 3 of u) and then took us over, with our luggage, in his little car, which can even be made into a bed. He ordered a special meal for us and invited us to return to his quarters after we were settled.

We purchased a bottle of white wine and returned to the Colonel's home. I gave the wife and the daughter each a lipstick and dad gave the Col. some cigars. They were pleased. Nevas got out some very old crystal goblets and we drank the wine. Then he produced some more wine prepared by the King's wine maker, aged, and in specially numbered bottles. Next he served small glasses of a special liqueur. Then Nevas made more coffee. (They always grind the coffee beans first and make separate cups.) We stayed until about 11pm and felt very welcome. Their lace curtains are 250 years old; their porcelain and crystal is 200 years old, the crystal goblets each have a different ring when touched. Their rugs are from Greece, trophies of this war adventures. He showed his mountain climbing equipment, showed pictures and told of his war experiences; his time spent in Russian concentration camps, his escapes; tour of duty in Greece, etc. (This has been a wonderful gesture on the part of Nevas Budou as her mother died yesterday at Trieste and she was unable to go to her family. Being devout Catholics she is supposed to go into mourning for a 30 day period and not even to go to market) Now they are talking of going to Venice with us if he can get relief from duty.

Monday Sept 24 1956. Col. Budou has to take his 14 year daughter, Mariaucchio, to Verona to enroll in school so asked Tom to ride in with him to see about a mechanic at the American

Garage. It was ascertained that the mechanics there were not proficient for requirements so Col. Raffeo Budou took Tom to an expert mechanic that he knew, they got the mechanic and brought him back to Pescherio. He started the car and drove it to his garage and fixed it. While the mechanic worked, Tom went swimming with Mariaucchio and her girl friend, Georgi Levi (She was chosen Miss Grace of the Trieste festival, she lives in Verona.) Tony and I had a short boat ride with Tom and the girls on Lake Guardia. After lunch at the hotel, we spent the afternoon in the Col gardens and courtyard, ate our fill of luscious grapes. Nevas and I manage to talk with the use of an Italian and American dictionary, plus help of what words Georgia and Mariucchio know. Tonight, the car being repaired, Tom took all of us, including the Budou family and Georgi, to the island of Simionie, to see the markets and a beautiful castle. This is a pleasure road extending out of it. We then drove to Verona where we had coffee with Georgi's mother in a huge modern apartment house. Beautiful furniture, crystal, paintings, etc. Back to the hotel where it was entirely closed up, even to the gate but we found a night bell in the read and finally got to bed.

Tuesday, Sept. 25. Again had coffee with the Budou's and bade them farewell as he could not get away so they could go with us. She presented us with peacock feathers, a weather barometer, a pot of everlasting carnations, seeds, etc. And he gave Tony a set of pictures. We drove to Verona where we picked up Georgi and her mother for a day of sightseeing. Visited the church of Romeo and Juliet. (Examined the magnificent metal doors) To the courtyard and balcony of Juliet; castle grounds and the amphitheater which we covered thoroughly, even to the underground runways. (I was horrified at the underground toilet facilities that we used. Tom and his father got into a worse one at the arena. Took Georgi and her mother to the PC at the Air Base where we had hamburgers and coca cola. Back again to Levi's apartment where we again had coffee. Their apartment is on the 4th floor with a balcony overlooking the street. An elevator takes everyone up. At 4pm we departed for Venice in a terrific rain, so heavy that the wiper would scarcely work. Arrived at the garage and Tom drove it up a circular ramp to the 9th floor where it was parked until we left. We donned our raincoats, took our luggage and embarked by boat for the Hotel. As it was full we were referred to a pension (a little boy about Jimmy's size insisted on carrying heavy luggage) We got nice rooms, had dinner and then walked in St Marks square, listening to the concerts and gazing into the windows which entirely surround the square. It started to rain again so we returned to our rooms.

Wednesday. It rained all night but Tom dashed out and brought back wonderful grapes for our breakfast. Finally rain stopped and we went out. The Church square was flooded and men were laying temporary bridges made of planks and saw horses, across the square. We would walk as far as possible as they kept building them ahead of us. Persons that were in a hurry were standing in small wagons being pulled by barefooted boys with their pants legs rolled up. We hired a gondola and then made a tour of the canals. There are 415 bridges in Venice. The streets they have are very narrow and circular. The post office fronts on the canal and the mail is brought by boats. The office itself is an open courtyard, surrounded by offices. We had lunch and then visited St Marks Cathedral which is enormous; all gold, mosaic, jewels, sculpture etc. We fed the pigeons in the square; there are thousands of them and Tony and I were completely covered by them as Tom snapped pictures. We had dinner at a sidewalk table. I ordered mixed fried fish and I had minnows, eels, oysters etc. My last mixed fried fish and Tom really laughed at me. We listened to concerts again and Tom sat in with one group to play for a while. He also met two of his buddies from the band. Back to the pension where Tom played cards (an Italian game) with our landlady and she served us some special wine.

Thursday Sept 27th. We watched the carrier delivering mail, he would whistle and buckets would be lowered from windows, he would place mail in them and they would be pulled back up. Everything is clean to the greatest degree, mats on every landing for feet to be wiped upon, so by the time one reaches their destination, their feet are very clean. Had breakfast at a sidewalk cafe and then took boat to the garage. Tom drove car down ramp and while checking out, we met Mr. and Mrs. Rey of Greenwich

Village, New York who were going to Padua. As it was on our way we took them with us. (They have written and illustrated a children's book and will send and autographed copy to Kym Meroa) Stopped at the PX in Verona for gas and lunch and as we drove towards Pescherio we met Raffeo and Mariaucchio Budou again. They insisted we stop for coffee so we spent several hours with them. He went out after special pastries which they served along with coffee, wine and grapes from their garden, giving us a large bag to take with us. We then continued on to Domodes-sella where we spent the night.

Friday Sept. 28th – Today we drove through the Italian Alps, it was breath-taking. Switzerland is fortified by cement caves, huge metal gates that can be closed instantly as the narrow roads are the only way of entry. The sides are so steep that every cow wears a bell with a different tones so that if he falls down the owner knows which one. There are herds of cows on the roads very frequently and all drivers have to use caution. Ther are church spires on all sides even in sparsely settled territories. On the top of Simplon Pass is erected a large statue of an eagle. As we journey on we find long tunnels and water falls flow either over or under them. Some of the tunnels are so long we wonder how the buses can pass thru them. We had trouble with the car heating as we climbed so retraced our road to a unique fountain by the road. (Remember the cows that surrounded us as they stopped for water?) Stopped for lunch at Montreaux and to make money exchange. We passed the Castle of Chillon which was built in 1240. Drove along the edge of Lake Geneva arriving in Geneva in time for dinner. Rooms at Geneva Hotel. Geneva is a beautiful city situated on the banks of Lake Geneva and half en-circled by the towering Alps and the Jura mountains. It was lovely gardens and flower decked promenades reflected in the blue waters, on which swim many beautiful swans. (These birds formerly were owned by royalty but have since been given to other privileged persons.) We crossed the bridge over the Rhone River and gazed at the beautiful city lights; enjoyed the floral clock in a beautiful setting of fountains, lights and flowers.

Saturday Sept. 29th – Today across the French border to Gex. Drove through the French Alps. Found our heating difficulty, a leaking motor connection which we had replaced in Dijon. Arriving here after dinner hour we had difficulty finding a place to eat. Finally purchased meat and bread and fruit at the market and took them to a cafe where they furnished wine and a knife, which we enjoyed at a table with the added attraction of music furnished by an orchestra. The car being ready we went on to Auxterre where we spent the night.

Sunday - We arrived at Fontaine Bleu this morning and made a stop at Napoleon's Palace. We entered the magnificent grounds thru the gate and walked thru the long gardens on cobblestone pavements to the entrance of the castle. We spent several hours going thru the beautiful apartments and galleries but had to leave in time to reach Paris by lunch time. Ate at the American Legion. (Tom joined this chapter while here. It is Genl. Pershing Chapter #1. He is very proud of his membership. After getting a room at the Paris Hotel, we went up the Eiffel Tower. Had to change elevators three times. Stopped for coffee at a table on the Champs de Elysees and then went to a movie "East of Eden" starring James Dean. Walked thru the Arc de Triomphe, saw the tomb of the unknown soldier and then had coffee at the Lido with Tom and Koko Chiengmai. Koko is from Siam and Tom had met her when playing here before. She has very dark skin and is beautiful, very slender, well educated and refined. She was wearing a green sweater and green suede shoes, making a very striking attire. She is a daughter of a Prince in Chiengmai, Siam. She lives with a French noblewoman and is very carefully chaperoned. She is a student at one of the colleges and also holds a responsible position with a shipping company. We all window shopped in the Lido promenade and then drove Koko back to her apartment.

Monday – Had brunch at the American Legion and then drove to the Church of Sacrecoeur which is a beautiful cathedral situated on a very high point, many steps leading up to the building. Afterwards we drove out to the Orly Air Base to get gas and visited the PX and made some purchases then back to Notre Dame Cathedral; Napoleon's Tomb and the Church of the Madelaine. Rainy weather. Had dinner at a Parisienne Cafe, enjoying Chateau Aubbrione. Then to Alan Roman's Bar. Alan Roman is a friend of Tom's and is a fine pianist and is in the top 10 French musicians. He played for us and also sent over a special liqueur for me. Rained all night.

Tuesday – still raining. Went to the American Express Company in a terrific rainstorm and really got drenched. Returned by underground. Stopped at picture show to see Danny Kaye in "Court Jester", a splendid picture. Then to American Legion and got tickets for "Casino of Paris". Had very good seats and the show was extra special, most beautiful scenes imaginable, gorgeous settings and beautiful girls, in all a very enjoyable evening.

Wednesday – Oct 3. Visited the Garden of the Tuilleries and then the Louvre where we spent several hours. The traffic in Paris is amazing; the use of lights and horns is prohibited. At night, everyone drives with parking lights. Cars park on the sidewalks on the Champs de Elysees and drive thru the crowds, gently nudging people to get around them. They are allowed for 1 hour parking so there is constant movement of cars. We started back for Germany and stopped beside some picturesque ruins and ate a picnic lunch. Got a room at the Goldenes Ross Bath House and then had dinner at a German cafe.

Thursday Oct 4 – Tom still has time off so we drove to Mainz and then out to the Air Force Base where we looked at some of Tom's colored slides. Went to Frau Hoffman's, a former landlady of tom's to see if she had an apartment for rent. It was interesting talking to her as she told some of her experiences during the war. She said the Russians moved in after the war, they came, dirty, with their feet wrapped in rages, some riding on oxen. They took possession of her home and threw all of her furniture out of the windows into the street and they slept on the bare floors. She said she cried to sleep in the basement across the street. How she despised the Russians. Then we picked up Erika and we drove out to Rudesheim, the home of the Rudesheim wine. The place was decorated with bunches of grapes and grape leaves; also red lanterns and guests wear tiny illuminated red lanterns, operated by batteries. The place was crowded and everyone was drinking Rudeshiem wines. German musicians were playing and everyone was dancing. The dance floor was raised with an abrupt jump off on the edge but no one seemed to get too near the rim.

Friday Oct 5 – We drove thru many small towns and looked at a house in the country but dad decided he did not want to get that far out and away from transportation. Then visited an agent that handled apartments where he gave us a list of six so we west house hunting. Every manager seems to live on the top floor so we climbed steps all day. Interesting to see interiors of German homes. Finally found an apartment on Leberberg Street which we rented for a month. (Price $45). Had lunch at the Eagles Club. Attended a picture show at Tanus Air Base and then went to the Gypsie Wine Keller. Gypsie decorations and musicians.

Saturday Ocy 6 – We moved to #4 Leberberg St Bornheimer and got ourselves settled in our new apartment. Met other tenants; a young couple, he is civilian A F employee and she is from Iceland. A German girl that speaks English; a Russian man "man without a country"; a German couple, he is very stiff and always bows and speaks but she never cracks a smile and we call her "Mrs Groucho". Our landlady we christened "Mrs 5x5", she speaks very little English. Our room is very comfortable with hot and cold running water. The bed is huge, two beds together and mattress is in three pieces. Linens and maid service is furnished; also use of the kitchen and dining room. There is a small store at foot of the hill and our landlady serves dinners, so we are well fixed. Stopped for lunch at a German Cafe and Tom drove us over to Frankfurt. It looks like an American city with all of its bright lights and signs. It has been rebuilt very modern. Spent the evening at a Bavarian Beer Parlor. Musicians all wore Bavarian hats and short, leather breeches. They picked various persons from the audience to lead the orchestra which made it very interesting. The enormous room was decorated with carved wooden figures standing on large wheels and balconies which moved all during intermission. The scenery on the stage, cows, other animals, etc. Also moved. It was a gay crowd, all friendly and no one intoxicated or obnoxious.

Sunday. Had breakfast in our room. It was raining. Went to the Kurhaus and had lunch at the Eagles Club as Tom had a rehearsal. He met us at 6pm and we went to Picture show "All

Boats Away". Dinner at Eagles Club later.

Monday. Shopping. Lunch at Eagles Club, Time with Tom.

Tuesday. Bought garnet ring and charms. Lunch at Eis Cafe, met Tom and went to a picture show to see "Miami Expose", then we picked up Erika and drove to Biebrach to check on Rhine boat.

Wednesday Oct 10. Noon dinner at apartment. Walked around Kurpark to home of Frau von Wullen. She wasn't home so left information with her sister and will call her later. Met Tom and had dinner at "Baba Brau".

Thursday Oct 11, our wedding anniversary. Had dinner at the apartment house, then went to Kurhaus to pay our Kur tax, for 3 weeks it cost 22 marks ($7.25) just for the privilege of staying in Wiesbaden. Of course we are privileged to attend concerts and use the Kur park; drink mineral water in the Colanda (if we could only read German and understand the signs it would help but we don't know where we are allowed to go or when). There are many ponds, some with fountains, also ducks, geese, gold fish, lily pads, all kinds of flower beds, band shell and chairs galore, statues everywhere (none of Hitler) and old Roman pillars. It must be a beautiful place in the summertime and is a popular health resort. (All towns having "Baden" in their name are health resorts and have hot springs.) We met Tom and went to Erika's house to spend the evening; met her mother, father and brother. Mr. Hoffman is general foreman of new American Hotel and makes 600 marks ($160) a month. They have comfortable modern apartment. Home about 2 am

Friday – shopping again; dinner at apartment; to American Express, purchased Hummell figurines. Called Frau von Wullen. Cold and damp.

Saturday Cold and drizzly. Dinner at apartment and went to football game. Sat with band while Tom played. Then Tom took us home as he expected to take off for Paris by plane to play a concert. We decided to walk down to find the PO which we did, but kept going and got nicely lost, walked for many blocks. Finally got back to our small Eis Cafe, had coffee and then home.

Sunday – Oct 13 – A surprise, Tom didn't go to Paris; because of fog the plane couldn't take off. Had dinner at apartment, picked up Erika and drove to Bad Schwalbach and other small towns, over mountain roads and thru forests. Had coffee in restaurant garden near a Monastery. To home of Herr & Frau von Wullen for tea. It is a lovely new home with beautiful china, rugs, paintings, etc. He is with the National Geographical Magazine. She had made a huge apple pie and we ate the entire pie. Her sister was with us. She is the wife of a Bulgarian office in Sophia she is on a limited pass and must return home by Feb 8 (She can't speak English). They told of her life in Sophia, how she is beaten and abused by other residents trying to covert her to Communism and I asked why she would return. If she doesn't return by the set date, her husband and son will be punished. The son is a prisoner in a Criminal prison. She said "Every day here is a birthday to me, I live it to the fullest". We took them to the show but seats were sold out, so we went to the Eagles Club where we had hamburgers, coca cola and ice cream sundaes. Later we went to the Baba Brau with Tom and most of the band members were there with their instruments and played part of the evening. The rest of the time, a German group played and Tom say in with them and played a tuba. It was a special festival and everyone was having a grand time.

One of the band members borrowed my horned hat and made believe he was a bull; one of the others got a coat and they demonstrated a bull fight. Then one of the German men asked if he might borrow the hate and he wore it the rest of the evening.

At the table with us was a Hungarian friend of Tom's. He was interesting to talk to, Also a tuck driver from Hamburg who spoke broken English but managed to tell us that he was a PW in Indiana in 1944-45 and was well treated. He prepared a card to send his wife in Hamburg and asked us to sign it also.

Monday Oct 15 – Shopping again. Tom had dinner with us at the apartment then we drove to PX and purchase projector for this birthday; went to his quarters and looked at slides. Later to show to see "Trapeze". Had bockwurst, torte and coffee on way home.

Tuesday Oct 16 – Tom went to Koblenz today for three days. Dad and I went shopping, bought ostrich purse and Dresden figurine and hots for children. After we returned to apartment, Tony became ill and was sick all night. No one could speak English and I couldn't find a doctor. I was frantic. What a night

Wednesday, Tom's birthday – Tony feels a little better so we had soup at apartment. Erika came over to make arrangements for trip to Koblenz and we went to town and bought "Underberg" which Tony took. Then we had coffee and cake. Check on Mrs. Manners dishes. Found a Masonic ring which we bought for our anniversary. To bed early.

Thursday Oc 18 – Had early breakfast and met Erika at Bus; went to Bahnhoff to catch train for Koblenz. The first one took us as far as Mainz where we had to change. They have tracks and steps like we do but before the Koblenz train arrived we had to change track 3 times and all the announcing was done in German. If Erika hadn't been with us we would have had a difficult time of it. Tom met us at the Koblenz depot and we went to his hotel for lunch. They were so slow that it took a very long time. Then Tony went downstairs to the toilet and was gone so long that I asked Tom to go down and see what had happened as I thought perhaps he had gotten sick again. Just then dad came up, wearing his hat but his coat and overcoat were gone and he looked so strange. He had locked the door and something had happened to the lock and he was locked in. There was a small opening over the door so dad climbed through it and got out, leaving his coats in the toilet. One of the hotel boys in the band marveled at dad's feat and had to see the place he climbed thru, one of them even taking a picture of it.

Then Omar Boggs went with us and we drove to the Castle at Stolzenfels. Had to park the car near the highway and walk up the long cobblestone grade to the top of the mountain. The castle is one of the best preserved castles in Germany today. The castle was first built in 1242 and was used as a customs house for trade in the valley of the Rhine. In 1688 it was destroyed. In 1802 the town of Koblenz presented the ruins to King Wilhem IV and was reconstructed in the early 1800s. In 1842 the King entered the castle with a big suite in "old German dress" and a torch light procession, along with his wife, Elizabeth of Bavaria. She stayed there a few times after the King's death in 1861. The house was preserved inside and out as a monument of housing culture and is of great value.

In the valley itself a passage thru a viaduct opens the way like a triumphal arch leading past a waterfall, artificially dammed dup, and a chappelike church. A second gate leads into the inner court. On the left rises the belfry or "rough tower" of the Middle Ages. The passage to the pergola gardens opens all the more surprising after the narrow court. Descending steps lead down the slope to the garden, centered by a well-basin. This nook is sheltered acoustically in such a manner that no noise can get through the high walls.

From this garden to the right a door leads to a large terrace in front of the dwelling quarters, leading into a large hall of blue and white and was formerly the archbishop's wine cellar. Then you enter the castle-chapel which was finished in 1845 on the older remains. This is adorned with beautiful paintings by old masters.

You then enter the Big Baronial Hall by a common staircase. Here you find a magnificent display of glassware and pottery, glass from Cologne in 1666; pottery from the Westerwald, from Raeren and Siegburg and a collection of arms, among which a Gothic shield is striking. You find glass paintings of the late 13th century from the Monastery of Wurtemburg; beautiful hand carved furniture and carved statues and figures; antique musical instruments, etc. And all within reach and can be touched. Nothing is roped off. The floors are all heavily waved (all inlaid) and everyone is required to put felt overshoes on and wear to the next exit where they are left and new ones put on at the next level. The winding stone steps are deeply worn and are designed in such a manner as to provide protection. There is a draw-bridge, moat and other fortifications.

As we descended the long pathway we stopped to wander thru the ancient cemetery and to inspect the church. Then Tom had to return for rehearsal so Erika, Tony and I took a street car to the Deustsches Eck (German Corner). It is amazing. It is a point extending out into the Rhine River and where 3 rivers meat, one being the Mousselle. There is a huge monument built there and we climbed to the top, up a circular stone stairway and then wandered thru the numerous pillars but as it was getting dusk we hurried down. It had been raining so we waded thru the water to look at all of the seals carved in the stone of a huge archway surrounding the monument. The crest of all the German provinces are inscribed here. The original statue was destroyed by tanks and was never replaced.

Several boat restaurants are anchored by the corner so we had cake and coffee in one of them. It was appropriately decorated inside and illuminated outside

When we returned to the hotel, Tom and Omar were waiting so we left for the concert, held in America Haus. Nine of the band had prepared this brass symphony of early music, composers of 1445 to 1695. This was sponsored by a champagne factory and held three days at different towns, the one at Koblenz being the last of the series. Bottles of champagne were on display and one was brough to us and we enjoyed in celebration of Tom's birthday, October 17

A large crowd of interested people arrived for the concert in spite of the terrible rain storm. The concert was splendid, and we were very proud of our boys. The German people are great lovers of good music. We returned to Wiesbaden that night in a bad rainstorm, stopping at a gasthouse for supper on the road home. (On the Autobahn).

Friday Oct 19 – Tom has a 3 day leave of absence came down and had dinner at the Apartment. A window had been broken in the car while parked in Koblenz, so they took car in to have window replaced and Tom and Tony went shopping for raincoat for Tony. Picked up Omar and his wife to start for Munich but she had to make visit for her mother first in an adjacent village. Had a long wait to get gas and the trip to her mothers was farther then we realized then brake trouble developed so it was decided to postpone our start to the next day. We returned to Wiesbaden stopping at a picturesque Gasthouse for dinner then to the Eagles Club for their floor show and then to Apartment where we watched television. As we got out of the car, Tony threw his coat over his shoulder and caught a woman passing, in the belt of his coat, embarrassing moments and apologies.

Saturday Oct 20. Agani picked up Omar Boggs and his wife and started. In Darmstadt we stopped at the Union Cafe and met

Tom's German friend, Max Reuss, who was having coffee with a group of other musicians. Tom met all of them and the bass player joined us at our table, along with Max.

Max then took us to see a Russian church, the most beautiful thing I have ever seen; the onion shaped domes are made of pure gold and the church is all marble, mosaic and gold. It was built in 1904 by the Russians and is Greek Orthodox. The Czarina was considered to be the Mother of the Church so her figure was used in all of the mosaics. Every stone in the building had been imported and the columns were made of material said to be better even then marble. These buildings were some of the last of the Russian architecture.

The Czarina was the sister of the Grand Duke and he had married a woman born in Darmstadt. They were married in 1905 and a chapel was built for the marriage. It is very modernistic and has a tall tower and numerous balconies. The building is also inlaid with mosaic and pure gold. The inscription reads - "Strength; Wisdom; Mildness; Humility" The buildings are surrounded with beautiful gardens, pergolas, statues and many columns. A large mosaic pool contains a lovely fountain. Many steps lead from various levels. One statue is called "Women Weeping" and shows the various stages of grief in women. Another is called "Evil Influence in Man" and has a profile of the most hideous man imaginable. The statues are all very modern appearing. Rasputin visited Darmstadt many times and had a great influence on the Grand Duke.

The Grand Duke and Duchess had a large castle in Darmstadt. In 1917, the royal family, including dukes and duchesses were all assassinated by the Bolsheviks so the churches remain practically unused today. There is a Russian priest there and 1 member of the church.

We then drove out to Kranichstein Castle, the royal hunting lodge, and its forest preserve. The forest preserve is 25 miles long and is completely covered with trees The grounds around the castle are beautifully landscaped, having many lakes stocked with fish, ducks and swans. Carved metal stags adorn the courtyard and the interior is a show place of trophies, door heads and antlers of many years past, all bearing the date of kill. An outstanding feature was the huge stove.

As we drove thru the tunnel of trees, Max told us facts about Darmstadt. It originally had a population of 400,000 people. It was bombed and a third of the population were killed in 20 minutes. Today it has been rebuilt and with a population of 140,000.

Max went with us for dinner at a Chinese restaurant. When the door opened it appeared as tho you were really in China; the ceiling was of bamboo, the walls were covered with cane screens and oriental decorations. Chinese food was served on exquisite Chinese dishes (very thin and real grains of rice showing thru). Our dinner consisted of shark fin soup, egg rolls with bamboo shoots, egg fooyung and jasmine tea. We bade Max goodbye and started for Gamburg.

As we drove thru the Odenwald forest it presented a beautiful picture, it was changing to fall colors of red, orange and yellow mingled with luscious green, one of the prettiest scenes imaginable, spreading over rolling hills. We drove thru tunnels of trees so dense that the road was as dark as if night had fallen.

It had been raining when we reached Reicholzheim and streets were muddy but Tom seemed to know where he was going. He drove up a very narrow street on a steep hill and stopped at a new home on the top. We found he had stayed there before and was the home of two spinster ladies and their aged mother. The house had been built in 1950, was roomy, containing two floors and a number of bedrooms. We had a very nice room, comfortable bed, feather quilts, hot and cold running water in the room. There was a very modern bathroom and delightful hot water for baths. After getting settled we drove to Bronnbach and had dinner at Ernest Lang's Gasthaus.

Ernest Lang and his wife seemed pleased to see us and invited us to return the following day. As they were very busy, we returned to the pension where we were staying.

It proved to be a most interesting evening. We purchased a bottle of wine from them and they joined us in their comfortable dining room. (All very old hand carved furniture, each chair having different designs carved on it. The china closet, filled with interesting old dishes, was all carved and very old. Lovely old hand made rug.) The mother (80 years old) brough in hot cinnamon rolls and we all say around the table. One of the sisters spoke a little English and Tom would translate what she couldn't say.

She told of their life in Karlsruhe where they had lived until 1950. She said that before 1950 the French Moroccans had come to Karlsruhe, that they had been living in barracks but made a pastime of raiding the homes. That all of their rings and valuables were taken by the Moroccans. She said they were like a bunch of animals and were whipped every morning by their officers.

She proved to be a very entertaining person. She works in a bank, teletyping replies to America on thermometers, which accounts for her knowledge of some English.

She said the thermometer or glass factory was a large place, employing 1000 persons, most of whom had come from behind the iron curtain as they had been given the chance to get out before the Russians took over. There is a large castle near in which beer is now being made for this whole part of Germany.

She then described a royal wedding that had been held in Bronnbach on September 13, 1956. They all had been eyewitnesses to the pomp and ceremony, and she mimicked the personages with great cleverness. It was the wedding of Archduke Joseph Arpad of Hapsburg and the Princess Maria of Lowenstein. Her parents had been married by the Pope himself. The young people had returned to be married at a very old church in Bronnbach and nobility from all of Europe was present. There were 800 guests and all had dinner at the old Lowenstein castle, which her family had owned for over 200 years. Among dignitaries present were ex-King Umberto of Italy and Archduke Otto of Austria. The wedding was held in this very ancient church, built in 1227, and also owned by the royal family. The bride was attired in gold embroidered brocade and the Duke wore gold mesh and a fur stole. The bride wore a diamond tiara and expensive jewels. Police were stationed every 3 feet and the country people were all interested observers.

The storyteller walked around showing how stiffly the royal personages held themselves, men wearing monocles, noses in the air, chest and fannies thrown out, etc. Women were all dressed in furs and feathers, silks and stains, long dresses, and abundant jewels. All were very stern faced, never cracking a smile. Men all wore full dress or uniforms, huge, plumed hats. Bells on the church toll every 15 minutes and for a long time on the hour.

It was very interesting to note on our return to Reicholzheim that the villagers were all scrubbing the muddy cobblestones. On Saturday nights it is the chore of the villagers to scrub the stone streets of the village and all assist, men and women alike, all busy with brooms and mops. There are hundreds of carts returning to the villages from work in the fields where every square inch of ground is cultivated. Carts are drawn by horses or oxen and all filled to overflowing with produce.

Sunday Oct 21. Again visited Ernest Lang. They took us thru their large gasthaus, a great many large sleeping rooms in very old building. The queen of Greece and her daughters all stayed here during the time of the wedding. Frau Lang said they were very nice and they had enjoyed having them there. Ernest took us thru the church where the ceremony had been performed and also told us all about it. The church had been entirely redone and every stone in it had been polished. The beautiful heavy carvings shone as did all of the wood paneling. It was like something out of a fairy tale. They served wine and cakes in their large dining room, afterwards showing us the grounds and gardens, a well-lighted patio in the rear.

We next went to Gamburg to see the old Ries home, which had been built in 1842 by Tony's grandfather Anton Ries. We heard two various versions of the original story. Herr Krug now lives in the house, his grandfather having purchased it from Tony's grandfather. (We had heard in the past that the house had simply been deserted and the other man had taken it over. There was a rumor that the Ries fortune had been left hidden in the house and the other man had suddenly come into unexpected money and had purchase the house later.) Anyway, Herr Krug said Anton Ries had built the house using funds of the city, of which he was the Burgermeister at the time. There had been an uprising and an accounting of funds had been called for. As he had a large family, he was not imprisoned but soon rumors were started that he was to be seized so and his family left under cover of night.

The priest later told a different story which I would more readily believe. He said the Ries family was a highly respected family of the community and were opposed to the high pressure tactics of the King and Queen and heavy taxation. Because of this opposition, the rumor had been started about Ries absconding with funds altho the truth was that he had refused to collect such heavy taxes from the poor people and he was to be punished for not getting in the sum of money he was told too.

The house was most interesting and we took pictures of it and the persons living in it now. We saw the interior of the first floor with its old woodwork and small rooms. The heavy wooden stee stairway leading upstairs. The balconies and carved figures adorning the exterior. Anton Ries name still carved in the stone above the door. Tony took the children of the house to a store and purchased candy for them, much to their wide-eyed amazement.

We visited the Priest that had given Tom the Ries and Lang family records. He was pleased to see Tom again and made us feel very welcome, taking us to his quarters and showing us the old records, so brittle they would crumble with carelessness. They dated back father then 1607 and he let me examine them.

He told us about the uprisings at the time of the Ries departure. Then told us about early uprisings. How many early records had been destroyed except for some that had been hidden. The Swedes had attached and burned everything in 1632. There had been a 30 year war, all the records had been burned, the church destroyed and all the wine stolen. There were two old towers, one being built in 1270 and one in 1525, and 3 tiers of walls. In 1570 the farmers had attacked the castle and great destruction had resulted.

The castle of Gamburg is still standing but portions of the tower have been destroyed. The very old tower of fortification still stands as a sentinel on the side of the hill. A new count had purchased the castle in 1946 and had paid the entire purchase price in doors.

While the priest was gathering some additional information for us form the old records, we walked down to Otto Lang's Gasthaus and ate dinner. He was not too friendly as he had a son killed by the Americans in the last war. His wife sat and visited with us for a while and we shook hands with him as we left. We met some other Americans in the dining room and visited with them

We stopped at the city foundation as we left. It had been erected by one of the Lang's and a friend, in 1906. It was inscribed "Noble civic minded people erected this in 1906 for water for man and beast. Around it was the following "Water flowed here for man and beast The best water from best well". Fountain erected in 1906 under directorship of Mayor Misselbeck".

Then we returned to the priest's home and received the data he had collected for me. He showed us where the church had stood that the Ries family had attended. It was destroyed by a fire but a new one has been erected in its place. He spoke of the Lang family, said Otto Lang had a daughter of 23 that was married 2 weeks before. Also that Ernest Lang had one son and one daughter at home and that one married son lives in San Francisco.

We drove up to the Gamburg castle which now houses "dependent children. Very narrow entrances but the boys directed us thru the narrow archways. We visited the main floor of the castle and by special permission, climbed to the top of what remains of the tower. We could see the entire country side and looked down on Gamburg and the old Ries home. Saw the old tower as we departed and drove across the Gamburg bridge. The children from the Ries house saw us and raced across the fields to wave goodbye to us.

It was late when we departed; drove thru Reichelsheim to see Liesel and her family but she was at a picture show. After a brief visit with her mother and brother, Rudy, we drove on to Darmstadt where Max was expecting us. His housekeeper had prepared a huge platter of sandwiches which they served accompanied by wine and beer. This was a very informative evening, as he was quite talkative. Some of his conversation was as follows:

Before the world war Germany was very self sufficient. Everyone had the utmost confidences in Adolf Hitler. He had told them that no places could ever appear over Germany. He appeared as a God to the people, no one ever said thank you, hello or goodbye, it was always "Heil Hitler"

Ot was a clear, sunny day and Max, himself was in swimming, when the sound of planes was heard. There had been a false alarm before so no one paid attention, because of their great faith in Hitler. As mentioned previously, out of a population of 400,000 one third of it was killed in 20 minutes. Immediate instructions were issued that no one should say they were enemy planes but were compelled to state that the entire city had been practically wiped out by their own planes.

This was the period that the German people lost confidence in Hitler. (It is interesting to note that with all of the statues and monuments in German, we never saw one of Hitler or hear mention of his name).

Max himself had served in the German Army and had been injured on the Russian front; both his shoulder and foot, the evidence of which he still carries today.

He is a musician, being a very efficient and well-known bassoon player. He is very adept at making his own reeds and showed us how they were made. Bassoons and oboes both use double reeds. The bassoon costs about $200 and $250 (about $1000 in the states) in Germany but is valueless without its reeds. The reeds are all handmade, requiring about 8 days to make. The reed is grown in Spain and southern France; it looks like bamboo; has to be cut and scraped soaked for hours, bent and shaped. It is very delciated work as reeds have to vibrate to produce the proper tones. Bassoons are very difficult to play, causing pressure on the brain and other vital spots. Expert players cannot play other instruments, or they lose their knack.

It got very late but they were reluctant to have us leave but we still had quite a long ride ahead of us. The fog was heavy and made the way home seem longer than ever.

Monday. Tom took the car to the garage for check over so we had dinner at the apartment and walked thru town and park.

Tuesday, Same procedure. On the way back we met a man who told us he was a Presbyterian missionary and had just been released from East Germany having been in a concentration camp for 8 ½ years. He was 54 and his mother had come with him, she was 74 years of age and in failing health. They had walked this far and expected to go on to Stuttgart, walking as they had no money. He said that 620 prisoners had been released at this time to return to their homes in West Germany. Said he had been working in an atomic factory. That there were still 2 ½ million in the camps although many had left illegally. He said they were not allowed to celebrate, sing, read Bibles, etc. They could not write letters to their families, consequently that when many of the men returned home, they found their wives had re-married thinking they were dead. Said his mother had formerly been a Gray Lady for the Red Cross but even that privilege had been denied her. No churches were permitted and that when the persons are released from bondage they are expected to remain there to make their homes and become citizens.

Wednesday. Tom to purchase clocks for us. Dinner at apartment. Went shopping for another figurine. Tom got his car and we had supper at the Eagles Club. Drove over to Mainz and drove thru town proper to view the many ruins. Tom parked the car and we walked around. The front of the buildings have been repaired and look like a thriving business district, then around in the rear and that ½ block will still be in ruins. The main street is well lighted and just in back, it is as dark as pitch. The streets are so narrow that Tom's car will not go through altho he could go thru them before when he had his Volkswagen. The houses are 4 and 5 stories high. Then Tom took us into a nearby cafe and everyone knew and greeted Tom. The lady owner came over and met us and so did the accordionist. The orchestra then played a Strauss waltz for us. When we returned to the apartment, Tom took 6 boxes to mail.

Thursday. Oct 25. We decided to go to the American Express Co, to see if they could notarize our election ballots for us. As they did not have the required seal they sent us to a Police station. What a time we had to find the police headquarters as none of the doors are marked and no one could speak English.

We climbed two flights of stairs and hearing voices from an inner office we waited for someone to come out. He spoke a little English and called another man for us. He took us down a long, narrow hall and found the man there was absent so then lead us down a flight of stairs, to the office of a woman that spoke English. She said they could not help us there as it was the criminal station and we must go to the Foreign Office. She called the foreign office and made an appointment for us, giving us a card with a man's name on it and giving us verbal directions as to how to find the building.

We finally located the building and entered an archway and found a door in the rear, climbed two flights of stairs, found two men that couldn't speak English but when we showed our card, they took us to a window and pointed to another door down the narrow alley, so back down stairs and another hunt for the door to get outside; down the alley and into the door, up two more flights of stairs and opened another unmarked door. We were given a seat and made to understand that we must wait. Then after interview by two more men, we were finally escorted to the Foreign Officer who spoke very little English. We finally made him understand what we wanted and after inspection and questions, we finally got the job done but each ballot required stamps, signatures, family history and a legal postage stamp. The family data was coped from the passport.

The envelopes were so marked up that we required an envelope so we went to the Post office, but they do not sell envelopes there. Tony inquired about the Postmaster and after many questions and assistance, we finally found him in an unmarked office on the third floor. He was glad to meet Tony but spoke very little English so called in an employee that could. The Postmaster had been in office for 42 years, they have 157 carriers; 50 to deliver telegrams and 50 to deliver money orders and C.O.D's Their mail is made up in much the same order as the states. Their carrier cases have about 40 separations that are individual to house numbers.

They had addressographs for patrons of the carrier routes. Their satchels are about 16" long, 10" high and look like big ladies pocketbooks. Their uniforms are dark blue with markings in colored braid. The carriers deliver money for the money orders to the patrons and get their signature for same. If no one is home, a notice is left and they must call at the post office.

They have closed cages in which they list orders and cages lock automatically. On return, they must balance out with the cashier for delivered orders and undelivered orders returned.

Could not ascertain the time of reporting but saw of number of carriers leaving the office with loads of mail at 4pm.

The Post Office lobby is all open and have no screen line of any kind. In the lobby are showcases displaying various kinds of merchandise.

The parcel post trucks are not as high as ours but are longer and are painted yellow.

The Post Office is an old building, having four floors and has housed the postal service since the population was 50,000. The population is now 250,000 and the building is still in use. It is more crowd that the Wyncoop office in Denver.

There are officials under the Postmaster who are assigned to supervise more than one function,

The employees are divided into three groups.

1. Officials, (They retire on stated pension at 65)

2. Workers. (Their retirement amount is not fixed and are subject to change.)

3. Employees. (These do not have any benefits)

I left Tony at the office where he had a two hour tour. Later he found a stationary store, bought envelopes and mailed our ballots.

I had an appointment for a permanent wave so I went to the Beauty Shop. My operator could not speak English but occasionally an assistant that could would come in for a few minutes. I was there for 3 hours but they were interesting. There were 12 booths in the shop and everyone seemed to work in all booths as students are always assisting. It takes 3 years for them to become operators and in the meantime they draw very small salaries. They spend all their time in the shop except for school hours on Wed. And Sat. Their hours are from 8 am to 7:30 pm

The shop was quite modern, having pink and gray chairs. They used Helene Curtis permanent wave; have plastic dryers that have heat regulators on the front; have movable basins and hoses for shampoos; the expert operators are working in several booths at the same time and the attendants do shampooing, taking out pins, etc.

My permanent was very nice and cost 18 marks ($4.50)

Tom came down and we went to the Eagles Club for supper. Tom had to play for a Foot Ball Rally so Tony and I got a table in the lounge and listened to the floor show. Cheer leaders led the group in cheering, introduced the team and the Football queen. This was followed by a fine program, soloists, acrobats, etc. We met a girl that sings with Tom's Combo and went out to her home in the American Housing Area. Her brother-in-law is a civilian employee and has the privileges of living in this quarter, use of commissary, PX, etc. Their home is beautiful and filled with Hummel figurines, Dresden and Meisen figurines, paintings, clocks, camel saddles, lovely rugs etc.

Before going to her home, we stopped at a picturesque wine cellar downtown, which we entered by going thru a long hall. The pianist here knew Tom and also played Strauss music for us. "Weyjets".

Friday Oct 26. The band played for opening of a new hotel today so Tony and I went down. The band played a concert outside first and we watched the celebrities enter. When the band went in Tony and I walked around to watch thru the mammoth picture windows and hear over the public address system. Who should we meet but Erika. She is to work in the new Gen'l von Steuben Hotel and had come down to witness the opening. We accompanied her into the hotel, met many of the personnel and guests, and made a tour of the hotel.

The General von Steuben Hotel is named for a famous German general who trained George Washington's Army in the American Revolution. It is a transient hotel for officers and important visitors on temporary duty in Wiesbaden. It is six stories high and contains 200 rooms. A winding stairway leads from the lobby to a beautiful mezzanine floor which has a parquet floor and mosaic pillars. This leads to a huge, glass enclosed ball room. A large bar off of the lobby and an enormous shining kitchen.

The new Earhart Hotel was dedicated next. It is a 400 room to be used for American women civilians working for the military in the Wiesbaden area. Occupation of the hotels will permit the Air Force to return to the German owners some requisitioned hotels in the resort city, where hotel space has been critical since the end of the war.

Erika's father was a foreman in the building of this hotel.

The Air Force Hotels were built from occupation cost funds thru the German Federal Ministry of Finance at a cost of 15 million marks ($3,571,000). This will return the Rose Hotle and the Schwartzer Bock Hotel to the German people.

Erika then accompanied us to the Museum on the Wilhelm Strasse which we went thru. It contains paintings dating back to 1400 and 1500. Also art treasures of Egypt and Byzantine, mostly dating B.C. Woodcarvings and figurines back to 1500. Many religious carvings and paintings.

Saturday (Oct 27) It is a rainy day and Tom was excused from duties so he came in after us, then we picked up Patty and drove over to Frankfurt where he had lunch at the PX. Drove around to see the city; the watch tower in the center of town, the city walls, city gates and all of the new buildings. Then we drove to Freiburg and Bad Nauheim. Here we saw the Hessen Sanitorium where Erika had been for a long time. It has the hottest hot-springs in Europe. A beautiful hot-springs fountain centers the town, surrounded by statues, arches, etc.

From here we drove to the top of a mountain (overlooking a monastery) and to a picturesque cafe where we had cake and coffee in an elevated garden patio.

As we drove Patty home, we passed a car covered with snow so Tom drove out north until we saw traces of snow, turned off on a road winding up a mountain which we followed to the top and drove thru deep snow. Tom parked to enjoy the first snow of the season, he and Tony had a snowball fight and then plastered the car with snow before we started our homeward journey.

We spent the evening in packing our leave taking tomorrow.

Sunday Oct 28, 1956. Up early and completed packing. Erika came about 9 am to bid us goodbye. When Tom arrived, we went after gas, dropped Erika at the Hotel, and started for

Holland. We stopped for lunch at Rasthaus near Koln. Koln proved very interesting with its tall, narrow houses with pointed roofs; the well known Koln Cathedral with its numerous spires brick streets; lots of street cars; flower markets and large bridge across the Rhine River.

Around Aachen we were impressed with the large number of different shaped bell towers; archways into the city and surrounding big mines. Near Aachen we crossed the Belgium border and went thru customs. The landscape changed and we see lower, stone or brick houses, green farmland and lots of livestock, sheep, pigs and cattle. The cows wear blankets made of material looking like gunny sacks. As we enter Liege we find wider streets. We looked for and found a hotel, settles and ate dinner there. We then joined the milling crowds to walk thru the business district which is all decorated with Christmas decorations, the store windows have beautiful moving displays; Red Riding Hood, Cinderella, Snow White, many other story book characters, all life size. Hundreds of beautiful toys, electric trains moving up and down circular tracks. Other windows show luxurious accessories, etc. On shelves that change levels continuously. One street housed a number of picture shows and the crowds completely filled the streets making it almost impossible for cars to drive thru. ($11 for rooms, dinner and breakfast).

Monday , Oct 29. Had breakfast in our room; a very rainy day. We started for Brussels noting many things as we travelled; the beautiful lace curtains in the windows; a lovely church and statue near Borgworm. Near Tongere we noted brick houses with tile roofs, with pull wooden shutters. Then odd shaped houses with thatched roof. In Brussels we find many new, modern looking and tall apartment houses. These were very signs and much street work so here we were lost for the first time. French is spoken here so Tom was at a disadvantage in making inquiries but eventually found the way out and headed for Antwerp. This is a seaport; has wider streets; a beautiful opera house and many windows have colored glass panes. In Brasschat we saw many thatched roofs. Went on to Breda and passed the customs into the Nederland's.

We arrived in Rotterdam at 3pm and went first to the

Holland American offices to see about checking our luggage. As it was possible we checked three suitcases to be put on the Maasdan, Went to the pension where Tom had stayed on his trip up and we rented two rooms. (Steep steps to 3rd landing). Then we started out to find where Jack Van Hoff was staying. It is a little town at the end of the dike, Cappelan, Issell. Tom drove over the top of the dike for miles with the ocean on one side and land, lower, on the other. It was interesting and Tom loved it but the narrow road was made of cobblestones and very slippery would have to find wide places to pass cars. When we found the house, Jack was in town and his folks could not speak English. They were very nice to us and we left a note and phone number for Jack. The brother-in-law rode back to Rotterdam with us and we dropped him down town. Then we went to a Chinese Cafe for dinner. Several U.S. sailors, submarine neb & men from a US cruiser were also there and Tom visited with them. The next day, we heard the fleet had been very suddenly called home and these men had to leave at once.

When we got back to the pension, Jack called and he and his nephew came over for the evening. We took them home and found a shorter road across the land, also went thru the Mass tunnel instead of over the huge bridge, a drawbridge and it looks very crowded and inconvenient. The Mass Tunnel looks very much like our Lincoln Tunnel and goes under the Meuse river, connecting the two parts of Rotterdam.

Tuesday. Had breakfast at the Pension and Tom had to get started back for Wiesbaden as he had to play that night, so he left at 9 am. The landlord offered to give us our dinners as there was no cafe nearby. It was delicious, soup, chateau aubrionne, etc. Jack came over and met us and we went by street car to Westlaan, by way of city park. Here we secured reservations for a boat to London. Went downtown to the shopping center. In a large department store we had lunch, pastries and coffee. Toured this store fairly well and visited several others; walked by beautiful fountain, courthouse and post office to the auto bus station. We also saw the large statue of the "Man without a Heart" which symbolizes the miniseries of the city had been destroyed. We left Jack here and we took street car back to our pension. The landlord served tea in our room.

Wednesday. Breakfast again at the pension. We decided to walk to the Holland American offices to check on our tickets home but it proved to be a very long walk and it was very cold. Fortunately we had purchased muffler and gloves the day before so we were dressed warmly. We walked along the dock it is the largest artificial one in the world. We met a retired sailor that had formerly worked for the Holland American line and he was going to the office to collect his pension so he showed us the shortest way. Tickets checked, we started back and again met the sailor. He told us about the marked which we had noted on our way so we left him and entered the center of the open market and walked thru it for several blocks, looking at all of the displayed goods, everything from flowers and food to clothing and lace curtains. The men working in the flower maker were wearing modern shoes.

During our walks we saw many horse-drawn delivery carts, such as milk; they also use motorcycles with small compartments. Bread is delivered, unwrapped, in a large baskets. We stopped at the bank to exchange our money and returned to the pension for a dinner of broiled beef chops and crepe suzettes.

We then walked down to get a better look at the Masas Tunnel. It has two parts, one for cards and one for bicycles and pedestrians. There are escalators to carry pedestrians. On our way back, I was almost hit by a speeding bicycle.

We had tea in our pension and then called a taxi to take us to the Muller dock and we boarded the "Batavia" for London. We had cabin #13. It was a terribly rough trip and the cabin was too hot. Tony tried to turn off the heat and flooded the floor. In getting into the upper berth, was thrown off ladder by sudden lurch of the boat, hurt his ankle and broke clasp on the door.

Thursday Nov 1. Had breakfast on the "Batavia". Arrived Tilbury at 8:20am , passed thru customs and took train for Fenchurch Station, London. Took taxi to the Bonnington Hotel where we secured a nice room. Walked down South Hampsten Row, Russell Square, Oxford Street to Charring Cross. Went to a picture show and saw June Allison in "You Can't Run Away from It", and Victor Jory in "Black Jack Ketcham". It seemed good to see and American picture and to be with people that you could at least understand.

Friday. Had breakfast at the Hotel and then took a sightseeing trip around London – Trafalgar Square, St. James Palace, Buckingham Palace where we saw the Changing of the Guard and also saw Queen Elizabeth as she came out in her coach and waved as she passed by us. Also Royal Cavalry Guard; Horse Guards; Thames River and Tower Bridge, went thru the Tower of London and saw the Crown Jewels; London Bridge; Scotland Yard; Blackfriar's Bridge; Monument; Bank of England; Lloyd's ; Bow Church (heard its bells); St. Paul's Cathedral which we went thru Fleet Street and visited the Old Curiosity Shop of Charles Dicken's fame.

Saturday. Breakfast at the Hotel. Went to Post Office to mail letters and to Lloyd's Bank to cash Traveller's checks. Walked down to Trafalger Square and the Pall Mall. Went to Holland-American offices to check on return passage and purchased train tickets for next Friday. Then walked down the Mall, thru St. James Park, past the Horse Guards, Houses of Parliament; Big Ben and along the Thames River. Went thru the Jewel Tower and Westminster Abbey, the Royal Tombs and the National Gallery; viewed the presentation of the Horse Guards; had dinner and went to see "Gun Runner" at a movie. Stood in front of 10 Downey St for long time.

Sunday Nov 3. At 10 am we took a Frames tour thru London suburbs to Chelsea, Putney, Bushy Park to Hampton Gardens and Hampton Court Palace. This Palace was built in 1515 by Cardinal Wolsey who present it to Henry VIII and it was favorite royal residence until King George II. The Palace contains many fine pictures and tapestries. Wren's Orangery is famous for its beauty and its paintings. It was the forerunner of modern greenhouses. The garden contains the well known Maze and are wonderfully landscaped. Fragrant lavender beds

Went thru Staines and Runneymede. It was here the Magna Charta was signed in 1215. In the shadow of Cooper's Hill stands the Runnymede Memorial to the British soldiers of 2nd World War. Green Meadow.

Then to Windsor Castle, a residence of Queen Elizabeth. We

entered the grounds by the main gate. We saw all of the buildings, the Royal Guard and grounds. The Queen was in the castle that day so we made our visit to St George's Chapel where we saw many graves, among them, King George and Queen Mary; Henry VIII. Also saw the banners and insignias of the Knights of the Garter. (On death of knight)

Stopped at Eton College which was founded in 1440, his statues is in the School Yard. It has 70 students that do not pay. This was the manner in which the school originally started. Now these 70 students are housed in the inner red brick building and each has his own small room. Previously these boys were house in one long dormitory and the upper class boys were house outside. The boys all wear morning coats and striped trousers, the shorter boys wearing Eton jackets. the boys range from 13 to 17 years of age. Until the war period, the boys all wore top hats but this is no longer a requirement.

Visited Stoke Poges Church which was immortalized by Thomas Gray, the poet. We saw his tomb and the famous yew tree, 1000 years old, under which he worked and here he wrote " Tillary Garden of Remembrance". The old church was built around 1200 and the original wood still remains in the ceiling beams and the door frames. It has beautiful stained glass windows. We saw Thomas Gray's pew and also that of Thomas Penn, bother of William Penn. The Penn pew formerly had curtains, cupboard and a fireplace.

Had dinner and then walked down town.

Monday. Went down to see the changing of the guard at the Horse Guards. Stood inside of the archway at the entrance. many children present, perhaps because it was "Guy Fawkes Day". Visited Trafalgar Square and then the National Gallery. Had dinner on Rupert Street. To see "King & 1"; had tea and went to "Strip Tease". Smoke low on streets when we came out because of bonfires celebrating "Guy Fawkes Day" and sounds of bursting firecrackers.

Tuesday. Went to the Post Office and Bank. Again to British Museum; visited the Mummy section and viewed the Parthenon sculptures. To "A.B.C." for lunch and took double-deck streetcar to Trafalgar Square. Went to see "Guys and Dolls".

Wednesday. Had breakfast at 7 AM and took tour to Oxford College. We visited Christ College which was founded in 1527 by Cardinal Woolsey. The tower is still standing and was built in 1220. The College of Liberal Arts has 7000 students, 6000 men and 1000 women. Oxford is composed of 22 colleges. From this college has come many renowned men, among them, William Penn, Lewis Carroll (who was a batchellor altho he wrote stories for children such as "Alice in Wonderland".) and Sir Anthony Eden. In all 6 Prime Ministers have graduated from Oxford. The first college was built in 1279 and the last one, St. Anthony's, was built in 1950. It was here that Penecillin was first developed and tried. The Tutorial System is used; each student has a tutor from whom he receives lessons. The students study in private rooms with their tutor. Lectures are given during the term and they are optional for the student. They all take examinations under the University Board. All subjects of Art and Humanity are taught.

We passed thru Milton Center, the home of John Milton and the Rev. John White of Plymouth. Passed Bleinheim Castle at Woodstock. Had luncheon at Warwick at the "Porridge Pot". Visited Harwick Castle, the home of the nephew of Sir Anthony Eden. Large paintings here of King Charles I and King Henry VIII, by Van Dych and Rubens. Went thru the "Great Hall", with windows overlooking the Avon River, Red Drawing Room, passage filled with armoury; the great dining room with its carved sideboards, crystal chandelier and inlaid marble tables; the State Bedroom and Boudoir and saw the famous Warwick Vast.

Saw graves of Queen Mary and Queen Elizabeth, sisters that didn't speak to each other in life but are buried side by side.

Visited Stratford-on-Avon and the home of William Shakespeare; a large, half-timbered house containing many of his relics; small room; narrow winding stairway and dark low ceilinged bedrooms, containing original furniture.

To Anny Hathaway's thatched cottage. It had a large stone & brick fireplace with hanging utensils; very old pottery and china; antique loveseat by the fireplace.

Saw Holy Trinity Church. Stopped for tea at Banquet Cross.

Back in London about 8 PM.

Thursday. (Nov. 8) Walked down South Hampton Row: Euston Place to Marylebone and visited Madame Toussard's Wax Museum. Had lunch on Baker Street. Went shopping in Selfridges, Oxford Street. To Piccadilly Circus. Had tea on Great Russell St. Had beer at Peter's Bar and then back to the Bonnington Hotel to pack.

Friday. (Nov. 9) Had breakfast and completed packing. Went to bank and checked out of hotel, leaving luggage in check stand. It is Lord Mayor's Day" and there is to be a famous parage. Walked down Strand, Fleet St. To Ludgate Circus and waited for the parade. The streets are very crowded and people stand for hours, waiting. Police men stationed every three feet. Aluminum is the subject for the parade and floats are made of or contain displays of aluminum, one had a mermaid with aluminum hair and tail. The two Lord Mayor's coaches are very ornate, all red and gold and drawn by 6 horses. Many different guards, each section in different costume; a Scotch bag-pipe band; Irish band; etc. Took an hour to get out of the crown when the parade was over, just moved by inches.

Back to the hotel, had lunch, and took taxi to Waterloo Station where we boarded the boat train for South Hampton. Boarded the Maasdam and had dinner on board.

Had a conversation with a man who said it was practically impossible for a Britain to visit the U.S. as they are permitted to only take 10 pounds of out of the country altho they could buy their boat tickets before hand. He said the exchange teachers could make it because they have an income to provide for them. He is interested in archery and would like to come to the USA to purchase supplies but it is not possible, Said they can't even import these things.

Also talked to a couple of exchange nurses. She said they come for 6 months period and draw $27 every 2 weeks. They are unhappy because of long hours and lack of freedom. Also they are looked down on by their superiors and feel very uncomfortable.

Saturday. Nov. 10 – On our way back to the U.S.A. Jack Van Hoff had seats in dining room reserved for us. His niece,

Arida, is also at the table. Sea rather rough. Arrived at Cobh, Ireland, about dinner time. Irish people came on shipboard with merchandise for sale. Movie - "The Proud and Profane".

Sunday. Nov. 11 – Sea is very rough and a great many are seasick. We are both fine. It was dreary and cloudy all day and ship rocks a great deal.

Monday – Not as rough but still cold. Bridge tournament.

Tuesday – Canasta tournament.

Wednesday – Sea is smooth and sun is shining. Made a tour of the bridge; saw automatic steering apparatus, water tight door controls; sprinkler system; smoke finder, charts and barometer.

Saturday – Will be a day late arriving so sent radiogram to Marylee. Tom is supposed to call her Sunday.

Sunday (Nov. 18) Thru immigration and doctor's office; thru customs after quite a delay; dock workers strike on but got luggage on Port Authority bus and arrived in N.Y.C,; taxi to B & O depot making connection with noon train. Arrived Washington about 5 PM, called Marylee and took taxi to their home where they had a grand chicken dinner all ready for us.

Monday – Marylee took the day off and we went sightseeing, visited the Mint, FBI, etc.

Tuesday – D.A.R. Bldg; White House; Pan American Bldg; Red Cross; Smithsonian Institute; Washington's Monument.

Wednesday – Taxi to us to Silver Spgs. Depot; checked out luggage and took bus to Washington, walked to D.A.R Bldg; then to Smithsonian Institute. Train for Chicago.

Thursday – Thanksgiving Day. Dinner at Depot. Went to see "The Giant". Very cold in Chicago.

Statement of Mary Ries

Tom's grandfather Adolph Ries was killed in an accident at the Cheyenne railyards at the age of 56. This statement describing the circumstances of his death was given by his wife, Mary Ries, Tom's grandmother, in 1922. It has been transcribed preserving the original spelling and grammar.

◆ ◆ ◆

Subject: PI&D of Adolph Ries, Car Repairer, and car inspector, Cheyenne Wyoming, d. October 22nd, 1907. Statement of Mrs. Mary Ries, age 65 years, widow, residing at 320 east 22nd, Cheyenne, Wyoming.

My husband was employed as a car repairer at Cheyenne, Wyoming, and was killed on October 22nd, 1907, about 9:00 or 10:00 PM. He worked the day shift, think it was from 7:00 AM to 6:00 PM. As far as I know he had not been called back to work that night. He came home from work about 6:30 PM, and went down town about 8:00 PM. It was pay day and he had gone down town to pay the grocery bill. He had not said anything that day about going down into the yards, and I did not know that he had intended going down to the yards that night for any reason. As far as I knew he had nothing to do down there. However, I will say that he had been in the practice of going into the yards often in the evening, he was very conscientious about his work, and when he got home he would often think of something that should be told the clerk, and he would go back to the yard and tell them. There was a great shortage of cars at that time, and he would often think of some car that was in good condition in some part of the yard that the office should know about. Although he had been going down there at night, I did not know he was going down there on the night he was killed. They telephone the house about the accident early the next morning, but my son had been notified the night before. As I understand it the accident occurred on the first track from the depot and just a little east of the depot. He was either run over by a switch engine or a car.

My husband was 56 years old when he was killed, and had

been in the service of the Union Pacific since he was 19 years old, that was sometime in the 70's, he started to work in Council Bluffs at that time, and worked there about six or eight years, and then was transferred to Lincoln, Nebraska, where he was car inspector and foreman for fourteen or fifteen years. At that time he had some kind of disagreement and quit, that was some time the last part of the 80's. He did not work for the company then for about a year, and then he came out to Cheyenne. As I think of it now I remember we came to Cheyenne in 1897, so the disagreement he had in Lincoln must have been about 1895. He worked continuously at Cheyenne as a car repairer and inspector from 1897 to 1907, when he was killed, that service was continuous. He has worked for the Union Pacific practically all of his life, ever since 1870 think was the first year he worked, he was building snow sheds west of Laramie then.

My husband was buried at Milwaukee Wis, and the company furnished transportation of the corpse and family to that point and return. I do not remember the name of the claim agent that was to see me at that time, he was a young man, quite tall, large boned man. I remember at that time I told him that I would settle it for $1000.00, but the claim agent told me that he could only make an allowance of $200.00, on account of the circumstances. I did not accept this amount. My boys though I should have at least $5000.00 but I do not know if they put in a claim or not. The difference – between the claim agent and myself was the difference between $1000.00 and $300.00. He said that was all he would pay, and I did not feel that I should accept that. No settlement was every made, and I have never started any law suit against the company, the matter just rested that way. The claim agent was only here one time.

Taken at my home at Cheynne, Wyoming, July 26th, 1922.

Appendix B: Thomas Family

Biography of Charles S. Thomas

Charles Thomas was the father of Tom's mother, Grace. He was interviewed in 1936 for the "Pioneer Wyomingite" series, part of a Statewide Historical Project to create a roster of all Wyoming pioneers. This interview has been transcribed from the original typed manuscript, preserving the original spelling and grammar. A copy of this document record can also be found online in the Wyoming State Archives at http://spcrphotocollection.wyo.gov/luna/servlet/detail/wyo~2~2~2386~165154.

◆ ◆ ◆

Pioneer Wyomingite, Businessman, Rancher, Stockman
By Ida Elizabeth Hintze

Charles S. Thomas has been an Indian trader, businessman, banker, rancher, and stockman during the years that he has spent in the State of Wyoming, and he has seen the country change from a barren extent of prairie inhabited by war-like tribes of Indians and a few settlers and traders, to a land of enterprise and business, where many towns and cities as well as large farms and ranches form the habitation of the people who call Wyoming their home today.

Mr. Thomas says, "I came out in 1880 as a trader with the Indians, and I should say there have been some changes! We, my brother and I, owned all the land north of the Union Pacific Railroad from Egbert to Archer Hill. George Gilland owned all the land south of the Union Pacific, and Burns is built on the Gilland ranch, although my ranch was included in the Golden Prairie District, that was opened up in 1906 and began the towns of urns, Carpenter and others. Talk of those days—people now days don't know what hardship is."

The busy life of Charles Samuel Thomas began on February 12, 1859, in Llangynog, Montgomeryshire, North Wales, British Isles. His parents were Cadwallader Thomas who was born at Bala, North Wales, in 1830, and Ellinor (Morris) Thomas who was born in 1833 in Llangynog, North Wales. The mountain country in which the Thomas' lived was very rugged but beautiful. The father farmed his land and for many years was a cattle dealer. He was largely interested in contracting, and has much extensive work to his credit. He was the superintendent of the construction of the largest tunnel in the world, which was the first tunnel made through the Alps Mountains, affording railway communication between Italy and Germany. It is nine and a fourth miles long through the Saint Gotthard Pass, and is called the Saint Gotthard Tunnel. He did this while a young man and before he was married. He supervised many construction enterprises in Great Britain and also in Europe.

The Thomas family lived in two places in Wales, Bala and Llangynog, and Charles went to school at different places in those parishes. The family left Wales in 1873 and went to England, where Charles and his brother, John, attended school in Leicester, where they lived for five years. After completing his grade school education, Charles matriculated at college and took a class of college training before coming to America.

In 1878, when Charles was nineteen, the Thomas' and their sons, Charles and John, came to the United States and settled in Cleveland, Ohio. The father became a merchant and was very successful in this business. He died in 1880.

Charles Thomas liked America. He worked for Joseph Gardner, a French-Canadian, who was a wholesale butcher, for one year. Mr. Gardner put him in complete charge of the meat market and also had Mr. Thomas make his home with them. This was a good job even if it was a busy, responsible one. People in Cleveland at that time were talking of Denver, the Capitol of the West, and of the opportunities that awaited the new comer there. Mr. Thomas wanted to go to Colorado. At last, in 1879, he turned his job over to his brother, John, and started on his way to the great city of Denver.

Mr. Thomas says, "I landed in Denver at six in the morning

on about the first Burlington train that came to Denver, and by seven o'clock was eating breakfast at the expense of Chamberlain, Archer and Clow, wholesale butchers who had one of the largest hidehouses in this section of the West, and who were located at Twenty-Fourth and Larimer Streets."

He worked for this firm for almost a year, being in charge of weighing the beef and selling the hides. He says, "I delivered the hides to the stockyards of Denver but after a while I found that the man receiving them was taking advantage of me. For this work, I was getting sixty-five dollars a month and my board and washing. Then I met James Tynan who owned the stockyards in Dever at that time, and who was a merchant and capitalist. He offered me seventy-five dollars a month and my room and board, so I went to work for him. I did not work for him long in Denver. He had a hide-house in Cheyenne and sent me here to run it in 1880.

"I came to Cheyenne in 1880 and managed the business house of James Tynan. In this place we handled cattle, hides and general supplies, and had a government contract to furnish Fort Laramie with beef. I had entire charge of this place for two years. During this time our business grew and expanded until it was one of the largest in the country. In 1892 I bought him out, and Mr. Tynan put ten thousand dollars to my credit in the Wyoming Post Bank so that I could continue my work and enlarge my business. M.E. Post was a big banker in Cheyenne, and was Territorial Congressman from Wyoming.

"In the meantime, in 1882, I had bought a hundred and sixty acres of land which lay west of Sterling, Colorado, and I kept on buying land at different intervals. I purchased government land also as every other section was government land, and I had three purchase of railroad land. I bought until I owned a hundred thousand acres in all."

Mr. Thomas hired foremen to take care of his ranches and watch over his herds of cattle, while he personally supervised the affairs of his merchandise business. This business in town had continued to grow as fast as did his success, and busy men were the Thomas brothers, as now John was in partnership with Charles. At this time Mr. Thomas also supplied Fort D.A.

Russell, now known as Fort F.E. Warren, and other posts with beef.

Mr. Thomas was acquainted with a Mr. Del Holiday who was the general agent of the Burlington Railroad in Cheyenne. He says, "At Mr. Holiday's statement that I could buy corn for my sheep much cheaper in Nebraska, I went to that state and stopped at the town of Curtis and later in Stockville. I found the men Holiday had told me about, and bought all the corn that I needed for my sheep from these farmers. It was in the town of Stockville that I met Charles Riggs. He had a lumber yard and a carpenter shop in that town and it was he who built a corn bin and many troughs for the feeding of the sheep. That was I November of 1891.

"Then one day I went to Mr. Riggs' shop to sharpen a knife and there I met his daughter, Meroa. I liked her at once and was very pleased a week or so later, when her father invited me to dinner on Sunday. On Sunday evening we drove to church, the four of us, and thus began the friendship that ended in our marriage on June 1, 1892. Her parents had come from the state of New York, and had settled in Iowa before making their home in Nebraska. My brother who was four years younger than I, married Meroa's sister, Alice, several years later. Mrs. Thomas and I made our first home in Cheyenne. We lived in Cheyenne for three years."

In 1896, Mr. Thomas sold the store, and the family moved on their ranch in the Egbert country. Both John and Charles had a home ranch where they each lived. In this venture as in his succeeding ones, Charles Thomas was again successful. He and his brother had also bought a hide-house in Cheyenne from Oburne Hoshick. They owned this for a number of years, and had James Barnes manage it. This was while the Thomas' were living on the ranch.

Ranching, however, had been Charles Thomas' prime interest, and he began in earnest to make a showing of this business, doing such a thorough job of it that at one time due to his large interests of cattle, he was considered one of the heaviest of Wyoming's cattle-dealers. He had a great many sheep also, and did much toward making this part of Wyoming at that time "sheep-wise."

Mr. Thomas relates of the experiences he has encountered during his life on the range, while in the cattle and sheep occupation, and of the hardships he and his riders endured while "on the trail."

In 1894 Mr. Thomas brought twenty-five hundred head of cattle from old Mexico. Most of the cattle in this country then had been brought here from Texas; getting cattle from Mexico was an unheard of venture to most of the cattlemen here, but Mr. Thomas did not let that stop him. He is glad that he was the first to trail cattle from that country. In telling about this event, Mr. Thomas says, "I went to El Paso, Texas, which is on the Rio Grand River, and went to see the Fenceler Brothers who were wholesale butchers there. They told me about the man who was the governor of Mexico, and of the fifty thousand steers that the had sold shortly before to one outfit. They said that he might sell some to me if I went to see him. His place was in the city of Chihuahua which was the capitol of Chihuahua state. They told me, however, to go to Mexico with my British passport as I would get better results than if I told him that I was from the States. This I did, and my British passport brought me what I wanted. Governor Trasus was very pleased that I came to him. I selected the cattle that I wanted at fourteen and one half dollars a head, to be delivered over the Rio Grande. The regular tariff was two dollars a head but the governor got them across at seventy-five cents each. I had paid an amount down, and after he had the cattle safely across, I paid him the balance. Texas Rangers helped fetch the cattle across the country to La Junta, Colorado, where we were met by my men, Ed Dolan, Emmett Coon, and others, who helped trail them to the ranch.

"We also drove cattle up from Greeley at three different times; each time we brought a herd of about five hundred head. One time my boys had brought the camp wagon, and what a time those boys had deciding who should be the cook. No one, it seemed, cared about the job. Finally my brother did the cooking, giving the boys to understand the first one who grumbled had to take on the job. He salted the coffee and gave it to them at meal time. Jim Barnes took the first taste. He said, 'Gee, this is salty!'

Then he happened to remember what John had said and he quickly added, 'but it's good, though.'

"I was very well acquainted with William Miner who was Senator Warren's partner and general manager at the ranch. I recall one time when Senator Warren bought some sheep from New Mexico which looked like goats, and was trying to get them across Crow Creek. There was only a little bridge there then, and the sheep would not cross. I happened to see his trouble and offered to put them across for him. He told me to go ahead. I tied a piece of bailing wire around the horn of a sheep and led him over the bridge. The others followed and soon I had the band on the other side. Senator Warren never forgot that incident, nor did I."

Mr. Thomas goes on to say, "During Grover Cleveland's administration, I brought a band of sheep to the ranch trailing them across the country from Oregon. The trip took six months to complete. We had twenty thousand sheep to look after. There were ten men with me, and we had three cook wagons. We just let the sheep graze their way over; letting them feed so much every day and then bedding them for the night. It was slow travel and a rather lonely as well as hazardous undertaking. There were few settlers. Not many people were in the country then, just a few freighters, miners and some traders. The Indians roamed all over in some portions of the country. We had no trouble with them, however. Whenever we came to rivers, as we frequently did, we would have to swim the sheep across. When we got to the division between the Laramie River and the head of the Chugwater, we called a stop and I rode out at break of day to locate where we were. While on my mission I met a man afoot. We greeted each other and I found that he was looking for his cows which had strayed away. His name was Shanton, and he had a place near the head of Horse Creek. They, however, called this creek, Shanton Creek. We talked a while and then we each went our way. The boys and I got the sheep home all right and very glad we were, after having been gone for so long.

"The strange thing about this meeting with the man, Shanton, was that twenty years later, Judge Matson and my brother, John, went to Panama to see the Panama Canal, and while there came into contact with the family of Shanton again. After they landed in Panama they asked a man at the dock about the best way to see the canal. He advised them to get a launch and go out, as they could then see the country as it was, as well as the natives at their work. He said that they could get the government launch at the governor's mansion. Judge Matson and he went to the mansion where the governor welcomed them. And who should it turn out to be, but the son of the Shanton that I had met two decades ago, searching for his cows in the hills of Wyoming. Governor Shanton had joined Teddy Roosevelt's Rough Riders and had become a captain in this army. He had a fine record for valor during the years that he served, and this it was that President Roosevelt appointed him the Governor of Panama. He took them to see his father and they had quite a chat."

Mr. Thomas says, "Back before McKinley was elected, we sold sheep out as feeders into the state of Nebraska. We did a lot of inter-state business."

He goes on to say, "Weather in Wyoming was cold, too. The winters were very severe and the blizzards made us take careful precautions to guard the lives of the cattle and sheep. It was cold work for the men. John and I dug two houses out of the rock for our riders and herders so that they might have shelter and food when they were caught out in a storm. These houses were one room and in each house was a place for beds and equipment for preparing meals. The houses were built in the rocks; one is eight miles north of the ranch in Wind Mill Hollow, the other is on Bull Springs. We came down every week to see how the boys were getting along and to bring the supplies."

Going back to his experiences in old Mexico where he went for some of his herds, Mr. Thomas comments on the peasant class or poor people of that country at that time. He says, "The morale of these people weas very low. They did not care what they did or how they did it as long as they got money for doing the deed. The poor lived together in small, tumbled huts, and marriage among them was uncommon. In order to get married, the Mexicans had to have about fifty dollars; but the country was poor and so were they. Fifty dollars was a fortune to them. They solved the problem by just living together. Their uncleanliness was appalling, and there was much disease. They did not bury their dead. They threw the bodies into some hollow and let the vultures eat them. Even the priest has privileges there that they do not have I other countries. They are also allowed to marry in Mexico. The morale of that country is worse, I believe, than at any other place that I have been."

Mr. Thomas recalls many of the encounters that he has had with the Indians. He tells of the time that he and Russell Tracy went from Fort Laramie to Salt Lake City to see the country. The Laramie and Platte Rivers come together at that point and it is in the fork of these rivers that Fort Laramie is built. The two of them were riding horseback with their guns on their saddles— Winchesters and repeaters, were the guns that they used—and they stopped to water their horses before going on. Three bullets struck the water near them, taking the men completely by surprise. They looked up and saw that three Indians were on top of the bank with muzzle-loaders in their hands. Mr. Thomas and his friend shot the Indians to protect themselves. Then they rode to Fort Laramie and reported the encounter to the authorities there. The troops then went after the bodies of the Indians.

"Camp Carlin, at that time was the headquarters of the railroad, also supplying all the other forts in this country, with provisions. Russell Tracy was the chief clerk there and was nephew to Major Lord who was the head man at Camp Carlin.

"Fort Fetterman was situated above the town of Douglas, Wyoming, close to the ranch home of Robert Carey. The freighters took their freight through there, and the troops were stationed at that place to protect the white men from the Indians. These troops also escorted caravans on their journeys over the prairies and through the mountains, so that they might reach their destination in safety, as the Indians had not yet been put on the reservations. Stages ran daily to Fort Laramie and the Black Hills, where the mining of gold and silver was drawing many people.

"The saddest sight that I have ever seen," says Mr. Thomas, "was one time when Mrs. Thomas and I were on this side of Hillsdale, coming on the south side of the Union Pacific on top of the hill near Atkins—now called Durham—when we saw a woman hitched with a cow, and hauling a barrel of water from the pump-house at Atkins. This was in 1896 and was the most pathetic thing that I have ever witnessed!

"While I was on the ranch I built several reservoirs on my places," continues Mr. Thomas. "That was forty years ago. The upper reservoir is on the farm now owned by Charley Louthe. "In 1906, I sold out to my brother and he in turn, sold the ranches to the Federal Land and Securities Company who were colonizing small towns and bringing homeseekers into this part of Wyoming. They also bought the George Gilland ranch and others, and called all this land the Golden Prairie District. There was a mortgage on the land when they bought it from use, but it did not stop the promoters from cutting the ranches into sections and selling these sections to the settlers—with the mortgage unpaid.

"After selling our ranches, John and I bought into the bank and were kept very busy with our duties there. My brother and I put up the Citizen's National Bank Building, and I, myself, went to Washington, D.C., to get the permit to build the bank. After its erection and after the bank was established, John weas named the president of the bank, while I was one of the directors. I was in the bank for fifteen years. Then I sold out and started a grocery and general store at Elk Mountain, Wyoming.

"In this store I carried everything that anyone ever wanted or needed to buy. Besides the general merchandise and groceries, I had dry goods, meats and machinery. I also had been appointed the receiver at Elk Mountain for the bank, and I handled the affairs for the Carbon Timber Company. My wife came for one week every month and did all my bookkeeping. I was at Elk Mountain for two years.

"After I sold my place of business there, I went to Memphis, Tennessee, and built the Union Stockyards there. It took nearly two years to build them, and longer than two years to bring the supplies in from other states. I did a good business at Memphis. Mrs. Thomas came several times while I was there.

"The Southern people were very hospitable. I never met with an unkind deed or a rebuff all during the time that I was there, and I went around to their homes often, collecting their products for market. One very peculiar thing that I noticed about the Southerners was that they lived and mingled with the negro servants, had negroes for cooks and nurse-maids, and yet would not allow them in their schools, churches, other affairs or in their riding conveniences. I could not understand it."

Since selling his business at Memphis, Mr. Thomas has more or less led a very active life. He owns many residences and business enterprises, besides having land and other property in and around Cheyenne, and in Laramie County. He looks after his many interests and investments himself, and although he is seventy-seven years of age, Mr. Thomas takes care of all of his rental collections and real estate with the aid of anyone.

Charles Thomas says that his life has been filled with many extraordinary coincidences, that years later hinged together to complete the experience.

Before his marriages and in the year 1880, Mr. Thomas was in the city of Jerusalem. While he was there he met a man by the name of D. D. Dare, whom he had heard of when they both had lived in Cheyenne, Wyoming. This man had been connected with the Cheyenne National Bank there. His partners in this bank had been a Mr. Collins and George Barid; Dare had skipped out of town one day with all the money that was in the bank, and had departed to lands unknown. George Baird and Mr. Collins, ruined by the dreadful act of their wily partner, committed suicide over the loss of the money. This man Dare had gone to Jerusalem and with the money that he had stolen, had bult a narrow gauge bridge from Joppa to Jerusalem. Mr. Thomas introduced his cousin who was with him and himself, saying that he was from the United States of America. Dare asked more specific questions regarding the state and city from which Mr. Thomas came, and was visibly frightened when he learned that Mr. Thomas was from Cheyenne, Wyoming. Mr. Thomas continues the story in his own words. "He asked me if I knew Mr. Van Tassel or Larry Bresnahen and I said that I did. I also added that I knew him. At first he did not know what to do or say. Finally he commenced to talk and he told me many things. He wanted to stay over but we told him that our ship left that day for the Suez Canal and we had to be at that ship or be left behind. I don't know what became of him., I never heard.

"I have crossed the Atlantic eleven times to visit my

relatives in the beautifully wooded mountains of my native Wales. I like to sail, and I enjoyed all of my trips. Mrs. Thomas went with me once on a three month visit. She completely captivated the hearts of the people with her charm and personality. On our return trip, however, the crossing was very rough and we were all quite sick. My last voyage was made when I took my daughter, Grace, over, giving her the journey as a graduation gift.

"Cheyenne, as well as other Wyoming towns, in the old days, was all wool and it was plenty wild. We got so that we didn't let the hangings bother us too much, and when the Indians got tough while we were out on the trail or on the range, we took care of the situation as we knew best, and trusted to Providence and to our trusty horses and guns to bring us through. There was much contention and strife between the different gangs in the town, and fights were not an uncommon occurrence. Freighters, settlers, traders, miners and many more of these as well as the riff-raff that always follows the opening of new towns or booming settlements, came to Cheyenne and had their day. For some, the day was very short. In most cases, the person's trigger finger decided that. Cheyenne as the "rip roarin' town of the West", had streets lined with numerous saloons, gambling joints, resorts where the dancing dolls lived, as well as its blacksmith shops, its livery stables and general merchandise shops. All these played their part in that gala day. In the post office was where the best people rubbed shoulders with the worst, as they all went there for their mail.

"The Great Western Barn and Corrals was situated where Twentieth Street is now, and between Bent and O'Neil Streets. The freighters stopped there for rest while their mules were turned into the corrals for feed and water. There was a place upstairs where the men could sleep, and the freighters would take their bedroll from the wagon and unroll it on the floor. Then they would lie down and get their much-needed rest.

"My brother, John, died in Laramie City, eighteen years ago," says Mr. Thomas. My other brother, William, died ten years ago. His daughter, Margaret, teaches in a college in Massachusetts; his son, Horace, is a professor in the University of

Wyoming at Laramie."

Mrs. Ellinor Thomas, mother of Charles Thomas, made her home with him after the death of his father. She died in 1899, having seen many years.

The Thomas family belong to the Methodist Episcopal Church and take an active part in its program. They are deeply interested in charity and give much help to the unfortunate. Both Mr. and Mrs. Thomas are members of the Republican Party and take a firm stand on its platform. Mr. Thomas takes a prominent part in the political affairs of this party and has been instrumental in helping to shape its policy in this country, although he is not interested in holding positions that they at times offer him. Mr. Thomas held the position of sheep and cattle inspector for a number of years, thoroughly discharging these duties with capable ability.

Charles S. Thomas is included in the volume of *Progressive Men of Wyoming*, which was published by A.W. Bowen and Company in 1903. The following concerning him is quoted from the book:

Charles S. Thomas

"One of the most prominent business men of the state of Wyoming, one whose energy, enterprise and business ability are rapidly accumulating for him a handsome fortune and giving him a place in the foremost ranks of the property owners of his section of the state."

At the close of the article the author says:

"No man in his section of Wyoming stands higher in the estimation of the people of the state, or could more easily achieve high public honors."

Mr. Thomas has traveled extensively all over the United States and old Mexico, as well as in parts of the Old World, and in his native British Isles. He is a well educated man, and this knowledge has served him rightly in his prolific climb up the ladder of success. He has seen this great West from Nebraska and Wyoming to the coast of Oregon and down to the Rio Grande, when that stretch of land was sparsely settled and Indians demanded the life of the white men as their booty for the loss of their hunting grounds. Hardship and work has been his master; his perseverance kept him at the goal that he has reached, and more than half of a century of living in the West, has not dimmed his enthusiasm of this state—Wyoming.

A Poem by Meroa Thomas

Meroa Thomas was the wife of Charles Thomas and Tom's maternal grandmother. She composed this poem describing the life of a young pioneer bride. This has been transcribed from a copy of the poem typed by her daughter Grace Thomas, Tom's mother, preserving the original spelling and grammar.

♦ ♦ ♦

A Pioneer of Wyoming

Imagine, how as a youthful bride
I came to the ranch with lots of pride.
How wild to a Nebraska girl Wyoming seemed to be,
And how lonesome at first it seemed to me,
when all alone, with miles of prairie to see
And having heard how on plains Indians roamed free,
I'd glance out the windows and suddenly see a post—
'Twould seem to be an Indian, or at least a ghost.
My heart would pound with sudden fright,
And I'd quiver and quake and take a second sight;
But gradually this new country I got used to
With duties so frequent to even feel blue.
Up we got when dawn tinted the skies,
Bread must be mixed and set to rise,
Bacon to fry and pancakes to mix,
Table to be set and breakfast to fix.

The duties of a ranch wife would get under way –
Water to carry and heat for the day.
The spring was down at the foot of the hill
And water had to be carried up pail by pail.
The chickens, geese, and ducks to be feed,
Then to get busy—the bread to knead.
Children to be combed and wash their faces
And start for the school house to find their places.
When all the men had left for work

Then I had to get busy and never shirk,
For there were dishes to wash and floors to mop,
Beds to make, and firewood to chop
To feed the small cookstove upon which to cook,
For lots and lots of wood it took;
Armloads of wood it took by the score.
Then waste water must be dumped out the back door.

The lamps were to be filled and wicks to trim,
The chimneys all washed so lights wouldn't be dim.
There was washing and ironing and cleaning galore,
And baking to do—for t'was miles to a store.
When children got sick or felt very ill
All I could do was to give them a pill
For the doctor was so far away
To get him--meant an entire day.
A telephone we did not have for years.
When it came, it did much to allay our fears.
The top wire of the barbed wire fence was found
To be a fine agent for carrying sound,
And it was a good way to get the news
And did a great deal to chase the blues.

Our nearest neighbor lived three miles away
And we didn't see each other for many a day.
Our latch string was always out for all
And we welcomed every call.
All visitors were asked to sit at the table
And to stay all night if they were unable
To reach their next stop before dark
With us they were always welcome to park.
Some politicians arrived one night at nine
And they were asked to sleep and to dine.
One of them was Ex-Governor Ross
Little we knew then that soon he'd be boss.

All travel was done by wagon or buckboard
For we had never seen such a thing as a Ford.

On Saturday we heated lots of water
With which to bathe our sons and daughter,
A real bath tub we did not have,
In the old tin tub each took a bath.
Or if the weather was nice and warm
Down to the creek we all would swarm.

We have oft heard Mondays spoken of as blue,
Down on the ranch this was certainly true
For not only did we use an old tin tub
But on the board we would rub and scrub
And into the boiler we'd plop the clothes
For Rinso was unknown in days like those.
Then all the clothes must be wrung by hand
For we had no wringer electrically manned.
Oh, for an electric washing machine
But those wonders had never been seen.
No electric switches that we could turn
No lovey gas stove that we could burn –

It seems I'm in an awful haze
When I recall those olden days.

Made in the USA
Columbia, SC
10 September 2024

83d60bd4-50fa-45e0-911d-da42257b848eR01